adDICTIONARY
of experimental language
Leanne Bridgewater

KFS

Newton-le-Willows

Published in the United Kingdom in 2023
by The Knives Forks And Spoons Press,
51 Pipit Avenue,
Newton-le-Willows,
Merseyside,
WA12 9RG.

ISBN 978-1-912211-95-1

Acknowledgements

Alec Newman would like to thank Lucy Hulton and Scott
Thurston for their help in producing this text.

In dedication to Snowy
In dedication to you
In addiction to words
In addition to the universe

Contents

Contents

Foreword by Scott Thurston

In 2011 Leanne Bridgewater (1989-2019) approached me about applying for a place on a Creative Writing Masters programme I was then running at the University of Salford. Little did I imagine the fireball of creativity that Leanne would unleash on the programme, nor that in ten years' time that I would be inaugurating a new prize for graduates from the programme in her posthumous honour. Nor, indeed, that I would be writing a foreword to introduce readers to Leanne's *adDictionary* – a project which started life as her final dissertation.

Leanne was a unique, complex and fearless writer who embraced creativity across all its forms in almost seamless continuity – working across drawing, writing, sculpture, film and performance. I would also include Leanne's courageous and committed work as an animal rights activist as something indistinguishable from the impulses governing her creative practice – whether sabotaging fox hunts or protecting badgers during the Warwickshire cull. She lived her life and made art in a wholly integrated way, refusing to recognise the standard boundaries or limits.

Within a few months of Leanne starting the course my office began to fill with the most remarkable objects and contraptions. The 'homophone translator' was a homemade console with a phone receiver through which you could listen to Leanne reading a text she'd translated into eight different languages, and then back into English. 'Alternative Anniversaries' was presented as a card spinner (an actual one you find in shops) stocked with her hilarious set of alternative greetings cards to celebrate events for which there are not usually cards ('congratulations on your accent change', 'the day of no electric', 'lazy day – be a couch potato', 'A day for Nature'). Finally, *Sentience* arrived as a five by five foot stretched vinyl canvas on which was printed a single uninterrupted sentence of over 7,000 words. Alongside these unique visionary objects, I was lucky enough to see Leanne perform several times at events like The Other Room and even witnessed her autodestructive performance of demolishing a ten-foot plywood obelisk (covered with words and drawings – I still have some souvenir fragments) at the Black Lion pub in Salford.

For her final Masters project, Leanne undertook the mammoth task of compiling a personal dictionary of 12,000 words to find a new way of sharing her unique and critically engaged view of the world, culture and history. The *adDictionary,* as it became known, sums up the essence of Leanne's enquiry in its very title: conveying the extent to which the dictionary was not simply about creating new definitions for existing words but also to create new words, often by colliding familiar ones together to form surprising and inventive coinages, for instance, **abacsoma** – a counted body; **paralist** – to make a mental list; **ubi tubi** – to be lost on the underground. Fascinated by dictionaries from a very early age, Leanne was driven by a utopian impulse – held in common with other historically unacknowledged legislators of the word – that is, if things could somehow be named in the right way, injustice, inequality and oppression could be made to vanish overnight as they become suddenly and irrevocably unthinkable because unsayable. As Leanne writes in her Introduction to the *adDictionary* (subtitled 'of experimental language'):

> In today's world, we have achieved interaction with words so much that we believe we are superior to animals who do not speak. Language was around before the word; in the spirit of sounds, visuals, gestures and movement. With this dictionary I aim to encourage people to create new paths, new insights, to discover unknown places inside of themselves.

During her time as a student, Leanne undertook an internship at the then nascent small press publisher, The Knives Forks and Spoons Press, who later became publisher of her first full-length collection *Confessions of a Cyclist* (2016). Leanne later submitted *adDictionary* to the press, but, weighing-in at nearly 1000 pages, it was not a workable proposition at that point. This special edition has been crowdfunded by twenty individuals who wanted to see this remarkable work in print, and supported by Leanne's family who gave us permission. Thanks to you all for your kindness and support. Special thanks also go to Lucy Hulton (the second writer to win the University of Salford's Leanne Bridgewater Award for Innovation and Experiment) for taking on the huge task of copyediting the manuscript and for her insightful design ideas and observations on the text. It gives me great pleasure, if one touched by sadness, to help present this work to new readers, with all its joy, irreverence and liberatory potential.

Professor Scott Thurston
University of Salford
November 2022

adDICTIONARY
of experimental language

Introduction

adDictionary (of 12,000 words) is an addition to the language we already have deep inside of our bodies. We must realise words are as real as a UFO: it is only when we take an unidentified object and engage with it and use it to engage with other beings that it becomes identified. In today's world, we have achieved interaction with words so much that we believe we are superior to animals who do not speak. Language was around before the word; in the spirit of sounds, visuals, gestures and movement. With this dictionary I aim to encourage people to create new paths, new insights, to discover unknown places inside of themselves. adDictionary is somewhat comical, with a warning of puns and plays on words. Afterall, we must never leave the playground. Ralph Walderson said that we should always live in our infancy. The purpose of this dictionary is to show that we are always learning and processing. Trying something alien will take you back to childhood; but the only difference is you choose the path, you are your child's parent. Never get comfortable – keep running, keep twisting. To try is to experiment. If we never try then we will never accept difference. Words are entries, doorways to reflections, reactions and realisations. In this spirit adDICTIONARY was born.

Using the DICTIONARY

Main entry words printed in bold

**Everything other than the definition
and certain abbreviations** placed inside brackets

An entry with more than one definition the " | " symbol
represents the start of a new definition

Additional information for inspiration of a word
- connectivity of words placed inside brackets with
  a "+" sign, e.g. [+ long]
- more insight into a word placed inside brackets
  e.g. [insp. *ramaria Formosa*]

Cross references shown in bold type,
e.g. **yam yam** [see **yam**]

Origins and meanings in brackets

Kic. Kiche	Fre. French	Na. Na'vi	Gk. Greek	L. Latin
Turk. Turkish	Hin. Hindi	Wel. Welsh	NZ. New Zeland	
Aus. Australia		Spa. Spanish	Na. Na'vi	Chi.
Chinese	Iri. Irish		*pic* Pictorial	

Abbreviations certain abbreviations that are placed before
a definition are shown in italics and abbreviations inside
brackets (after the definition) are shown in regular font

Additional keys
| a new definition
+ add/and
e.g. for example
insp. inspiration
oppo. opposite

Aa

A *pic* a ladder from far away | a step ladder | a mountain

AA and alive

AAA three in a row [see **O's and X's**] | triple A battery

AAAA four in a row [see **FIAR**]

AAAD an apple a day

A&E ask and estimate

aback to go back (there)

abacsoma a counted body

abacud to cuddle many times | to hug a number of times

abacus to count bullets [insp. **gun**]

ABAD a banana a day

aballity the bounce of a ball | the ability to play a good game of "catch and throw" | the time it takes to solve a problem

abarredown a boarded up pub when you really need it to be in service

ABBAcus to curse ABBA

ABC angry blood cells

ab can to exercise going in and out of different consciousness [insp. **ub con**]

ABCD a brilliantly crap day

ABCDeffort the effort of writing | the effort of filling out forms

ABCDEFGHI to read everything somebody is writing or has written

abcdefghijklmnopis s to slur words after intoxication

A,B,C,D,E,F,G,H,I,V the teaching of sexually transmitted diseases

ABCDEFGHIVise to remember the safe sex alphabet

A B C dese to gesture the two fingers in a cursive manner

a-b-clergy group of infants in education

abdomino to have a 'spot' of abdominal pain

abduce the London underground subway – of how it moves people in and out of the central lines

abduct'n'dive to take a punch for someone

abduct tape to have lost its stickiness | for a bond to be lost

A,B,E,D,C look, we will rest here

abeepbeep to forget what you were saying | the act of dementia

abeer-ji a social drinker [Jap. abere–ji: average] [+ beer]

abe vigoda a grandpa with vigour [insp. *Abe from The Simpsons*]

abhoratus abhorred apparatus

ABI a bad idea

abishbash violence

ablaskat a black cat [+ Alaska] [insp. **alascat**]

ablouse a top which has offensive writing or indecent images on it [abuse + blouse]

abondle a group of spies | spies in a crowd

A book the book you are currently reading

aboot about a boot

aboreal original truths [+ aboriginal]

abover one above

abpi building work

abracad to learn how to talk [abracadabra + ABC]

abradub to dub another language | to make up a translation

abrainsion to split the head open [brain + abrasion]

abrase a minor crack [+ abrasion]

abray to perform stomach exercises

abru cadabru an unexpected bruise of unknown birth

abs the city cabs | the muscles | to ease 'getting around'

abscorption to absorb or take in too much that it kills you

abscription abscorption by overdosing on prescription medicine

absentence a person convicted of a crime who does not receive a sentence

ab sloot a slow goodbye | when somebody is dying you visit them knowing it may be the last time you say goodbye

absol very hot [absolute + sol]

abso loot to rob everything

absolut an absolute utter(ance)

absorbet to be won over by sweets | to be bribed with sweets

absort loot to rob nearly everything [+ 'sort of']

abstale to eat food too quick and feel the effect

abstrick an illusion [abstract + trick]

abstrict a one-track mind [abstract + strict]

absubtract to scrap an idea | to remove a view

abundle-duct to take too much | the act of gluttony

a bundle-of-nerve flowers to give somebody a bouquet in hope you are forgiven

abuse to pringle

ac animal collective

ACAD a chocolate a day

acadenims formal-looking jeans

accamodate to have a date online by webcam | a chat with a new friend on webcam [accommodate + camera + date]

accelary food which is high in water content [accelerate + celery]

accelebration of how dates come round fast, e.g. the birthday is an accelebration when you get old, so much it stops being a celebration

acceler rate the rate of speed

accelerights the need for speed

accelery to eat celery fast [accelerate + celery]

accell to break out of a prison cell | to break loose [accelerate + cell]

accessarts intriguing and artistic accessories, e.g. a rubber ring worn as a belt

accessence the essence of things being easy and available

accessence axe for **accessence** to be axed | for something to stop being **accessence**

accessore broken access

acchord sing praise to

accomodera reasonable accommodation [+ moderate]

accomplush to successfully grow hair

accordion according to

accramp to feel a cramp coming on

accrimp when your hair starts to frizz in wet or windy conditions

accumole-in-hole definite profit [accumulate + mole-in-the-hole]

accure an accurate cure | the correct treatment

ace's in pot the rise and fall of fortune [insp. *the game 'Ace's in The Pot' where fortunes rise and fall quickly*]

aceness awesome

acenest an awesome home

achive to make a chive sauce | to season [achieve + chive]

ACID a call in demand

acidick a sour tasting dick

acid rain very sour juice from a fruit

acid-said to have said something with sourness | said with hate [*acid is a compound usually having a sour taste*]

acoustic nerve the tuning of an acoustic guitar

acoustic nerver to never be in good tune

acquiz to question a skill | to question a way something is done [acquisition + quiz]

acreager still playing the field [+ acreage]

acre baker the mass production of wheat and its intolerance

acrobatch a team of flexible workers [+ acrobat]

acrobet to bet only for entertainment [acrobat + bet]

actcont to act as if you hold the answer to everything [+ contact]

activote to activate a vote | to vote on something

actrivial trivial actions

AD and dead

ad access denied

adaptoire an adaptable repertoire

ad-choc to eat chocolate for diabetic reasons [ad-hoc + chocolate]

add commercialism and consumption of ownership | luxury of products and new artificial foods to suit chemical appetites

addias to add days

addiol to dial the wrong number

addis ababa another child | another baby [*Addis Ababa is a place in Ethiopia*]

addistinct adding distance makes something more distinct

addo to add another

addradate to aggravate a date

addrisk a dodgy internet address

addro to type the wrong address in on internet and a peculiar site comes up

addye to add a dye | to add a colour

adell a person called Adele using a Dell computer

adepot to adopt a depot | to make temporary housing out of a warehouse

ad hockey a play in ad hoc

adidas as I said

adivase a vase with a tribal pattern

ad libera to impro | to drift away from set instructions [ad lib + liberate]

ad-libido role play | sexual improvisation

adlog when your alarm clock goes off and you set it again at a later time in order to have more time to sleep

admirror to admire the appearance looking back at you

adollt an adult doll

adollterer a man committing **adolltery**

adollteress a woman committing **adolltery**

adolltery to commit adultery with a doll

adope to be doped | to become dope, e.g. the idea was adope

adopetion adopted by dope

adrows drawn on eyebrows

adrift to feel drunk | to have lost it

adull a dull adult

advans more room [van + advance]

advent to breathe again [+ vent]

adventilations the hype of certain calendar days [advent + ventilations]

advento the start of an adventure

ae animal equality

aeride to travel by plane

aero aeroplane

aeroar the environmental effects of aircraft [+ **aero**]

aerodrummage when your ears pop

aerogrump a moody person on a plane who will complain and rant about bad service [+ **aero**]

aerosion to break off a relationship when on a plane | to fall out with someone when on an aeroplane [+ **aero**]

aerot a planes engine comes on fire causing the plane to explode in the air [+ **aero**]

aerota a timetable of flights [+ **aero**]

aerow to fly a boat | or to let a boat sail itself | to let the wind be in control [+ **aero**]

aerscare to be scared of travelling by air [+ **aero**]

aerusty a rusty aeroplane | an old aeroplane [+ **aero**]

aesthetuck suck in the aesthetics

afelder to send an elder away from their original surroundings, e.g. afelder the elder to a care home [afield + elder]

afer dri to be in a different state from the one you were in before drinking

affair a hat worn to the side

affcotdeath when you fart in a public place and hope for people to ignore it and keep talking but they don't and there is complete silence [insp.

*Roger Profanisaurus:
'affcot': the sort of fart
you hope people will
talk after*]

affear to inflate the
cost [oppo. **affork**]

affen after then

affens to talk about
the olympics in a
negative manner
[Athens + affend]

affiction fiction with
affect

afflask for a body to
always be a warm
temperature [affluent +
flask]

affluent with ongoing
flu | to have an ongoing
illness

afflunk comfortable
in failing [affluent +
flunk]

affoe you have so
many friends you could
do with making some of

them enemies [afford +
foe]

affork to put a hole in
it | to fork it, e.g. affork
the pie to let heat get in
[afford + fork]

afreaka oh my!

afried to be in so
much fear your brain
fries

afro to go after

afrodisia to be an
aphrodisiac for afro
hair

afro duck when you
only see a head pass in
the window

afterm the post
terms [+ after]

ag again

agar aug the change
of colour from white to
pink to yellow [insp.
agaricus augustus]

agar bis to brown slightly [insp. agaricus bisporus]

agar bit almond-like smell [insp. agaricus bitorquis]

agar haemo to flush blood-red [insp. agaricus haemorrhoidarius]

agar mac aniseed smell [insp. agaricus macrospores]

agar pla to avoid [insp. agaricus playcomyces]

agar sil to stain pink [insp. agaricus silvaticus]

agar silvicola the change in colour from white, to yellow, to orange [insp. agaricus silvicola]

agar xan to stain yellow [insp. agaricus xanthodermus]

age agenda period of the agenda

agendamen people who are top of the agenda

agendate date of the agenda

agendocide to not have done the list of things you were supposed to do

agenera the time of a generation

ages usa the pork industry in the USA [+ sausages]

aggest to gesture anger | to express anger [aggressive + gesture]

AGI a good idea

agnos tick to not believe in time | to not live by conventional time

agob to talk about love | to talk of love

agrainst to have your skin against a rough texture, e.g. your face was agrainst his stubbly face [against + grain]

agrin to carry on smiling [again + grin]

agun ability

ah not secure

ahoy a good sleep

AHS all hail snail [see **AHW**]

AHW all hail whale

AIDS retro virus [insp. *the retro generation*]

AIL animals in laboratories

air bloom a garden in bloom [air loom + bloom]

airper to try and tidy up air pollution [+ repair]

airplan a plan (up) in the air

air play breathing exercises

air player person who performs or joins in with breathing exercises

air stair a level of breathing

aka uncreative [oppo. **maka**]

akimboat to akimbo but placing the hands in changeable ways on the hips as if posing

akra pregnant [Na. pak.ra: soil (fertile)]

al animal liberation | alphabeat

ala a good girl

alahcrity godspeed
[alacrity + allah]

alan sugar a
commercial sugar
brand

alarm cock to insert
an alarm cock into the
anus or vagina and wait
for the alarm to go off

alas lost at sea again
[see **las**]

alascat a white cat [+
Alaska]

alasgators sensitive
teeth | to take longer to
eat

alaskar a cold car

alaskat a black cat [+
Alaska] [insp. **alascat**]

alba to scoop
[*wandering albatross
scoop squid from the
sea*]

albertus all be good
until it hurt us

albin a white bin
[+ albino]

album a series of
bums [*an album has a
series of songs*]

albumen a group of
dirty albums

albuster to dress up
as a ghost | to give a
ghostly look [ghost
buster + albus]

alce back

alcohey to socialise
on alcohol

alcohola the good
feeling of alcohol

alcope to cope with
having no alcohol after
being addicted to it

alder an older
pregnant woman

alearnt to have great
interest in [alert +
learn(t)]

ale-long a while after drinking

alemon ale having a lemon taste

alev at (a) level

alev trev at a friendly level [insp. **alev**]

algae a good pain [insp. **algosh**]

algae bra a bra worn for too long and shows signs of dirt or bacteria

algebra a bra which comes undone or is difficult to undo

algim to pretend to be in pain [see **algosh**]

algore-rithms gorey algorithms

algorise for a pattern to show

algosh the hurt | the experience of pain

alice in winterland *Alice in Wonderland* walking in the winter wonderland

aline alien but conventional | strange but understood [oppo. **a line nation alien**]

a line nation alien to find the linear alien | to find something strange in which should be unstrange | to find something in an area it should not be in, e.g. a mug inside the stomach is a line nation alien

alist to name

alkaida a drunk kaleidoscope | to have blurry eyes from drinking alcohol [insp. **alkite**]

alkite a drunk kite; one which does not fly very well or is over the air limit (or would it be under?)

allaid having sexual intercourse with friends [allies + laid]

all-am love for all [+ amore]

alleg clock a prisoner's kerfew time [(prison tag on) leg + alarm clock]

allergy an alluring allegory

allergy tablets printed allergies (usually in the form of a book) [see **allergy**]

allevibrate to carry on the sorrow | to spread sorrow [alleviate + vibrate]

alleycats backstreet boys

alley key a short cut

allie to share a lie

alligato to take a short cut by going down an alley [alligator + alley + gate]

allinear to be part of the trend | to follow the trend

allined to join the line [allied + line]

all-kite high-flying | all about status

alloaf to try out a different bread

alloan to look at different loans

all oar nothing it all means nothing

allob to throw something different (into the mix)

allocal a different local

allog for a bird to move from one perch to another

allord a different lord
[+ allo]

allotrend to have a
different trend [+ allo]

allowand to be
allowed something
special

allowd allowed to be
loud

allowed zone

all spice ill space

all wall no way out

allympic when there
are too many people
down the **back street**

alo a good boy

aloan in debt

aloe lonely

alor to say hello [+
oral]

alore lost love

aloss lost

alphabet spaghetti
never grow out of being
a kid

alpha decay when
teeth begin to feel furry
after drinking or eating
sugary produce
[radioactive power +
alpha decay + decay]

alpha spag alphabet
spaghetti

alpha-sprout one who
is beginning to learn
the alphabet

alquerque roof tile
[*Alquerue is a game and
its boardgames lines are
incised into the roof of
the tiles of the ancient
temple at Kurna, as an
honour*]

als store [insp. **alsa**]

alsa restore [insp.
sassafras]

alsas sandals [insp. sandalwood]

alternating currant to eat fruit for nourishment | to match fruit on a fruit machine [+ currant]

alternaval to roll the belly | to belly dance [alternate + naval]

altgr to grow alternative(ly)

alturd altered

aluss lust

aly always

alycal to expose a bright red patch [when *the alydus calcaratus bug takes flight it exposes a bright red patch on its abdomen*]

am mornings

am a fist amethyst

amanda palmer to have a man eat out of your hand | to have a man wrapped around the finger

amarry the combining of the colours red, white and blue [America + marry]

ambalance for an ambulance to go speeding round a corner [+ balance]

ambidexter a debate [+ ambidextrous]

ambigoon an ambiguous goon

amblaze to start a fire

ambolt bell an alarm | an emergency sound | a siren [+ amber]

ambrr oranges lacking juice

ambulant a casualty in an ambulance

ambulanterns the lights on an ambulance

ambulend an emerging helping hand

amcoc rarely seen out of doors [insp. *the american cockroach is rarely seen out of doors*]

amen our men

amentalc to put on a holy mentality

amer-amore to love America

amgrand I am old, but grand, I am history, I am respected, live long respected (grandma)

amino not at all mean

amish a mission

amishmash to try out living the Amish lifestyle [+ mish-mash]

amitation the action of an amateur [+ imitation]

AM, like PM? the amore of passion inside me is questioning

ammoneia battery cage farming [ammonia + money]

ammonia-lisa when fast-food businesses add ammonia to children's foods [+ Mona Lisa]

amoodment the amusement of being in a mood

amoreamore double love

amountain a big amount, so big you gasp for air

ampar protein [insp. avocado]

ampere-shaped a sound problem | to have blown a fuse

amperspam unnecessary additions [ampersand + spam]

ample crumble a piece of technology on its last legs (near to being dead) [ample + apple crumble]

amplesand more than sufficient

amsterdam tiles the nightlife in Amsterdam

amsterdazed to be high on cannabis in Amsterdam

amulot a lot of good luck [+ amulet]

amuseum a place of old laughs | laughs about the olden days | the atmosphere

anaconda blunder to feel as if the whole world has eaten you up alive

ancest pest an evil family member

ancestory a story about the history of a family

anchin a long chin [+ anchor]

anchor a bit of weight

anchord to leave at the correct time [anchor + chord]

anchore the chore of being in authority

andacon and a conundrum

andaid to hold hands

android to refuse to andaid

andyhandle a handy handle

andypan a handy pan

andypant a handy breather | a needed break

anecdate a date as an anecdote | a medical appointment

anec-do an anecdote in action

anecdoh a failed anecdote

angelina bell arena a classical dance and music arena

angelinear innocent | a do-nothing-wronger

anger manger a box of dark magic | voodoo

angio both female and male, e.g. the top was angio so I shared it with my brother [*angiosperms have both female & male trees together and separate*]

angola own goal

angristle the energy of an angry person | of an angry situation

angrr to walk away in anger [Na. ngrr: root]

angry blood cells deathly fights in prison cells

animal a prisoner

animat to roll up a mat

animawhom a human who does not know they are **humanimal**

anime flat shoes

animillions millions of animals

animossity to hate using a toilet if it's not your own [animosity + moss]

ANIS available now in stores

anise cap blue-green

ankle banner a prison tag

ankult converse

annail a nail in the anal

annar not a female now

anni not a male now

annilav the love of light coloured spaces [+ vanilla]

annorack no cleavage

announcindered to be announced as cindered, e.g. at a funeral the body would be announcindered

anocon to make a snowman [L. build: condo]

anoint to place semen in a vagina or anus [anoint also means to smear a sacred oil on a body]

anonessential nonessential is not essential [+ anon]

anonynom to be unaware of what you are eating

anoracksick when an anorak is too tight and makes you feel sick

anosoma another body

anotam a woman who is knowledgeable in anatomy

anotim a man who is knowledgeable in anatomy

anownen always now and then

anstarticas starshaped icicles

anteeshire one who does not wear or is against wearing teeshirts [+ anti]

antelobes big earlobes

anteloop to crawl around in circles [antelope + loop]

antennerve when the body shakes after having caffeine [antenna + nerve]

antholo yo to collect sponsorships [+ anthology]

anthon hand

anthony hands

anthroax a bad throat

anti pants to not like wearing underwear

anticipation the working of ants in a team

anticipatron a patron of anticipation

antick a well-played trick [antic + tick]

antique olive a dried up bogey left on a surface

antisimo to jump and stomp on crunchy autumn leaves

antisipotion brewing anticipation [+ potion]

antlurgy to feel your way around in the dark [antlers + lurgy]

AN:US available now: udder sin [insp. **ANIS**]

ANY are not you

any ing any doing

any ling any audio story | any lyric

anybodyna desperate for any body | desperate for anyone

AOAD an orange a day

A ok are you ok?

AOYSTER being ashamed of yourself soon turns energy rotten

apachike bike to get around | to have anyone for sexual companionship | to have everyone for sexual activity [Kic. apachike: whatever] [+ 'local bike']

apachike like to like whatever | to be able to like anything | no highstandards [Kic. apachike: whatever] [+ like]

A (past) one letter past Z, two letters past Y, three letters past X, four letters past W, five letters past V, six letters past U, seven letters past T, eight letters past S, nine letters past R, ten letters past Q, eleven letters past P, twelve letters past O, thirteen letters past N, fourteen letters past M, fifteen letters past L, sixteen letters past K, seventeen letters past J, eighteen letters past I, nineteen letters past H, twenty letters past G, twenty one letters past F, twenty two letters past E, twenty three letters past D, twenty four letters past

C, twenty five letters
past B

ape cape a very hairy
body

apen to write with a
pen | to handwrite

a pick-pocalypse the
end of a world when
something is stolen, e.g.
what a pick-pocalyse it
was when you got your
bag stolen which
contained your flight
tickets to get back to
France to get married

aporeatus a skin
cleanser [apparatus +
pore]

appara disability
aids, e.g. a hearing aid
[+ apparatus]

apparat apparently
they have rats

ap-parent
apparently, the one in
charge [+ parent]

appeal to peel an
apple

appelsap to find
water

appendick feels like
something is sticking
in the appendix | feels
like the appendix is
sticking out

appendixie pixie to
add something to make
it more magical

appinch to steal an
app (a mobile
application)

apple energy

applegut a gut full of
apples

apple-pay bed to pay
someone to make beds,
e.g. at a hotel [see
apple-pie room]

apple-pie room a
way of tidying a room to
prevent the person from
messing it up

apple score the main score [+ apple core]

applie apple pie

applus a good response [plus + applause]

appolo for an app (a mobile application) to be in constant use

appre to be a representative for an app (a mobile application)

appropoet a mainstream poet who is studied in schools

appunch to get rid of or bad mouth an app (a mobile application)

apricot to appreciate rest [+ cot]

aprigut a gut full of apricots

aprong to pick up something using tissue [apron + prong]

apse to go ape

apt opt for an application

apu a shop keeper [insp. The Simpsons]

aqualung to be able to hold your breath for a long time under water

a queue a waiting room with no chairs

ar animals rights

arabia a ray of bi/bia(s)

arcade fire the rage of gambling

arcav an underground shopping centre [arcade + cave]

arcave a house of archives | a museum

archaecoli to look around for signs of ecoli poisoning [+ archaeology]

archaeoli to look around somebody else's house or work area for evidence [+ archaeology]

archivade a well lit up archive | a well organised archive | an exciting archive

arcode copper and silver

arcor serious gambling [arcade + hardcore]

arctic monkeys polar bears

are our

a red worm a hot link | an important connection

are hola to touch the breast area [areola + hola]

a-re i the space of the person [Jap. a-ra: measure of area] [+ RE: (subject) + I]

argos wait until your number comes up | the objective of a raffle

argy badgy meaningless statements [argy bargy +badge]

arial to find out which direction the phone is ringing from [arrow + dial]

arishuttle to philosophize when walking [+ *Aristotle*] arizona fresh air

arm army

armadillo arms up in the air

armash to fit out a shop | to shelve

armask to fit out a kitchen [insp. **armash**]

arm bra an arm sling

army arm

aroma neu the prediction of a tumour [+ neuroma]

arose a rising flower [oppo. **erose**]

aroxy slippy rocks upwards

arran to run in a direction

arrest to have something safely leaning against the wall or surface

arriva arrive at

arriver to arrive at a river

arrow a bird flying towards something or somewhere

arrow away to go in the opposite direction

arrow-row to row to a certain direction

arrow row row to row following the arrow of the compass

arrows point to come together

arrust to be left to rust

arscichive an archive of science

arsy sweeten [insp. clove]

art and literature brown [insp. *Trivial Pursuit colour*]

art bear a soft touch

artchive an archive of art

artet fungal | dry [insp. alerce]

artheritis art which is unable to move and is hard to take in [arthritis + art]

artic seal silver and white | grey and white

artistrial for an artist to be on trial

artition an art exhibition

artive to move into art [+ arrive]

artnam no mantra

art sake because it looks good

artshma for a piece of artwork to be too crowded | a piece of artwork unable to breathe

artword image and text together | the pictorial of text

arulil to tell children

to be aware of [insp. arum lily]

as association

asbestoe an infected toe

asbestos as best as

asbethos a poisonous point | a toxic area [asbestos + ethos]

ASBO and still be 'oh'

ascillic the ascent of acidity levels

ASDA a sunny day awaits | as that is

asdf to have learnt qwert [see **zxcv**]

asec by two, e.g the animals went sec asec, hurrah, hurrah

ash burgers pates of dead beings [+ ash burgees]

as jazz as it goes

as jive as it dances | how it moves

as jizz as it flows

ash not as it used to be

ashbody a burnt body

ash mellow when ashes are scattered

as in ass quiet way for saying "assassin"

ask and estimate buying from stalls – to ask the price then estimate its value

ask dafter to 'ask after' by asking daft questions or in a situation where the ask after is irrelevant, e.g. it would be an ask dafter to ask how Jay is because we know cancer means unwell

as long as a tape measure not as long as a piece of string | a set duration [oppo. 'as long as a piece of string']

a snowman in the sun an unworthy product

aso and so on

aspar uncommon

asparagraph an aspiring paragraph

asparagus a spare paragraph

asparagust to aspire with disgust

as path pathetic

aspathetics pathetic aesthetics

aspiratus the aspiring apparatus

aspirint a fast acting aspirin

as plus an extra

as ply implied

as pus weeping (from a) wound

ASS a sock society

assalt when there is too much salt on the food it wrecks it

asse assess the asses

assembroid to leave an ass print on glass [ass + embroid]

assisted bounce to be bounced on a bouncy castle by someone else's bounce

assk a half-arsed question | to not ask properly

assorbet to make pudding [assort + sorbet]

asstray to sit on glass [+ ashtray]

astep to have a dream about falling

asterisk the risk of 'and'

asthma after the mass

astick time for cooling the skin [acetic acid + as tick] [see **lacetic**]

astrolug to drag the feet, walking around with no energy, scuffing the shoes, hoping to fall into another space where you will float and cycle like the moon

astro nought no gravity

a-sukarma the earth's lifecycle is yours too [Jap. asukara: earth colour] [+ karma]

at ambient

atari threatened with imminent capture

ated to talk someone around to avoid any problems [+ tred]

a tent tion an attention-seeking tent

athird by three

athleak to sweat from exercise

athro the back of the throat [see **bethro**]

athsoma an athletic body

at-hum in melody

atlass a lady who travels globally

A (to) one letter to B, two letters to C, three letters to D, four letters to E, five letters to F, six letters to G, seven letters to H, eight letters to I, nine letters to J, ten letters to K, eleven letters to L, twelve letters to M, thirteen letters to N, fourteen letters to O, fifteen letters to P, sixteen letters to Q, seventeen letters to R, eighteen letters to S, nineteen letters to T, twenty letters to U, twenty one letters to V, twenty two letters to W, twenty three letters to X, twenty four letters to Y, twenty five letters to Z

a toaster for a teacup when water runs dry

A to B car an old car which just about works

atmoatsphere the aura of an inner circle

atomat a cherry tomato

atomato a red atom

aton banan backache | slipped disk

a-tool anything that can be sat on

at plus spare

atslantis a cold stroke [atlantis + slant]

attainer a pregnant woman [+ attain]

attax the attack of paying tax

attendon to move the tendon [+ attend]

attenshun to dislike or turn away from attention

attention spam to pretend to listen

attint to only express a hint of attention

at-tire tired looking clothes [attire + tired] [oppo. **attoyr**]

attitude at a latitude of

attouch to make two things touch [attach + touch]

attoyr quirky clothes, e.g. a picture frame for a necklace [oppo. **attire**] [+ toy]

attrack on the track to becoming attractive

attrain to get on a train [+ attain]

attrickt fool someone into being attracted to you | to pull someone in by being devious

attuc to steal lunch [attack + tuc]

au burn burn when a fire begins to stop burning and there's a brown colour [auburn + burn]

au haiku a haiku based on the autumn season

au volt a teacher of electronics [*au vol is a cry used to encourage a hawk to fly*]

auckland awkward [*Auckland is an island of New Zealand*]

audance to interact with the audience

audig to dig out a problem in an audit

auga to have thick flakes of dandruff or a dry skin condition [insp. kauri]

aumehanol automatic melancholy [see **mechanol**]

aunt sue a souvenir shop in a family museum

aura or a

auri auri unattractive [insp. auricularia auricila-judae]

auri bori to carve your name into wood [*'bori' means any of the various Japanese techniques for carving and engraving*] [+ aura]

ausatrail Australia

ausco withstand [insp. palm lily]

auski threat [insp. black gin]

authorn for somebody to bad-mouth an author

autism the autumn holidays of halloween and bonfire

auto autumn

autumn to walk

auxa survive [insp. grass-tree]

auxalaugh to laugh with someone | an additional laugh [auxiliary + laugh]

avant-garden the art of experimenting in the garden

ave age par age

average par

avernue a new par

avoid laundrette wear your clothes inside out

avoil to avoid ale

awe some some dread

awhailable highly available [+ whale]

awham and away to be blown away by a sound

axedent an accident

which was really on purpose

axeno a strange accent [Gk. xeno: alien]

ay aren't you

aya raw spirit | natural energy

ayar when a scarf is so long it touches the floor | sweeping the earth with warmth

ayax space

azerbaj has a badge

azerbajon has a badge on

azu haw blue spots [insp. *the azure hawker dragonfly has blue spots*]

Bb

B basic | blue

B *pic* sunglasses worn on a 90 degree angle

b2f back to front

ba basket-case

ba-ba basket-ball

BAB build a boat

babaskint a poor child

bable a miniature bible

babnormal an abnormal baby

baboat a little boat [oppo. **uboat**]

baby a four legged being

baby bat a little black

babysit to look after the earth

baby spice a little spice | mild

bacarden to put something back in the **den**

bacardi back in the garden | to put a jacket (e.g. cardigan) back on

bachieve to compose [achieve + *Bach*]

back alce

back-bank a dodgy finance dealing

back-book a book which is put to the back of the shelf | a book of which is rarely read

backet a soiled nappy
[back + bucket]

backhandaid to have
damaged the back of
the hand

backpack to sit on
someone's shoulders

backsigh to sigh
without a person seeing

back street a side
street | an alley way

backstreet boys
people who hang round
the back streets [insp.
back street]

bacterri the power of
bacteria [+ battery]

bad an uncomfortable
bed

badapt to not adapt
well

bad-aware unable to
sleep well due to the
bed being **bad**

bad-bid a bad vote | a
bad act

badda budge when
something bad will not
go away

badder to be
desperate for the toilet

badess a bad female

badet a bad male

badger gert

badger baiter a
murderer

badgit a gadget
attached to the clothes
or bag, e.g. a spy
camera

badissimal bad
medication

baffer the machine in
a public toilets, e.g. a
tampon machine or a
condom machine [insp.
buffer] [+ bath]

bag luck and skill [insp. *the game 'Backgammon'*]

bagafer to transfer bags

bagaferris for a bag to break and so you try and catch the falling shopping

bagag to be given lots of agro

bagam a game of chance [+ 'Backgammon']

bag ears ears with big lobes

bagel a morning swim in a rubber ring

baggy trousers lucky trousers

bagoggle to be getting lots of attention

bagogglue to give a lot of attention | to give fixed stares

bagpoise carrying bags

bagpuss a cat carrier

bagpuss bagpoise to not be happy with **bagpoise**

bagree to agree a lot | to nod a lot

bagroom cloakroom | cubbyhole

bagtag the brand of a bag

baguette a bag of food

BAH build a house

baharma light harm [+ Bahamas]

bahe bad head

bah lung to smoke

bah lunge to smoke a lot

bahrain to feel sheepish

bahummer bugger one who eats a lot of hard sweets and mints

bailey bail

bailord one who is behind on bills [oppo. **billord**]

bain multi [insp. tree aloe]

bainblut dirty bath water

bake-bike hot steel | hot metal

bake-bread to put on weight [oppo. **break-bread**]

balkan bulk many accordions

ball a good time

ball-ache the ache after exercising

ball bladder to curse

ballboard an up-todate billboard [+ 'on the ball']

balldoon unable to make friction

ball-dozer one who bores when talks | a very slow talker

ballet for a balloon to float in the sky

ballimic to throw the ball up (in the air) [+ bulimic]

ball-joint a good connection

ball lot an array | a pile of balls

ballo to play a different game

balloat for a balloon to burst

ballof a league

balloi to blow up a balloon to a very big size

ballooney a deflated person who suddenly becomes hyper

ballow to blow up a balloon [blow + bellow]

ball-point a good point

ball-point pen a written essay where intriguing points are made

ball-polar up and down times [+ bi-polar]

ballquet a bunch of balloons [+ bouquet]

ball-rallet fast ballet

ball-room (to be) slow on the feet

balls soon to become round

ball-to-ball from cogto-cog

bally cat for a cat to stand on two legs

bally dog for a dog to stand on two legs

baloose a blouse too small around the breast

balti a locked door [+ bolt]

bambelt a very thick, heavy or big belt

bambi a piece of cloth used as a belt [insp. **bambelt**]

banack to have a bar in the back [+ knack]

ba na na cannot come (in) | is not welcome | cannot come due to a ridiculous reason

bananandsand bright yellow sand | extremely hot sand

banchor a bank loan
[+ anchor]

bandada to walk
across **bananandsand**

bandage bondage
gone wrong

band-bond to get on
with someone due to
having similar music
taste | a relationship
built on musical
interest

bandem metallic
green blue and yellow
colours [insp. *the
demoiselle dragonfly:
the male has metallic
green or blue body and
the female has green
body and yellowish
wings*]

banditto an equal
prohibition

bandrage to have a
hate for a certain band

banged-up nose to
have a wounded nose

banguet a banquet of
loud music

banjoke a comical
song played on a banjo

banker a baker who
uses currants [insp.
currency]

bankip to build up
dreams | to have more
sleep

bankit to cash in

bankitty to store it in
the kitty | to put money
away

bankle an ankle
bracelet

banklet a discount
store

bankuet to choose a
loan [**banquet** + bank]

bannistairs stairs
out of order

banquet a list or
collection of
prohibitions

ban shud to ban the husband from the house

banta thankful banter

BAP build a portfolio

bapi to release fire | of fire [insp. the jack pine tree]

baqa to drink plenty of water [Kic. baq: thin]

bar barry

baramadamn to eat when you are not supposed to

BARBERS bring a radish, bring every radish sprout

barcade a bar and a casino | a place of betting and drinking

bare banjo a stringed instrument without its strings

baredigrae a face which only expresses mardi gras

barf a scarf too warm or too thick that it makes you feel too hot, suffocated or sick

barge a bar that sells alcohol to under-aged persons

bark a security guard [*bark is also the outer protective layer of the tree*]

bark chew chewing gum

bark door to put something in the dark | to put something on stand-still until a more convenient time

bark hark a call of joy

bark zirk a bizarre call | a bizarre noise

barlow (to be) low on barley

barmy a bar full of crazy and up-forpartying people, e.g. The Clements is a barmy

barn bowl indoor bowls in the evening

barn dunse a bumpkin who knows nothing other than barn dancing

barney purple and green, e.g. I'll have a barney (a grape and kiwi) drink please (see **mr blobby** for another refreshing option)

barret to dance on a bar surface

barrk different textures | different characters [*bark is either rough, smooth or fissured*] [see **bark**]

barrot a wheelbarrow left to rot

barrot pot to use a barrot as a plant pot

bar-row to bar someone from borrowing something | to bar something from being borrowed

barry bar

bartandem an arrangement made at a bar

bartend to sell alcohol

barter to try and get served at a very busy bar

base-in the main supply of water [basin + base]

basemount a mountain base

bashette a travel kettle

ba sil a person with quirky character

basin a bucket which never moves from an area

basink an over-flown basin

bask contain

baskee to contain balls

baskervault to jump up [basketball + vault]

basket containet

basket-ball a good team | a good finding | a good catch

basketcase to have a (court) case

basket-ville a mini supermarket, e.g. Tesco Extra is a basket-ville

basket wedge to get pleasure from having a wedgie

baskins tight socks [buskins + basque]

baski-vile terribly tight clothing

basstard an annoying bass sound

baste the taste before the current taste

basun an area for somewhere to dry or where something dries in the sun

bat a boat sailing at night

bata eternal life [insp. yew]

bat & ball to serve a good conversation | to be of good service [Hin. bat: speech]

batch people speaking at the same time [Hin. bat: speech]

batch-clutch two or more people holding each other tight

batchmania the collection of a batchmanic's items [see **batchmanic**]

batchmanic the act of buying items in bulk

bath lab

bathaw to dive deep [Gk. Batho: depth] [+ thaw]

bath boom an over flown bath

batherage a beverage in the bath whilst bathing

bathermath laidback calculations

bath gaf a lifeguard supervisor

bathlantic the flood of a **bath boom**

bathought deep thought [Gk. batho: depth]

bathquet a swimming pool centre with more than one pool

BATHROOM big apples talk hoods rivet orange or mint

bathtermath math more relaxed | an estimated calculation

bathtub relax

bathtub of ice-cre relax and pig out [+ icecream]

bat hung when everything is 'upside down'

batman man with a bat

batoo in too deep [Gk. batho: depth]

batsibicalat sabbatical

bat-smack to strike hard

batter fosh battered to fosh

battery pay as you go

battle to bat the eye lashes

battlefat a war on food | a war against food

battle of ghastings battle of the haste and the ghastly

batty batter

batwoman woman with a bat [insp. **batman**]

bauhaus a barmy house ("bah")

bawonasmi smiles all round

baybe a beach babe (female)

bayboy a beach babe (male)

bay con to look through the window

baylet a little view of the sea [insp. **eyelot**]

BB be brave | be beautiful

bbb three in a row [see **O's and X's**]

bbbb four in a row [see **FIAR**]

BBC newspope

bb car a street racing car

BB goon an owner of a BB gun

BB gun a 'bestbefore' date

B book the book you plan to read after the **A book**

BC before crystals | a bar code

B car business car

BD before dime

b-ding-ding butler service

be being

beach bitch

beacone for a fire to rise high, flames form into a point [beacon + cone]

bead a bed

beady eyes *come to bed eyes*

beakonomics financial bills [beak + economics]

beakshelf a food shelf

beard be hard

beardare a light dare

bear hands hands that massage well

bear hug tight gripped hug

bear off after negotiation [insp. *the game of 'Backgammon'*]

bear on in negotiation [insp. **bear off**]

beartruth a light or fluffy truth

beary big and cuddly

beast be a star

beaten eaten too much

beatroot the place where your beat came from | your musical interests

beautiful simful

beauty sim

beauxeno beautifully strange [Gk. xeno: alien]

becks a pecking beak

bed kipper | breed

bed-aware to be aware [Lit. bad-awar: windbrought]

bed-a-wars arguments brought on by the current situations, e.g. recession [see **bedaware**]

bedbank to pay for a bed for the night

bedbug a despised bed companion

bedgie a room in a budget hotel

bedigator a person who is snappy when just woken

bedigrot to tuck the duvet under the feet and wrap yourself in

bed in a shed currently not looking for a relationship

beditor a lazy editor

bedkin a child asleep

bedouin soundclash a clash of alarms – when more than one alarms goes off | to be woken up by somebody's snoring

bedroam to look for a place to sleep

bedrolm a temporary sleeping place [realm + roll-out-bed]

bedwetter to not be able to get well

bedwomb to plan to get pregnant

beef big

beefi disease

beeG's a group of grateful people [insp. BG] [+ bee]

bee gee broken glass

beers bias

beesness business in Manchester [*the bee is the animal of Manchester*]

beet the buzz of a bee

beeth baby teeth

beetle largest order [*beetles are the largest order of insects*]

beet route where are you located? | where is it located? | it is to be located

bee wee a beetroot coloured wee after eating lots of it

beerwhile a long time drunk

beerwig to spill or pour beer onto someone's head | to throw a drink in someone's face

befear to fear before even trying

beforce the force before the current force

beg egg to desperately want a baby

begloved gloves that are dearly loved

beg nei to depend only on luck | to happen only by luck [insp. the game 'Beggar My Neighbour']

begrin the beginning of a grin

begun to be available

behe bedhead

behoney became

beirut a beach [*bay'root: root of bay: sand*]

belate blatantly belated

belay to rest the head on a stomach

belb belly button

belch a toilet [+ bench]

beleaf to believe something is going to fail | to believe something is going to fall

beleave to disacciate from what you already know [+ believe]

belgium bell shaped

bella bell service

bell base bell on the hour

bell covert to ring a bell and nobody comes

bell-jangle the 1:00 AM bell

bell one the"quarter-past" bell

bell overt to ring a bell and somebody comes

bellow a "brilliant yellow" colour

bell pepper to be awake at night and hear the bell, and be shocked at the time - "a visitor to the ear at this time?"

bell peppered for decibels to perpperspray your ears

bell three the "quarter-to" bell

bell two the "halfpast" bell

bells to it balls to it, it has nothing to do with faith

belly the movement of bells | vibrations

belly flap stomach flab rolls

belongong a background sound in the home environment, e.g. the boiler's hum was a belongong

belt waist line

beltable for something to have to be tight (and perhaps can be loosened after)

belter viz to be cheered up from reading **Viz**

belunge to grab your belongings [+ lunge]

ben ten minutes [insp. *duration of the game 'Beggar My Neighour'*]

benchmark time for a break

bene a benefit lacking fitness

benjam a sweet sauce

bergen to score in points [*'Bergen' is a point scoring game*]

berk a curb made of bark

besee to curl into a ball

besemen worthy of making a child [+ beseem]

best be(there)st

bestil best 'til

best of cluck said before pregnant person biths child – as cluck is what hens do, and they lay more than anyone

best of clutch best to take it one step at a time | to wish well before a driving test

betastock a second delivery

betch a pedigree(d) woman on the arm of a man who bets high amounts at casinos

bethel organic | nature

bet-hell mcdonalds [*bethel* means '*house of god*']

bethro the front of the throat [see **athro**]

betrayal to take somebody's tray or plate away from them

better a letter of good news

bever age over eighteen

beverly hill a row of pubs

BG bee gee | be grateful

bheith be here with [Iri. Bheith: existence]

bi a person | someone | somebody

BIAS bed in a shed

bias beers

BIC because it's crap

biccy a bin attached to a cupboard door

bick to hiccup and burp

bicket a tin of biscuits, e.g. put the luppers in the bicket and there sprout a bourbonny lass

bickit a dust pan | a vacuum [+ bit]

bicyc-oil to oil a bike

bide a bird that is domestically dependent [bird + abide]

bieber no hate

biesk to hitch a bike ride [+ busk]

biffer a fibber

big beef | pie

big-bag a big mouth

big brother CCTV

big-mug hold requires using all fingers

big red dog big and gentle

bi hay to day dream [see **hay**]

bihe big head

bik the cycle of a book [+ bike]

bil to look up who a piece of work is by

bill too hot [ill + boil]

billabong someone who encounters many problems but bounces back with solutions, e.g. has the aballity to billabong | one who will never stop using a bong

billboard sucker one who is sucked in and easily brought by advertisements

billet doh letter of bill [billet-doux + doe]

billord one who is always on top of paying bills [oppo. **bailord**]

billsy to be released [+ bills]

billusion the cost of an illusion

bin to be looked down upon

binformate to discard information, e.g. the satellite navigation told us where to go so we told it where to binformate itself

bing being

binge to eat from bins or skips | to look in skips for useful objects or materials

binged-up nose a red nose from being in the sun

bingo-wing to be winning at bingo

binstinct to discard an instinct

binterface to not see an edge | to not notice the step [bin + interface]

binvit to bin an invitation | to refuse something

BIO big investment organization

biofuel good energy

biold old biology

biologo DNA cells

biosoch to gag

bip bipolar

bipsyche a psychotic cyclist | a chaotic cyclist | a changing of energies

bira a hard shell [insp. bunya-bunya]

bird sight as the primary sense [*as it is for most birds*]

birdate date of birth

bird in a cage trapped | prison for life

bird in a rib cage trapped to death

birka an all-in-one body suit (to hold the fat in) [+ bra]

bisc-quite rather like Robert Crumb

biscuit brows stubble from shaving the eyebrows

bish a broken dish

bishmit unlikely to be confused with any other [insp. *the bishop's mitre bug is unlikely to be confused with any other*]

bishop diagonal [insp. 'Chess']

bishy a little basic

bistroll to take a walk after eating

bi-ted to talk someone into more than one thing

bit bed bits in the bed

bithrise the body with its 5 senses [bi + thri + rise]

bitter it better be

bitty dust | crumbs

BIYC ball's in your court

bizart bizarre art

biztro a bistro visited by celebrities [+ showbiz]

bizz-buzzard a buzzer in constant use

BK be kind

bk backwards

black and decker to fight and give someone a black eye

black box a british cab

black-cabbage a black cab working all hours

black-eyed bean a dangerous possibility | a possibility of danger [insp. *the black-eyed pirate*]

black flag piracy

black screw a bent
screw

black shoes formality

black sick not
looking good |
something is wrong

blackstop to bang the
head off a wall [insp.
*the game 'Craps' where
a backstop is for the
dice to bounce against*]
[+ black]

black-tail to perch on
a rock or the ground
[insp. *the black-tail
skimmer dragonfly
perches on rock or
ground*]

blackulb for a bulb to
go out and for the room
to go dark

bladdered blood red

bladders wet
ladders|wet trousers

blad red dark red

blaggage the weight
of lies [blag + luggage]

blahcause always
because of the same
thing

blake to cook near a
lake [*William Blake* +
bake]

blakes bakes food
which has no artificial
flavours or
preservatives [*William
Blake* + bakes]

blamish a spot of
blame | to tell a white
lie

blammenstrual to
moan at everything
when it's that time of
the month

bland band a band
lacking oomph

bland date a date of
doing something bland

blandee a bland moment [+ blunder]

bland-gland one who only likes mild food or always eats the same foods | one who never ventures from their comfort zone

blanguage words only spoken to give the person a status

blank tiles any letters [insp. *the blank counters in the game 'Scrabble'*]

blarry tongue the singing of drunk people (especially karaoke)

blasphlegmage wicked phlegm

blast a cheap plaster (one which barely stays on)

blastards to curse and bad mouth about the **blast**

blasteroid to drift back and forth out of a daze

blastick to hit with a stick [+ blast]

blatant to know when/where someone/something will stop

bla wra an inflated bladder

blax a funeral more relaxed about the colour code, allowing people to dress in other colours other than the limitation of black

blazen good hell, hell yeah

blazer hellish

blazer lazer when a bright light hurts the eyes | the cause of light sensitivity

blazure a blazing blue flame [+ azure]

bleak an oil leak ['*b*' *for black*]

bled led poisoning
bledspec blue and red

bleducation to be educated in the understanding of blood, to know how to fight someone to his or her death | to know how to remove a blood stain from material

bleech a blood sucking leech

bleeper a signal

blelhelium an extremely high-pitched voice [Scot. blellum: an indiscreet talker] [+ helium]

blend date where days roll into each other and turn into weeks

blessaid to have given blessings

blessalt to throw salt over the shoulder

blessoma a blessed body

blest-list a bible

blime extra lime

blind date when an event or special date soon turns into an economic comercialisation, e.g. christmas or Wimbledon

blind hughie fast and fun

blindman's huff to guess [+ blindman's bluff]

blind wind to close your eyes when a grit truck passes

blinguist a pieced tongue [bling + linguist]

blip lips dirty lips cheaply speaking

blipponent the opponents of dirty words

bliss is good

blist a long list [+ blister]

blisted to be given a long shift | to have completed hard work [+ blist]

blister a butcher

blisting the pain of working long hours when one minute feels like an hour

blisturn to have taken a wrong turn | a bad choice

blixeno blissfully strange [Gk. xeno: alien]

blizzard a white lizard

blizzness showbiz business | glamour

bload to have blown a load

bloat a boat with too many passengers

bloated a flooded lake

blobnoxious obnoxious for no reason

blobster a dead lobster

blocab to hold on to a taxi so no one else gets it

blocake a square cake

block maria to be blocked by police [*black maria is british slang for a police van*]

block-a-choc to block out chocolate [insp. **chock-a-block-ice**]

blockade the drama in the neighbourhood

blocktipus nowhere to go

block-tongue to watch what you say | to restrict conversation

blodom for the remaining to be distributed [insp. *'Block' dominoes game*]

blog a log with the letter 'b' carved into it [see **clog** and **d'log**]

bloggotry bigotry of a blog

blogster a daily writer who publishes stories and information on the web

blood-beat to be beaten until bleeding

blood-bet a high risk of danger

blood boat a pillarred letterbox swimming down a canal

bloodice a bloody body

blood on your hands if you buy products that are tested on animals

blood-stock injured people | A&E patients bloodsuck on it

bloomering-rang the dance of a flower in bloom | the growth of something colourful

bloom-stock seasonal flowers

blootstrimes blatant rhyming words at end of a poem

blossummon to summon excitement

blot to sit alone on an edge | to sit on in a corner alone [insp. *in*

*'Backgammon' any
piece that sits alone on
a point is called a 'blot'*]

blotch a watch worn
but does not work or is
not set to the correct
time

blottire for alcohol to
make you tired

blow va

blow a kiss va va
voom

blowbillord one who
does not care much
about keeping on top of
bills as is always
behind because he/she
will spend money on
other things than bills

blow bluff to pretend
you lost | a made-up
misfortune

blowest when a ball
heads to the left

blowit when a fielder
does not catch the ball

blowki to puff out
smoke from a cigarette

blown van

blowoff jo the noise
of a creamed penis
getting a handjob

blowout when a ball
is out

blowquet to stamp
on flowers [blow +
bouquet]

blowright when a ball
heads to the right

blox ski and trump
when you are in a
queue and you try to
hold in a fart

blub a wide range
[insp. *the blue bug
feeds on a wide range of
insects*]

blubber boat the
place they keep wine on
a ship | a fishing boat

blube the street lights reflections in puddles

bluce geography [insp. *'Tivial Pursuit' colour*]

blucov blunder cover

blue lube

blue flag calm air

blue hair a river flow

bluemonia feeling ill from feeling blue [+ pneumonia]

blue pear unusual

blue tongue to have swallowed poison

blue-stock dead bodies

bluetube the porn on Youtube

blug a blood sucking bug

blugent an urgent blur

blumble to gargle the water and to make bubbles from doing so

blummer a bloomering bummer

blunder to walk into a wrong-doing

blunder boot under to sleep in your shoes

blunder cover to blow your cover

blunder-snail to be in a deep sleep

blunge to decide to jump at the last minute | to jump too late | to not jump far enough [lunge + blunder]

blunket a blanket for a bunk bed | a singlesize duvet cover

blurbs and the bleeps one-sided insights [insp. *'the birds and the bees'*]

blurdigon wearing a cardigan of blur | not seeing properly | to walk around in a haze

blurgen god knows why it is an emergency

blurrage glazed eyes | blurry images | to not be fully known

blus blue bliss | to pass time traveling on a bus | passing blues | emptiness which will soon shift

blusher an embarrassed leader [+ usher]

blushere to blow something away, e.g. we would blushere the pencil shavings and then on birthdays we would blushere the flame

blut blue and black

blut rut in a rut of feeling blue

bluve unsure love

bly tall, dark and handsome

bly(f)ummy a belly that sticks out more than the butt [belly fluff + tummy]

BO bottle opener

boa a boat

board game to see how fast you can do the ironing

boarded-up window to have no view

boat time has flown

boatabitat habitat of the boat | to hear only the water and the birds

boat-coat a life jacket at sea

boatmeal wood chippings | scraps of wood [+ oatmeal]

boatyar yacht

BOB bee on blossom

bob a part

bobbin scrap parts

bobble part dreamlike

bobble snobs people who think it is low or cheap to wear big bobbles or child-like hair accessories

bobbulk a big part

bob-sledge to have a bobbed haircut where one side is longer than the other

BOC baby of creativity | blend of cultures

boccy a bottle

bock a bike lock

bocket a sick bucket [+ **boccy**]

bodabull to not believe in the **budabulb**

bodims dominated bodies

bodoni a donned body

bodpart to sell a body for parts [see **bodprice**]

bod price to price how much a body is worth (dead or alive) [see **bodpart**]

body-bath a game where you see how long you can hold up your body by gripping onto the sides of the bath with your hands

BOGOF big only gets one fear

boggage swamp

boglong a long time on the bog [+ oblong]

bog tree bug when a bug creeps into your bum whilst you are squatting outdoors

bohemedica to reject pharmaceuticals

bohike a bohemian hike

bohome a bohemian home

BOI burst of inspiration

boil mo to over-power a piece of technology, resulting in it burning out

boils kettles

bol bad striated [insp. iletus badius]

bol cyan to dive into a deep blue sea [insp. boletus cyanescens]

bolder to hold in a wee [hold + bladder]

bolders uptight shoulders [oppo. loosders]

bol ery red spots [insp. boletus erythropus]

bol fla slimy [insp. boletus flavus]

bol gran slender [insp. boletus granulates]

bol lut to not dry [insp. boletus luteus]

bol sat red veins | a gastric attack [insp. boletus satanas]

bol sub ribbed [insp. boletus subtomentosus]

bolsovereign to think you are getting more than you actually get, e.g. a diamond ring, 56 ct gold, but instead a silver ring with one gemstone, a bolsovereign

but at least it's your
birth gem-stone

bolt to freeze | to
become speechless

boltel to be locked out
of your hotel | for a
hotel to lock its doors
after a certain time

bolterfly a butterfly
trapped inside and has
no way of getting out |
unable to express
something

bolt gun the big bang

boltooth to be locked
in a large place
[Scot. tollbooth: a town
hall]

bolts the material
holes on a belt

BOM back of **the
mind** [oppo. **FOM**]

bombarge open fire
into a tunnel | to
bombard a barge

bomber whacket to
throw explosives [+
bomber jacket]

bomlys the discovery
into symbols and signs
| the semiotics

bomtomb a bunker
[bomb + tomb]

bonawir to look-out
for a rainbow | to
search for a rainbow

bon born 'I wish you
a good birth' | to be
born again [Fre. bon: "I
wish you"] [+ born]

bonerve to hit the
bone and for it to hurt

bones sweets

bones voyage a
dangerous voyage | a
voyage which may lead
to death

bonged-up nose to
have a bunged up nose
from taking powdered
drugs

bon greed, mal greed whether willing to be greedy or not [Fre. bon gré, mal gré: whether willing or not]

bonjourney happy holidays | happy travels [Fre. bonjour: hello] [+ journey]

bonneeds bonny needs

bonnet a bony bottom

bonnice a nice trunk | a nice bum on the bodice

bonoose a spare hanger [bonus + noose]

bont to bounce a ball hard and for it to carry on continuously bouncing

bontanicle to plant an idea

bonzebra very simple [Aus. bonzer: very big + zebra]

BOOB be open, open be

boob hoax

boobade a fire brigade where the people of the service are giant boobs

boobalti to dress your breasts in spices

boobe to obviously boast

booboo a blue balloon

boobskint so annoyingly bobskint that it becomes silly

boob tube Youtube videos of people singing and talking at their computer

booby trap to get the foot caught in a bra

strap, e.g. I know the booby trap is an at(ta)c(ke) of(f) the bra

boodle to doodle a body

booj time just gone

BOOK but obviously others (are) kind

book buck

book antiqua a book over one hundred years old

book bait either 'information' or 'research'

bookends cranes

booket a box of books [+ bucket] | a book case

book et and spray the adults version of **bucket and spade**

book it bucket

bookle up to get reading | to get studying

book-lice to work with paper [insp. *a booklice feeds of paper and moulds*]

bookman old style a person who makes books by hand using no machinery

bookshop medicine self help books

bookteeth people who read out loud

bookteria the mould which develops in an old book

boom to bump into one another, e.g. 'we boom we did, we boomed, we mushaboomed'

boom box when you boom into someone and you square dance verticle and forward, you both seem to be choosing to go the same way – the dance is a box

boomering when you call someone the same time they are calling you | when you think about calling someone and 'hey presto' - they are calling you

boomkinder young bumpkin

booshket a groove

boo-shy with fear

boo'sy when a blurry eyesight makes up scary visions

boot to run

boot-clout to hit someone over the head with a shoe

booth a baby tooth

boother to stand in a booth for a while

boother bog a booth as a toilet

boother spill to urinate in a booth, usually a phone box

bootroot the place where your shoes came from

bootswag foot prints

bootswagger a trail of footprints

bootswago to follow bootswagger

bootswig to get rid of foot prints or finger prints

bootylicious lots of room in a car boot

booze to walk around in boots

BOP birds of paradise

bo-peep a person who hides away [see **miss**]

bo-people people who hide away

boprey birds of prey

borack artificial breasts [+ borax]

borack obama the politics of **borack**

bordeer when a deer loses its antlers the deer becomes a borderline deer, a bordeer, as antlers are the symbol of the deer

borders stiff trousers [insp. **bolders**]

boreadom the boredom of reading a piece of text

bore row a row which doesn't raise an eyebrow | an unneeded argument

boreder line to wait in a boring queue

bori & bonsai Japanese arts

boringring an unwanted phone call [+ "ring-ring"]

bornament to make stiff | to turn into a statue

borneo a bad knee

borneon born bright [+ neon]

BOT beans on toast

botan a bit of a natural tan look due to eating lots of betacarotene, e.g. too much carrot juice makes botan

botch-clock a badly repaired clock

bothem bother them

bother brother a close friend who fusses a lot, or bring a lot of bother to your doorstep

bothrmouth when your bath water becomes cold you also become cold

botshot a small bottle

botswana the boots want to, e.g. botswana walk

bottall a tall bottle

BOTTLE beans on toast, tomato, lettuce: evolution

bottle of the sea to gargle salt water

bottler a glass bottle used as a candleholder

BOTTOM beans on toast, tomato on me

botty bottle

botyacht a boat that has sunk to the bottom of the sea

boudoor the bedroom door [+ boudoir]

bough cough to cough up [insp. *bough is a large branch of a tree*]

boughne a broken leg | a broken arm [see **branch**] [+ bone]

boukeep to accept a bouquet of flowers

bouleyard a car park [boulevard + yard]

bounce wave a backand-forth hand wave

bounce-base a basketball court

bouncy castle the journey of **up and down** [see **up and down**]

bourbon a secret word for poo

bourbone to have a deep love for chocolate spread on bread

bourbonnet a brown hat

bourn dark [insp. Bournville chocolate]

bout about now?

bout-and-bout completely spread everywhere

bout-boat to get about by way of water

bout pout a kissing place

bow & sorrow pretty sad [+ bow and arrow]

bowel to crash into something [insp. tenpin bowl]

bowelsac the stomach

bowel wall the stomach lining

bowel well healthy bowels

bowind to keep bowing

bowler hat a fishbowl as a head piece

bowler hatted to have a bowling head on

bowl hat to crouch when bowling, ready to roll

bowlinger to walk around the block

bowlingo to roll the tongue| to talk without real meaning

bowl-of-bananas a basket-case

box to tame [insp. box tree]

boxflo when a group of males surround one

female [insp. *the flowers of a box tree*]

boxhook to hold onto an edge by gripping onto it tightly

box realm to live by a timetable | to keep in a box

box set a display or collection of TV's

boyoyo an 'up and down' feeling

boy red boy troubles

BP battery powered | boiled potato [see **MP** & **HP**]

B (past) one letter past A, two letters past Z, three letters past Y, four letters past X, five letters past W, six letters past V, seven letters past U, eight letters past T, nine letters past S, ten letters past R, eleven letters past Q, twelve letters past P, thirteen letters past O, fourteen letters past N, fifteen letters past M, sixteen letters past L, seventeen letters past K, eighteen letters past J, nineteen letters past I, twenty letters past H, twenty one letters past G, twenty two letters past F, twenty three letters past E, twenty four letters past D, twenty five letters past C

br brecht

bra a bar

brac-bit trinket

bracelist many

bracelists worn

brackets warm layers

bradar to guess a womens brasize | to see if a woman is wearing a bra

brae a gasp [+ breathe]

brag a bag that brags | a designer bag that only brags and doesn't really better the human

bragain cheap underwear [+ bargain]

bragues brogues which have different coloured tips

brain cust helpful people at customer services [brain trust + customer]

brakin to be busted due to a joke

bramble to move into a complicated situation

bramble bee the stinging of brambles [+ bumble bee]

bramble gas tear gas (how it stings the eyes) [bramble + bumble bee]

bran bland but healthy

branches the arms and the legs

brandana a branded bandana

b-randy branded sexual advertisements [brand + randy]

brandy christmas equivalent to tea | a brass chandelier

brandye hardcore 'til death

brass knowledge

brass knuckles laborer's hands

brass lass a well looked after porcelain doll | a person who has studied well

brass loss for a **brass lass** to have lost the brass

brasshard a brassard showing opposition

brassi ja to feed on seeds [insp. *the brassica bug feeds mainly on the seeds of jack-by-the-hedge*]

brattle one who is in danger of losing friends due to being a brat [+ brittle]

brawfood excellent food

brazenith to have reached a levil of zen

brazil to not wear a bra [bra + zilch]

brazilch no nuts

breaccount to terminate having a shared bank account

bread bed a stomach stuffed with bread

breaka to break down [+ aka]

break-bread to lose weight [oppo. **bakebread**]

break down a massive breakfast [oppo. **break fast**]

break fast a light breakfast [oppo. **break down**]

break up to sick up your food (especially to sick up a **break down**)

breathirst short of breath

bre aviation to be breathing through a nebuliser

breef small | brief [insp. **big**]

breeze-block a big breeze

bren a local favorite

bresch torso [breast + chest]

breta weapon [insp. californian yew]

brevin to inhale a little

brevitaliy short of vitality

brew drink

brewcolage to brew your own alcohol [+ bricolage]

brewdy to be broody for a brew

brewonge orange and brown

breyu (with) character [insp. the joshua tree]

brible a corrupted story [bible + bribe]

bri cha li to be very clever

brice boiled rice

brick to undercook vegetables

brick-book a heavy book

bricket a loud band [ricket + bracket]

brickoli to undercook broccoli [insp. **brick**]

brickplayer a bricklayer who likes to get laid

bridali a bride who has been stood up, and now melts in her hearty tears

bridish a British dish

bridge-bodge a sluggish connection | a half-arsed DIY job | something not built safe

bridge fudge not able to go across | no direct access to the other side

brigbrag to brag about a situation where you were took hostage [+ brig]

bright charisma

bright eyes eyes looking directly into the sun

brilload to fill up on cleaning equipment

brillo-pad not brilliant | tough

brin bread bin

brink brown and pink

brink basin on the edge of suffocation

brinkst to feel the lips with the fingers [brink + midst]

briskit to look through a manual

britain to maintain brittleness

brith after birth [oppo. **girth**]

broad bean a broad possibility

broad-body to hide in reeds or bushes [insp. *the broad-bodied chaser (dragonfly) perches on reeds and bushes*]

broadleaf broad (fat) from healthy foods

brochurn when a leaflet or brochure brings on bad feelings [brochure + churn]

brock solid

brock wall a solid wall

broke bike to not go

broken-dawn when morning tasks do not do go plan and start to run on into midday

brole to reduce surface area [*short for broadleaf*]

bronchi bronze or copper [insp. *the bronze shield bug has a bronze or coppery head*]

bronchi brella a croaky or nervous voice

bronchi poncho to have a soothing voice | a relaxed and mellow voice [bronchi + poncho]

brond bronze and blonde coloured

bronze to be ready for sleep [insp. *the green shield bug is a deep bronze colour in late autumn (before going into hibernation)*]

bronzest a browning lemon

brood-band to wish for faster broadband

broom Birmingham | Brum

broomers rumours intended to brush people up the wrong way

broquet a bunch of broken things | damaged goods [broke + bouquet]

brothello to pay for any kind of greeting [brothel + hello]

br-ouch for a brooch pin to stick into the skin

browbeat for people to be worried about 'beat' poetry

brown art and literature [insp. *'Tivial Pursuit' colour*]

brown bob to hit the surface of the swimming pool [insp. *the brown bobby bird*

*dives into the water
from a low height,
therefore hitting the
surface at an angle]*

brown shoes
interesting

brownze brown and
bronze coloured

brows conventions

browspecs glasses
with brown lenses

browsure conventions
[closure + brows]

brr-ring a sales call

brr-ouch when the
cold gives you illness |
pneumonia

bruce burnt rice |
narrow strip [insp. cape
york red gum]

brucey burnt rice in
the sea [+ **bruce**]

brucey shell burnt
rice in the sea shall [+
brucey]

brucey shell bee
burnt rice in the sea
shall be [+ **brucey
shell**]

**brucey shell bee a
ten** burnt rice in the
sea shall be when still
hot and for to have
burnt the tongue like a
sting from the bee it be
[+ **brucey shell be**]

brude to cross a
bridge and you are
weary about whether it
is strong enough to
take your weight
[bridge + grudge]

brue lippy having
purple or blue lips from
bad circulation, cold
weather or from being
dehydrated

brug to find lice in a
comb

brui a bad cup of tea
[brew + bruise]

bruisier for more
bruises to appear

bruit fruit the main
gossip

brum broom

brunch to stretch the
branches [see **branch**]

brussel brothel to
steal sprouts

brussel sprout a
small green bush

brutool a brutal tool
| brutality as a tool

BT brush teeth

bt biscuit tin

B (to) one letter to C,
two letters to D, three
letters to E, four letters
to F, five letters to G,
six letters to H, seven
letters to I, eight letters
to J, nine letters to K,
ten letters to L, eleven
letters to M, twelve
letters to N, thirteen
letters to O, fourteen
letters to P, fifteen
letters to Q, sixteen
letters to R, seventeen
letters to S, eighteen
letters to T, nineteen
letters to U, twenty
letters to V, twenty one
letters to W, twenty two
letters to X, twenty
three letters to Y,
twenty four letters to Z,
twenty five letters to A

bub a baby birthed in
the water | a half-arsed
bubble

bubblegut full of gas

bubble squabble to
fall out with someone or
argue with someone in
a dream

bubblur to get high
from having too much
sugary drunk

buck book | money

buckaroo contract work where the buck is unknown

buck case loose pages [see **booket**]

buckerknuckle to fight over money [insp. **bunkerknuckle**]

bucket book it

bucket and spade kids holiday necessaries [see **book et and spray** for adults version]

bucket-cluck a bath too hot

bud a cosey bed

budabulb the light of Buddha

budapest an annoying friend, e.g. the bud's a budapest

buddance to dance with a friend | to have a friendly spirit

buddha burger a burger containing no animal

buddhapast to have had a good life so far

buddhi to be greeted with vegan food

buddhive a place where Buddha is worshipped

budgie a budget

bud on your hands to be holding something good | to have great wisdom

buffeet a buffet which looks, smells and tastes of feet

buffer a refreshments cart on a train [+ buffet]

buffoon comic

buff tether to buff teeth | to buff the car | to buff the floor | to shine

bug baby

bugee to beg on your hands and knees

bugger a burger

bugi a big hug

buglue when flies feed off of each other

building-dong a building soon to be knocked down

bula bus lane

bulb a tuft of hair [insp. **bulbhead**]

bulbhead a baby's head (having only a little tuft of hair) [insp. pulgaric]

bulcer somebody who openly tells lies [bull(crap) + ulcer]

bul-de-sac to be in a gro(o)ve of made-up talk and having no way out [+ bull]

bulgaia to not believe in the gaia

bulgar wheat god damn, crikes, why me?

bull when tall people have to dip their head down to get through the entrance (like a bull ready to charge)

bulld bulldozer

bullet belt in unneeded angst

bullets beads [insp. **abacus**]

bullhip to bump hips with someone | to bump the hip against something

bulloy a bully's weapon [+ alloy]

bullquet a bunch of (f)lies [insp. **ballquet**]

bum bulimic

bumble to move around

bum-cheek clap only a little clap [oppo. **clap-of-thunder**]

bumerang to not come back when expected to [bum + boomerang]

buna to bump the head

buna curry to buna and lose memory for a moment

bunanaza an area where many rabbits are sighted

bundull a dull bundle

bun fight a tea party

bungaloot one layer of loot [insp. **bungalow**]

bungalow a 'one-level' law

bungeese when geese open up their wings [+ bungee]

bunjive to dance by bouncing up and down | to hop like a rabbit [bungee + jive]

bunk'n'trunk a male to pick up another man for sexual interactions

bunkbed to bury a body on top of another buried body | a shared grave

bunkerknuckle when two knuckles collide in a fight

bunkle two single beds [insp. bunkbed]

bunnet a group of bunny rabbits [+ punnet]

bunny bail a rabbit never let out of its cage

bunny doe to hop on board an investment scheme

buntab to fix up bunting [+ tab]

bunya-bunya [insp. aboriginal sacrament]

buoy to make something more colourful

buoyach for a boat to be in line with a buoy

burban the crumbling of an urban area [+ bourbon]

burbur a sudden birth

burdent to carry braces in the mouth | to have temporary braces in the mouth [burden + dent]

burger on baptism modern age and Christianity

burglare to steal a stare [burglar + glare]

burgun-stone a reddish brown stone

burlesque staged porn

burnitoes the writings on gravestones [Fre. burino: graving tool]

burrough a rough area [+ borough]

bur sari to be granted protection [bursary + sari]

burshi half red [insp. *the birch shield bug has the front half of their scutellum red*]

burstrang stuffy atmosphere

bury plant [see **loon don**]

busaclust to be in between big objects

busage in between use and abuse

bus blabbus rabus blabbus on a bus [see **rabus blabbus**]

bus bustle to play with breasts on the bus

buscovado a talk on the bus with a stranger

bus flare to pay less bus fare

bush-cricket flightless [insp. *the speckled bush-cricket*]

busher somebody who ushers others through bushes

bushiness organic business

bush latte a milky herbal tea

bushush a quiet walk in the wilderness

bushvelvet a bush that has velvety leaves

bu shy a native person who is not used to socializing

buskerville a place with many buskers

busquee when a busdriver tackles a sharp corner

bussard a person using an old bus ticket to save money

bus-surfing a game where you stand on the bus without holding on to anything, and see how long you can keep balance

bust an empty bus

bust buzzard a barely used buzzer

busto bus stop

bustard custard pigeon poo [bustard + custard (the fluidity of the poo)]

bus-tea a builder's cup of tea

bustile to dress up the breasts, e.g. tassles

bustle breast play

busy body a person who smells of wee or poo on a bus

but like 'ply wood there are stronger woods, like the law?

butcher evil

butchurn chub

but-t a seated 'but': one which won't shift from being a butt for a long time

butt butter

butt cherry to sit on something too hot

butt chilly to sit on something too cold

butter slime

butterant to butter up

butter cup a solution | an improvement [+ but]

butterfly soya spread

butthole a button hole

butthole surfers surfers who surf in shorts too big for them

button the anus

button eyes a person skilled in textiles

buttonhi for a button to come off

buttrest the seat part of a chair

butt-smoke the odour of a fart

buttwo zig-zag [insp. *the buttonwood tree having zigzag branches*]

buwoflo deep red [insp. *the flowers of a buttonwood tree*]

buxta nearly friends

[buster + juxtaposit]

buy to empty

buzzard a buzzer

buzzcock an alarm that won't go off (and keeps on going on even when it's off)

byay to excitedly say goodbye to someone

by-bye to be near to leaving

Cc

c connect

C *pic* a round ear | a bear's ear | pacman without a mouth

ca capra

cab yellow and black

cabal to call for a cab

cabar a strip bar

cabaret to strip or have sex in a taxi

cabbag a green bag

cabbage a cab

cabbage pitch a field of cabbages growing | a lousy football game | a queue of taxis waiting for customers

cabbage warm a person who is too lazy to get out of their sleeping bag [insp. *the cabbage warm caterpillar feeds on cabbages*]

cabballet the story tell of the cabbala

cabeam to move a problem out of sight [Scot. caber: a pole or beam, especially one thrown at strength]

cabinary a small area | a small amount of numbers [cabin + binary]

cabinot a cabinet for 'what-nots' (bits and bobs)

cabinote a filing cabinet

cable having only the ability to watch television | a person who spend every evening watching the television

cable-bodied those who system themselves through tv – the news, the soaps, the dramas, the football [insp. **cable**]

cabloke a taxi driver

cabrasive to clean a vehicle (especially public vehicles) [abrasive + cab]

cabstain for a taxi driver to refuse to take you [+ abstain]

cabus blabbus rabbus blabbus which takes place in a taxi [see **rabbus blabbus**]

cackle to talk with the mouth full

cacklean a brittle broom end [cackle + clean]

cacoe cocoa an irresistible urge for chocolate [cacoethes + chocolate]

cadave the common type of corpse [insp. *Dave is a common name*] [+ cadaver]

cadavergo to look dead when very sick | to feel like a walking corpse | to look like shit when just woken [vertigo + cadavergy]

cadental the sound of a dentists instruments being used

caduck an old duck

cafelic leisurely Catholic [+ café]

cafederal nero the mass governance and power of Café Nero [+ federal]

cafeka a multi arts venue which is also a café [insp. Kafka]

cafeteria bacteria in a kitchen | mouldy food

cake sweet

cake & tea selfindulgence | fanciness

cakecake 'sweet is sweet' [insp. **toothtooth**]

cake can a pack of sweets

cake go to sick up cake

cake god a sweet tooth

cakerwo for one person to eat a whole cake

cakerwo go for a **cakerwo** to spew up the cake

cakerworm for two people to eat a whole cake [insp. cankerworm]

cakie a soft cookie

cakles brittle bones [insp. **cacklean**]

calab a callous label [oppo. **valab**]

calculator gun

calcull to kill a calculation [+ cull]

calender to call for the end of something

calf veal

calibra a sweaty bra [+ California]

calikes things you like which make you feel safe and comfortable

calithorn a hot prick [California + thorn]

callord the person who always calls

calm peace

calmaculture the belief in peace

calm arm a peaceful army

calseagull to have lost the flow of a calculation [insp. **calcull**]

calu scaly with age [insp. pepperwood]

cal utri either entirely white or cream, e.g. a wedding is normally cal utril [insp. calvatia utriformis]

calypsort to change the rhythm [calypso + sort]

cambodia for something to appear daily [came + body]

cambria via Cambridge

camcorderhoarder a hoarder of camcorders

came honey [insp. river red gum]

camel heel the camel toe of a knicker line

cameli the way the weather alters our moods

camel mal to have the hump with someone

camel spit to have a fly or something in the mouth and to get it out by spitting

camel thuds the sound of heavy feet coming up the stairs

camel thumps marks on the skin from being abused

camelon the camel toe of visible nipples

camera-culture a culture of only representation | a culture lacking originality

cameraloss to not visualize

cameralust to look at porn

camera toe to always be taking pictures

camhoarder a hoarder of cameras

camma a visual comma

campanion a camping companion

camparts camping necessities

camp placid a commune | a peace camp

can gun, e.g. he went to shoot the cans and suddenly wondered how it was possible to do this because the can he planned to shoot was the can he was shooting from

canado to swim in a canal

canalog tunnel vision

canalysis narrow analysis [+ canal]

canapé no hope

canasta some skill required

cance dance the spreading of cancer

can cell a high ceiling prison cell

cancer-banter popular news spreading

cancer bats cigarettes

cancern an illgrowing concern

cancers artificial foods

candeladrum the flickering of lights [candelabrum + drum]

candelta three lit candles

candenzen falling into the rhythms of Zen

candera a time of candy

candie the rotting of the teeth

candlestack to look down at all the lights from a hill top on a dark night

candlestick to get stick because you are religious [+ **stick**]

candoe honest earnings [cadour + doe]

candy creativity is vital [insp. *Charlie and the Unicorn – The Candy Mountain*]

candy can to do the can can whilst eating sweets

candy cane sweet punishment | to have got off lightly

can dy cane creativity is the growth of the seed

candydate a volunteer of sampling sampler of sweets

cankerworm for two people to destroy something [insp. the cankerworm moth]

cannabiz a cupboard full of canned food

cannibalism free loathe

cannotation a collection of comments [can + annotation]

cannote a prohibition sign

canny ring-pull

cantain contents of a can | the can contains

can-teen a cooking class

cant inf fold-like [insp. cantharellus infundibuliformis]

canvaroo a moving picture [kangaroo + canvas]

canvey to show determination [+ convey]

CAP come and play | come and pray

cap to think

capacite to think big

cape cocaine to cover yourself from the snow

cape of good hope a favourite jacket | a graduation gown [*Cape of Good Hope is a place in South Africa*]

caph one that is the most-grown | the most popular [insp. canary palm]

capi invasive [insp. bean pitch pine]

cap kip a 'ten to twenty minute' nap

capluck chance of making capital

capp to limit the use of an app (mobile application)

capscratch to scratch the head as if trying to remember | to try and remember

capseize to have to take your hat off [+ capsize]

capsize for a penis to not be able to stiffen

capsize casino to be in debt due to gambling

capsilk when kinesis takes over the mind

capsoul a person who relies on Western medicines [+ capsule]

captivities teeth firmly gipiing on

capward to carry on thinking

car age the age of a car

car age gar age the length of time the car has been sitting in the garage for

caramel for something to be light to carry

carble a car rolling backwards because somebody forgot to put the break on

carbonnet car bonnet

carbuncle to play around in the car **Carcinogenic**

cardigan game an old game of cards

cardigran a love for cardigans

care woven to be treated with care

caread without a book [L. career: to be without]

carear to be without a back garden [L. career: to be without]

carest to quit caring for a while | to give the occupation of caring a rest

car-go for a car to drive off

cark park a time of worry [+ cark]

carma driving with karma – allowing people out and driving with good manner

carnage to eat cars

carnogon a dirty jacket | unwashed clothes [+ cardigan]

carod to open up a card

carous to go round slowly (like a carousel)

carpat to touch or feel **carpit**

carpatch a patch of stubble

carpenter's lot cuts of wood

carpet a beard you get attached to and it

becomes the new domesticated pet

carpit stubble

carpraise to praise someone for growing their hair [insp. **carpet**]

carprick a fraudster mechanic

carrag fan-shaped, [insp. carragheen]

carraid to be taken away | to remove an option from the menu [+ corrode]

carrisk when you carry something that puts you at risk, e.g. a bag of weed, a toolbox full of tools or a kitchen knife in the sock

car rot a car on fire | a burnt out car

carrusk to always carry a snack | having something to nibble on or eat if you get hungry

cart a car without its wheels

cartage the time when wagons were used for transport

cart cell a prison cell on wheels

carter to hold onto a car when it is moving

carton a car without wheels

carton cell a small prison cell

carva lava a love for carving

casinoe a narrow sail to winning at casino

caskettle a dead kettle

cassette a played case

cast to walk wonky

caste to situate [insp. **castle**]

castle situation

castnet curt to call for a curtain close

casualty casualness

cat stimuli [insp. betel]

cata four-legged

catabolt to stop shooting [catapult + bolt]

catapelt hailstones

catapult to say it straight out

cataput to put it straight | to put it right there

cataract to act like a cat

cat chat to wash one another

catch the bell to listen out to see what time it is

cat cot a cat's sleeping area

categore a bad selection [+ category]

cater invasive [insp. indian almond]

caterpillarbox a pillar box which is soon to be emptied [*the caterpillar will be in cocoon state until it becomes a butterfly*]

cat flat cat to supply a public house for cats

cathe a tea room in a catholic church

catillac a big cat

cat la tin a tin of cat food [insp. **dog la tin**]

catman a man with cats [insp. **catwoman**]

catmush canned cat food

cato a prickly or strong odour [insp. californian nutmeg]

cats chalky [insp. white hemlock]

cattle big cats

cattell cursing eyes

catwoman a woman with cats [see **catman**]

cauliflower patch an area of the ear containing earwax [see **sunflower patch**]

causerium the core of the cause [+ serum]

causin a related cause [+ cousin]

cavaedium minimalism

cave woven a domestic house wife

caviar to abuse a child | the sheltering of a cave

caving peeling paint

cavoc havoc in a cave

ccc three in a row [see **O's and X's**]

cccc four in a row [see **FIAR**]

c c c c something crack(l)ing

C chord the average

CCTV big brother [oppo. **citv**]

CCTV camera scamera

CCTV moat CCTV security | highly secured

CCTVisor electronic evidence [+ vision]

cd chindogu

CD crumb a damaged CD disc

CD dum to throw away CD's, e.g. perhaps start CD dum the **CD crumb**

CD pimp to keep changing over CD's | to swap music over so quickly you never get a proper feel a song

CD pomp a pompous CD collection

CD romp to put a CD in the CD rom, and then later, out

ce creat(e/ivity)

ce ce to fa fa back to back, then front to front [insp. **F2F**]

cecile! cramp in leg

cedat angled upwards [insp. atlas cedar]

ceefax an old computer

celaboration success
of a promotion
[celebration + elaborate]

celbough sellotape
[cell + bough]

celeditty ditty
celebrity

celedizzy to be
infatuated with
celebrity's lives

celefray to get away
from a celebration | to
escape a celebration

celegritty a gritty
celebratory

celery to be in prison
for doing a good cause
[cell + celery]

cellar below

cellaugh a deep belly
laugh

cellirst the first to go
low | the first to fall to
sleep [cellar + first]
[oppo. **lofirst**]

cellotape to be stuck
in prison for a long time
[+ sellotape]

cellular phone to
talk to another when in
different rooms

cellulaugh to keep on
laughing

cellutility body cells
| cells in the body

celofame to be
wrapped in a celebrity
lifestyle

cemental insane
material |
groundbreaking
bizarreness

cen lut translucent
[insp. *the front of the
abdomen of the
centroptilum luteolum
mayfly is pale and
translucent*]

centre-punch to
punch someone in the
stomach | to make a
hole in the centre

centrifle a sweet centre

cepi high altitude [insp. arolla pine]

ceramock a fake ceramic [+ mock]

cerebran wholewheat bran [+ cerebral]

cerebrawl an overruling thought | a disturbing thought | when something its playing on the mind [cerebral + brawl]

cericirca from pink | from an area of pink

cesbra to hold up [+ braces]

cevent to blow in the middle [L. venter: to blow] [+ center]

cf McCaffery

c-hab to walk when you have a hip problem [+ crab]

cha change there is change

chafore cooking that is cold or has not been cooked long enough [chaufe + thaw]

chafter cooking that has been overcooked [chaufe + after]

chair a table with a back

chairy a chary chair | a person scared of being sat on or suffocated | a fragilelooking chair | wary about sitting on something

chaka demus and pliers to undo a bad DIY job with pliers

chake to choke on cake

chakra sight-seeing

chakrabanc a fraud [insp. **chakra**]

chalk nothing is forever

chamag adornment [insp. champak]

chance race [insp. *race games are dependent on chance*]

change pellets

changel when a vending machine gives you extra change | to find free money in the 'change slot' of a vending machine

changer-up to get brutal

chant the most used [insp. **chanterelle**]

chanull nothing to watch [+ channel]

chaos a free-spirit being free

chaotick the wellbeing of chaos

chaotock a time of chaos

chaottack the attack of chaos

chap-chop a haircut for men | to cut your lip

chaplet a pile of beaded necklaces [chaplet + lot]

chaplot a rack of hats | a stack of hats [chaplet + lot]

chapped book a bad chapbook

chapstick a dildo

chapsule a car that does not work becomes only the shell [chap(ped) + capsule]

char to burn

chard to choose to do something the hard way [oppo. **cheese**]

charge mood

charger contract

charicket a loud character, e.g. the exclamation mark is a charicket although not as much as the people to the left of me

charismat a mat used to lean on when praying

charist to wear the heart on the sleeve [charity + wrist]

charmer a charmed chamber having candles, petals, and champagne

charmur-mur charming whispers and sweet-sayings in the ear

charrot to set a car on fire [**char + car rot**]

chart to burn data

chartcoal the start of a positive gradient | the start of something good

chase-town a place where everybody is after each other

chatterbox post box

chaura the aura of the character

ch ch chat a chat on a train

ch-chooze to snooze on the train

che change thanks for the change

cheap-jack a cheap lead (normally one for the computer)

cheat to keep a straight face

checker to give way

checkoslavakian a check-out person

check-shirt a lumber jack

cheek squeak when an elder pulls at a child's cheeks

cheerish to cherish with cheer

cheese to choose to do something the easy way [oppo. **chard**]

cheesee y/m

chemical artificial insemination

chemical brothers people who take drugs together

chemicauldron artificial (flavourings)

chemin de fer an hour to a whole evening

chemmitre a chemical to clean wood | to build something out of wood [chemical + mitre]

chepper a Chess player ['Chess' + player]

chepper vespa an exhilarating game of Chess | an exhilarating Chess move [oppo. **chopper vespa**]

chera a delicacy [insp. cherimoya]

cheran delicate [see **chera**]

cherare to cherish the rare

cherrie cheerful and merry

cherry cherry pom pom

cherry pick to pick at a scab

cherub to rub and cherish, e.g. I cherub the Buddha ornament every week

chess black and white

chess cat a black and white cat

chess-clock to limit game time

chess dog a black and white dog

chessre warfare

chessre cat a cat fight

chestwatch the body clock

chew-moo a grass eating cow

ch heck to have to check over a wrong doing

ch hit chat a violent chat | a conversation involving violence

chi flow

chic stabilize [insp. cocoplum]

chi che of various time [insp. *the game 'Chinese Checkers' has varied duration time of play*]

chicken to push

chief beef the gang leader

chiju ridge [insp. chilean wine palm]

child loompa [insp. oompa lumpa]

childrent the money you receive for having kids

chill pave

chilldaze a cold look

chilled pavement

chiller to shiver

chilly con carnage chilled flesh

chime chosen time

chimerit praise for doing the unreal | praise for trying something different [chimerical + merit]

chimes good news

chimnees dirty knee [+ chimney]

chimnese burn a chinese burn from a chimney | a burn from a house fire

chimney breasts dirty breasts

chimney sweep to stroke the chin

chimpsport monkeying around

chinatzy decorated with cheap chinaware [+chintz]

chin burn a chinese burn on the chin | a chin on fire

chin check a sixpointed star [insp. *the game board of 'Chinese Checkers' takes the form of a six-pointed star*]

chinchilla a cold chin

chineat the formalisation and strict rules of China | nothing out of place [China + neat]

c hip cracked or chipped hip | a crisp

chip lazy

chips chipped hips

chip flask hot oil | to sweat from heat

chipgut a gut full of chips

chip-proof an independent body | one who does not let things get to them

chippy chipped glass

chipship the game where you watch people opposite a chipshop and for ever person you see you have to decide if they are going to the chipshop or not | when chips go cold

chip slop postsickening fastfoods

chir-hapsody to perform a rhapsody in sign language [Gk. chiro: hand]

chiroar to use your hand to gesture 'stop' [Gk. chiro: hand]

chiroast to warm the hands up [Gk. chiro: hand]

chiro-cheer a highfive [Gk. chiro: hand]

chiro palmtree to hold seeds in the hand | to show good fortune [Gk. chiro: hand]

chirough rough hands from doing physical work [Gk. chiro: hand]

chirp a quick positive noise meaning 'ok' or 'fine', e.g. the teacher would chirp as she chalked and so we chirped back

chirpchip to wait in a chip shop hungry for food like a chick chirping for food from its mother

chirpe energetic

chirupert a person who always wears a scarf [insp. *Rupert the Bear*] [+ chirpy]

chiseller a sales
person | a cold-caller
[chisel + seller]

chi tea tai chi

chit hit a good
conversation

chit that to talk
about 'this' and 'that'

chloride cat a
domestic plant

choarder a song
which uses an extreme
amount of tones and
chords

choc temporary
energy

chock to check the
clock, e.g. we chock
more than clock checks
us in game of check
mate

chock-a-block-ice
when shock-a-block-ice
huddle up or curl into
the body and try to get

warm [see **shock-a-
block-ice**]

choco-black dark
chocolate

choco-block for there
to be chocolate
everywhere

chocodile a crocodile
covered in mud

chocolate barge a
long narrow chocolate
bar (in the shape of a
barge)

**chocolate coated
sour cream** to have a
split personality

chocollage a display
of different chocolates
[+collage]

chocoon to live in a
habit of eating
chocolate every day

choco-too-late
melted chocolate which
has lost its shape

chogut a gut full of chocolate

choiet a low volume [insp. **choir**]

choir almost too quiet to hear

choking on cotton having bad dreams

chomby wrong [insp. clam]

chomed to laugh hard [comedy + chrome]

choo-charge a person in charge of trains

choo-choo side to side

chookle a nervous laugh [Aus. & NZ. chook: hen or chicken] [+ chuckle]

choo lace the joining of trains and carts [choo choo + shoe lace]

choo stew stuck in a train of thought

chooth the chosen truth | to choose the truth

choo true a train of good thought

chooze the satisfaction of being able to choose [+ ooze]

chop book a bad chapbook

chopper vespa a dissatisfying game of Chess | a dissatisfying Chess move [oppo. **chepper vespa**]

chork to be encouraged to do work [cheer + work]

chow mine I'm confused

chrim crack a fivepointed star [insp.

chin check and the christmas star]

chrim trim the christmas trimmings

chrisange to lie with your back on the floor and your arms and legs spread out

chris pud christmas pudding

christmas pudding very rich

chromatopaz very dazzling

chromecca to worship shiny objects | very clean and shiny

chronick&nack to wear the same pants and pair of socks for a long time

chub butchurn

chuck-a-block a room filled with laughter

chuckleberry to chuck berries (or even to chuck a Blackberry phone out of the window)

chuf poof to positively say 'phew'

chug chewing gum

chuggle a warm chuckle

chunlare to launch [+ launcher]

church tile a religious party | a religious celebration

churing an awarded ring [insp. churinga]

churn preacher [+ church]

chutzpahney the love of giving [*Chutzpah brooches were given to partners in relationships as a token of love*]

chym the ringing of
bells [chime + hymn]

cidarette of alcohol
and cigarettes

ciderblab to talk
nonsense when drunk

cider blob to twist
your words when
intoxicated

cider broom to clean
under the influence of
cider | to empty your
house of cider

ciderbulb when
alcohol kicks in

cigarments clothes
which smell of
cigarettes

c in a circle
copyright

cindra dragon [insp.
dragon tree]

cinest to design the
interior | to decorate a
home

cinnamoney
earnings from selling
sweet foods

cint to burn money
[cinder + cent]

circumfluentrance
a door that stays open,
e.g. a church used to
have circumfluentrance
but nowadays it is Spar
(the 24-hour
Convenience Stores of
the city centres)
[circumfluent +
entrance]

circumslance a
negotiable
circumstance [+ slant]

circus maximus the
largest circus [*must be
a human circus as a
circus using animals is
not a circus, it is a place
of cruelty*]

citrine to sit in urine
| to soil yourself when
sitting down

citv little brother [see **CCTV**]

city disp let it be displayed in the city [insp. *cito disp: (in prescriptions) let it be dispensed quickly*] [+ display]

cl Columbian

clag a slow clock | time passing slowly [Iri. clog: bell, clock] [oppo. **clig**]

clairsavvy one knowledgeable in clairvoyance

clairveil to show the workings of clairvoyance

clairvoyage the voyage of a clairvoyance

clam to be turned down

clamate hot climate

clamore ongoing loudness [+ clamour] [see **clamouge**]

clamouge to put the clamour in a morgue by wearing earplugs

c-lamp a clip on lamp

clamp to put your hands together

clampompous not able to give up being pompous

clamposse to be stuck in a gang

clampspar a strong grip

clampus to be stuck in an institution

clam sneeze bizarre

clanavalendinner a communal dinner [clan + naval + lend + dinner]

clancer a group of people with cancer

clandle flame-gazers

clanger to communicate through unconventional sounds

clanguage the sound of metal and steel being struck

c-language cursive language

clap-of-thunder a massive applause [oppo. **bum-cheek clap**]

clapper fast moving hands [*'clipper' in pirate language is a fast moving ship*]

clappy ears to hear the odd sounds | to hear the distorted

clapsize to clap at wrong time | to clap when you are not supposed to be clapping

clarks'n'clerk plain

clarust when the clear becomes unclear [L. clarus: clear] [+ rust]

claser when a laser light draws closer

classter a group of the same class [+ cluster]

c-law the claws of law

claw danger

claws scratch marks

claw slice to accidently make a ladder in your tights

clawsuit a tight cat suit

clawyer a lawyer with claws | ready to take

clay to play cards

claya climbing space

cleanada not clean

cleanfidence how being clean brings confidence, e.g. seeing flies dead in the bread bin gives you a lack of cleanfidence

clearant a catch up on gossip and rumours

cleat right breast

cleathes clean clothes

cleft the left breast

clement element vitamin C

clementime time spent under the orange we like to call 'sun'

clemint the horrible taste of when you drink pure orange juice after washing the teeth [+ clementine]

clesoma a clean body

clevbev a good choice of drink [+ clever]

clew to fly

cliché hat a drinking helmet hat [insp. the cloche hat]

c lick to lick windows

clicke easy, you know what buttons to press [cliché + click]

clifell to fall off a cliff

cliff fanger to get something stuck in the teeth

clig a fast clock | time passing quickly [Iri. clog: bell, clock] [oppo. **clag**]

climat to be highly thought of yet treated badly

climb to spider

climbing frame a digital picture frame

climbing trees
going wild [insp.
climbing walls]

climbing walls
going mad [see
climbing trees]

clims clumsy limbs

cling film a film with
much attraction

cling-clang an
unforgettable sound |
an unforgettable saying
| a ringing in the ears,
e.g. the gig left me with
cling-clang

clinicall a chat with
the clinic on the phone

clipriq to clip your
nails on the floor [prick
+ risqué]

cliptonite one who
wears no coloutful
clothes [+ kryptonite]

CLIT cancer leaves its
terror

cloak to hang up a
coat

cloak li to only see a
little | to not get the
whole picture | unable
to process the (w)hole of
it [look + layer]

cloat a layer of blood

clob a group of bullies
[lob + club]

clobberish to clobber
for no real reason

**clock en spoil
glockenspiel** for
another sound to
disturb the voice of the
bells

clock gok en spiel
the time when a Gok
show is on

clock-it to open and
close using a key

clockroach a clock
which moves in its own
time [+ cockroach]

clocktopus an octopus shaped clock

clock wok en spiel the time when a cooking show is on [insp. **clock gok en spiel**]

cloddle to coddle a lot

clode a dress code, e.g. no hats

clo dip to live in a ditch [insp. *the cloeon dipterum mayfly breeds in ditches*]

clog a log with the letter "c" carved into it [insp. **blog**] [see **d'log**]

clopat just over 15 minutes [insp. *the duration of the game 'Clock Patience'*]

cloppy ears ones that are tired of listening

closed bracket a 'zipped up' jacket

close-lipped rather silent | for something to be kept a secret

closet privately sat

closoar to have blocked nasal holes and sore nostrils from blowing too much [+ closure]

closort to sort out the closet | to clean out a cupboard

clotterpillar a caterpillar that will never become a butterfly

clothed closed clothes

clothen open clothes

clothermo to wrap up warm

C loud average loudness [**C chord** + loud]

cloud a crowd of people (passing by)

cloudicont always passing [content + **cloud**]

clouds sheeps

clout a sky without clouds [+ drout]

cloutch to clutch the crotch area

clowd a clown passing by (like a cloud)

clown-around to sit on a red nose

club-tail swollen [insp. *the male (dragonfly) club-tailed skimmer's abdomen at the end is distinctively swollen*]

cluck an alarm clock

cluckle when cups clank together

clucky horse shoe no sign of luck

clud to be given a weapon [insp. *the game 'Cluedo'*]

cluedo six suspects [insp. *six characters in the game 'Cluedo'*]

clump bumper a clumpy bumper

clutch unable to catch

cly involving tears

cm comical

C minor the average minor

co communication

coast a cost

coaster a person who lives on the coast line

coast illumination the lighthouse light

cob Bob Cobbing

cob on a corn the works of Bob Cobbing

co op cry over

coal a cold kill

coast the cost of a holiday

co-ated to **ated** a company or group [see **ated**]

cob-bab a small-sized cob

cobbing to find patternations in sound

cobbler to poetically experiment

cobblert to break out into tears in a street (preferably a cobbled street)

cob-blob a large-sized cob

cob-bob a mediumsized cob

coble a round table [+ curve]

cobra a cold bra | a wet bra

cobran to crawl on the stomach in a hurry [cobra + ran]

cobwad a batch of cobs

COC code of conduct | cup of coffee

coca-cola-caine the world's addiction to coca-cola

COCK can ointment cure kin? [see **DICK**]

cockle to be dumpy [insp. the cockle]

cockler a tricky sexual position

cockroach a penis containing huge amounts of bateria, so much that it is possible the penis may just crawl off [insp. **sockroach**]

cockscrew to have a bad start to the day [cockcrow + screw]

coclo come close

coco Co-op! Co-op!

cocoa rage to crave chocolate

cocoa rags to get chocolate on your clothes

coconut to travel hundreds of miles (just like the coconut)

coconut alliance the group of people who talk about something different but are still

understood *[the coconut is a fruit, not a nut]*

coct correct

COD change of direction

code demorse to unlock a code | to break a code

coff front [oppo. **alce**]

coffee cough 'E'

coffee jab a need of energy | to spur fuel

coffice only an office and coffee, nothing else

coffin out of caffeine | the come-down from having (too much) caffeine

coffoe a hater of coffee (both taste and smell)

coff rags to get coffee on your clothes

coffsoma a caffeinated body

coga to work something out [cog + yoga]

cog cot something which used to work

cog dust industrialism

cog toga to wear something out

coherentry to try and make sense

cohorse a horse kept in a yard or small space [L. cohors: yard]

coi ride [insp. **coi-ill**]

coi-ill ill from going on amusement rides [+ coil]

coil beats electro music | vibrations | shock-waves

cointoss to throw

money at something | to fund a project

coi-scine to do more than **kiscine** at the cinema [Iri. Cóiscín: condom]

cokra crispy (burnt) okra

cokra cola cokra with cola gravy

coke rake to gather phlegm from drinking coke

cokerape to drink all of the coke

col five to seven years old [insp. *the game 'Cows & Leopards' having five or seven pieces*]

cola a cold 'ola'

col mine oh my, it's cold

colco vibrantly clothed

coli crust

cold culled | ice

colden could not,
e.g. it colden handle it

colders hands that
turn blue or purple due
to temperature or poor
circulation

coldplay to play
outside in the snow | to
play around with
substances

colett different
shades of green [colour
+ lettuce]

colgate murder

col gate a college
gate

colk a remote place
[insp. *the collard
kingfisher most evolved
in relative isolation on
remote pacific islands*]

collapse to leave
college before expected

collies college
students

collinger to wonder
what to do after
studying

colord the master of
vibrance | one who
wears the most colour

colourage how colour
effect the mood
[courage + rage]

colourdy when an
image blurs and you
can only see a colour [+
cloudy]

colourfray to lose
colour

colourful dresden

columbake to try out
worldwide cuisines
[insp. Columbus]

columbathe to swim across the channel (not a TV channel)

COM climb onto me

com abo to come about

comabustion when a comb breaks | to split into two

coma comma to put the use of commas on hold | to not use commas for a while [see **gertrude**]

comba-dog-clean to brush dog hairs off the clothes [insp. **combaclean**]

combaclean to brush bits off the clothes

combacne to brush dandruff from the shoulder area of a jacket [+ acne] [insp. **combaclean**]

comber culture keeping a comb in the pocket

combin to fall into a ditch together| to both be in a bad situation

combus a stuffy bus [+ combustion]

com dar a black triangle [insp. *the common darter dragonfly has a black triangle on the thorax*]

comea to nibble flowers [insp. *the common earwig is common in gardens where it nibbles flowers*]

comedia comedy about the current events

comedie dark comedy

comediedre when a comedian is not funny [+ comedie]

comeplex to ask for the complex version [insp. *calyx: outer leaves that protect a flower bud*]

comeplicated when a complication is welcomed [+ come]

comfotbell a familiar sound

comgro to not reach beyond [insp. *the keel of the common groundhopper does not reach beyond the tip of the abdomen*]

com haw yellow stripes [insp. *the common hawker male dragonfly has 2 narrow yellow stripes on the thorax*]

comican the humour in comics

comican-pelican a lolly pop light with a smily face drawn on

comic sans comic stands

comjun medicinal [insp. juniper]

comlamp the light the computer lets out

comma-mercial to write for advertisement

commasoma half of the body

commendatory for it to be essential to use commas [+ mandatory]

commercialism x factor

commint a new comment

commoc the same length | the same both ways

commoney shared money [+ commune]

communchal a dinner party

communicat a cat
who meows a lot [+
communicate]

communicate
measure

comp computer

compan to rest food
on your computer
keyboard

companini a
company who sell
sandwiches [+ panini]

compass not knowing
the way

compeat for a
computer to have eaten
a virus

compenny a
company with
insufficient funds [+
penny]

compenslate to not
receive full
compensation

compensuit a
reimbursement [+
compensate]

compentine to nonstop
type

compleat to be
finished with eating

complaymence the
game of complimenting

**comp like and
hated** the love and
hates of technologies

complywood to be
not be happy with
complying

comp moat
computer security

composset in
possession of
something composite

compound to ponder
a bargain | to think
about an offer

compte rendull the dull proceedings of a dull meeting where dull points are made and dull chairs are sat on [computer + render + dull]

compust wet compost

computer comp

computubby a massive computer screen [insp. **teletubby**]

conast how nasty [Iri. conas: how]

conbone a joint [+ combine + connect]

con brillo pad removing hard bits | the the magic of the brillopad

concluster a joint decision [conclude + cluster]

concourt for people to be on the same level

concrate a heavy crate [+ concrete]

concreep every foot that creeps will soon make a noise

concrete bed inappropriate

concurse to also curse [+ concur]

condom onion, garlic or any other food that makes the breath smell

condom amore lovingly and protected (from vampires and close contact) [con amore + **condom**]

condomcave a condom-wearing penis in a hole

conducktor the duck who makes the most noise [+ conductor]

cone a tent

cone and only
there's only one point

confedpad a police
station [confederal +
pad]

confedped a police
motorbike or bicycle
[confederal + pedal +
moped]

confishgate to take
somebody out of their
location | take
somebody out of the sea

conflu ill with
confusion

confor cold and dry
[insp. *conifer forests
dominate only in cold,
dry, mountainous
regions*]

conformula to
conform to **formula**
[insp. **formula**]

confract to work out
a fraction [+ contract]

confresh confess | to
come clean | to wash
the teeth

congesture
mixedmessages

congratratrats
congratulations; rats to
it

coniferrous for a
conifer to hit you on
your head

conjuggle to start up
joinery [conjugate +
juggle]

conjunction the
pollution of
conjunctivitis

conman a
conventional manner

connect join

connection joint

conneticut a deep
cut

conny can anybody hear me?

conof on-and-off connection

conse to let the wind blow you away, or move you [insp. *conifer seeds are usually dispersed by the wind*]

considry an old judgement that is not relevant any more [consider + dry]

consistantrum with regular outbursts [consistent + tantrum]

consortina six tasks [+ concertina]

conspiracy to put a glaze over the world, to pretend this is reality, to feed people drugs to stop them from telling others of what is really happening, to section people so they can keep the ones who know

controlled in this glaze of reality, to pretend dreams are made up and not real when they are the most real ever, to kill a certain side of us, that side, our chaos

constanza to constantly rhyme or make music

constellas a group of people drunk on Stella [insp. constellation]

constantrum a constant tantrum

constella a constellation of people drinking Stella

construck to load a truck with goods [+ construct]

consummer a travel agents [consume + summer]

contain bask

container to hold a prayer

containet basket

contigenius a high achiever [continuous + genius]

continull to discontinue

contra bri most sophisticated and intellectual [insp. *the game 'Contract Bridge'*]

contrace to trace contrasts | to find difference

contract charger

contrash an alternative to fashion , e.g. wear a bin-bag for a PVC coat, a banana peel for a hair accessory, a piece of net from a punnet for a top and a ring from a wrapper

conundrum skin to phase out a riddle

conversatile to have more than one conversation at the same time, e.g. on Facebook we may conversatile

convertsation a conversation which converts into another conversation

converse the commerce of indie footwear

convertigo to translate dreams| to chat to **dizzy**

convery to carry a lot from one place to another

convery ferry a ferry that is carrying its maximum weight

convextra to have an very curvaceous figure

con vince a magician

convoyage to carry around suitcases and bags when travelling

convoy-wage travel insurance [convoy + voyage]

coo-coo eyes to think too big | to think small as massive

coo-cot a bird house

coo-fee a bird who is non stop cooing as if it has downed coffee

cookernel roasted nuts [cook + kernel]

cookie a baker

cookieduckie a fat duck

cookie jargon to talk whilst munching cookies

cookiejoey a fat kangaroo | an extra large coffee

cookjoey a fattening coffee – one with cream and marsh mallows

cooktail an experimental meal, e.g. beetroots and onions in icecream pie

coo-pon a cheap date

coon food eaten when hiking or camping (usually dried fruit or canned foods)

coot death the use of eggs for human consumption [*the baby dies*]

cop to thank

copenhagana hoping to **copenhagen**

copenhagen to be able to cope

copepper bits of copper [+ pepper]

copi to stay closed (for a long time) [insp. the beach pine tree]

copter a flying policeman

copyright a c in a circle

cora juvenile [insp. the cook pine tree]

corbel a loud ringing sound

corden hairy and triangular [insp. *the coriomeris denticulatus bug has a hairy antennae and a hairy triangular protonom*]

cordinnaire one on a cord or lead, a baby still attached to cord

cork the end of a penis

cormar of a larger size [insp. *the coreus marginatus bug is larger than its similar species*]

cornament a corny ornament

cornear near (the) corner

coronation street a row of coronations

corporal pun a witty gesture or clown-like movement

corporation clouds silver cars

corpserate a corporate corpse

coshort the cohort's life was short

cosi the change of copper and silver left on a surface

cosmoke cosmo plus smoke

cosmonan an elderly hippy woman

cosmonorde far out

cosmonun a woman who believes in scientology

cosmooch love for the cosmos

cosmopa an elderly hippy man

cosmosoot dark space

costa that'll cost you

costa wreaker to cost a smelly lot, e.g. the costa wreaker wreaks [+ Costa Rica]

cost-host a product on the market

costol the overall cost

cost-plush to be laid back about making a profit on something

costs ace the mass selling of Costa coffee

cosu corrosive substance

COT cheese on toast | cup of tea

COT death death by cheese on toast

cot to have a drink of alcohol to ease you into sleeping [*the term 'clap of thunder' in pirate language means a strong, alcoholic drink*]

cotacoat a small coat [Iri. cóta: coat] [+ cot]

COTC corn on the cob

cother to have it covered | there-there

coughederal one who turns a blind eye to an offence | an officer who lets crime off the handle [cough + federal]

countercook a cook with a deadline | to cook with limited time [oppo. **whilercook**]

counterprops the props needed for a certain event

countershade to make someone feel rejected | to exclude someone

country tiles the nightlife of the country side

county mathematics

coup-quid to have no money to go out

courage broth power food, e.g. alfalfa sprouts

courier service a funeral | a send-off

courset an intense course [+ corset]

courgette coor, **icbi**

cous-ine to eat at a cousin's house (or to eat couscous off their roof)

coven a cold oven [oppo. **hoven**]

cover poncho

covederal a friendly federal

covertigo covered in sick

coving the borders

cow bark graffiti on a tree

cow hands leather gloves

cow pitch a field for cows

cowrapt corruption disguised

cow's back a cowskinned sofa

coy a bit sacred | to be grateful for the small things (in life)

cp common points

C (past) one letter past B, two letters past A, three letters past Z, four letters past Y, five letters past X, six letters past W, seven letters past V, eight letters past U, nine letters past T, ten letters past S, eleven letters past R, twelve letters past Q, thirteen letters past P, fourteen letters past O, fifteen letters past N, sixteen letters past M, seventeen letters past L, eighteen letters past K, nineteen letters past J, twenty letters past I, twenty one letters past H, twenty two letters past G, twenty three letters past F, twenty four letters past E, twenty five letters past D

cr character

crab-apple to curse

crabe to pinch someone [+ crab]

crabgrass crickets in the grass

crabies crabs and rabies

crabin a tight squeeze | a cabim lacking space

crabitat a small habitat

crab mouth a paper shredder

crabstract to look at something sideways on

cracked actors comedians who use the same act over and over

crackerjack one cracker (no cheese please, but you can pull the other side... hat please and you; toy)

crackhood a place where there are lots of pot holes

crack willow to drop things | to be clumsy | to have problems in understanding or doing but you always get there in the end [insp. *the willow tree drops twigs which eventually stick in wet mud and grow*]

cradle creeks people who sleep on floors

cradlegnat to talk in baby talk

craig david to spend time browsing craigslist.com

craig dayvid a week [+ day]

crall to call someone you don't really want to call [+ crawl]

cramberry and graspberry to try and learn a lot in short amount of time

cramp a bad/broken/badly sounding amp

crampage a skate boarding or BMX injury [insp. rampage]

cramp wank to wank someone so hard that they have to walk with a limp

crampedals feet too big for pedals, or pedals to small for feet

cranchor a crashing anchor

crane-fly slender with long legs [insp. *crane flies are slender with long legs*]

cranes bookends

crane-um to hold a thought [+ cranium]

crange a range of cringe e.g. a crange of fur coats

crank bank a bank with very bad customer services

crankle to not want to age | paranoid about wrinkles

crank wank to get a pissed-off wank, or to only wank someone to stop them from moaning

cranumb a numb brain | a dead cranium

crap genetically modified crops

crap mouth a bin

crapper hatch a very dirty toilet which contains flies

craps no official rules [insp. *there are no official rules for the game 'Craps'*]

crashberry squidgy

crass grass dead grass

crass'n'craze when a craze dies out | to calm down from hyperness

crass-rid to get rid of stupidity | to be only serious

crastove to dry out from too much heat

cratom to be tired of carrying crates of stock

craven arms arms which want to reach out and give a hug [+ crave]

crawl cruel

crawlful crawling with awfulness

crawling eyes eyes which like to see everything | to never want to miss out | eyes always looking elsewhere, e.g. your man has crawling eyes, my man has crabs, but atleast I know they are from my crawl and not his, your mans crawling eyes like to catch anything going, even a ball in mid air

crayon to stack crates on top of each other

creact a create response [+ reaction]

cream of tartar the creaming in on good manners

creativity zone psychiatric section

creature a small significance

creature-features baby features

credge at the edge of having credit or losing credit

creditto to have the same amount | to have paid the same amount

creek cradle the bed of a floor

creg a disqualified driver [+ registration]

crem'n'crime to have commited the crime of killing [crematory + crime]

crested tit for one tit to hang lower than the other [insp. *the crested tit can lower their crest feathers slightly*]

criarisp when a crisp has too much seasoning and you end up choking from it

crib half an hour [insp. *duration of the game 'Cribbage'*]

cribbage
partnership games |
relationship games | to
see how many friends
you can make in a
certain length of time
[insp. *'Cribbage' is
popular as a
partnership game*]

cricket sound of the
night [see **crabgrass**]

crickettle the
clicking noice of a kettle
| a cricket in the kettle

crike trike a
problem, but it can be
fixed

crikumber crikes,
that's big!

crimpleats
unattractive pleats in
clothes

cring a nervous
phonecall [ring + cringe]

cringerm a passing
on of cringe or fear

crispit a bed having
lots of crumbs in (due
to someone eating in
the bed)

criticunt one who
criticizes another's
performance

crive to want to cry |
to want to have emotion
[+ crave]

crochet pet to put a
little pet on a lead [Fre.
crochet: little hook]

crocodial for
someone to be snapping
at you (like a crocodile)
when on the phone to
them

crodom to take up
less space [*this is what
the game 'Cross
Dominoes' also does*]

croke rake to scratch
the throat | for the
throat to be scratched

crook-book a book
that is priced far more
than it should be

crooked-leg of
unequal length

crooket to hear
noises at night time
[crook + cricket]

crookid a kid having
an issue

crookie a really hard
cookie

croquet the game of
counting birds |
birdwatching [+ crow]

crows curved rows (of
seats)

cross fingers to prey

crossbone poaching

crossbowl to offer a
game of crossbow

crossed arms a war
memorial

crosshuff for two
people in a relationship
to be fed up [+
crossruff]

cross-key, allen-key
to change the locks on
a house so someone
who has a key is now
not able to enter

cross-leg to feel
within

crossriff for two
people to share a tune |
a married couple's first
dance [+ crossruff]

cross-soction to put
on someone elses socks

crouch when you
position yourself into
a ball shape for
protection and things
feel a bit better

crownology
technology that is flying
off the market and
making good sales

cruddly to find sleeping rough **cuddly**

cruel crawl

crum when you cram too much in and end up breaking something [+ crumb]

crumbpet a pet who eats anything

crup-ted a vandalized teddy

crus to run low on stock

crush to have plenty of stock

crush curbish to have a crush on someone when already dating someone else

crushendo to have a crush on a musician [+ crescendo]

crushion a casual crush

crush'n'cran squeeze

crussuminoose because some is in use | be curse some in noose

crust crossed

crusto coli

crustom for custom to dry up [insp. **crusto**]

crystal stilts crystals and pistols

cs Chomsky

CSS summer sale clothes

ctenation endangered species[Gk. Cteno: comb] [+ nation]

ctenover a comb-over [Gk. Cteno: comb]

C (to) one letter to D, two letters to E, three letters to F, four letters to G, five letters to H, six letters to I, seven letters to J, eight letters to K, nine letters to L, ten letters to M, eleven letters to N, twelve letters to O, thirteen letters to P, fourteen letters to Q, fifteen letters to R, sixteen letters to S, seventeen letters to T, eighteen letters to U, nineteen letters to V, twenty letters to W, twenty one letters to X, twenty two letters to Y, twenty three letters to Z, twenty four letters to A, twenty five letters to B

ctrl clock time, reality line

cub to kill a child

cubel a square shaped bangle

cuberg to hit a problem in convention | for a convention to declare it unsuitable [+ iceberg]

cubideformed one who watches too much TV that they lose their life to it [cubiform + deformed]

cubique for everywhere to be square [L. ubique: everywhere]

cubolt a square lock

cubs cold bubbles

cuc-coon a mental institute where the patients are not allowed to leave the premises

cu-cu cover up, cover up | to hide quickly | to cover up quickly, e.g. ah swear words, cu-cu the ears, cu-cu cu-cu

cucumbers bright eyes

cuddash when cutlery falls on the floor

cuddleast the least cuddliest

cuddly pleasing

cudland a land of love [+ woodland]

cue bid to provide information

cue bod to provide your body | to give yourself | to give something your full attention

CUF cut off from

cuffa tea tea stains of the cuffs of a shirt

cuiscene a restaurant feel

cuiscine to play footsy under the table [cuisine + **kiscine**]

cui sine wave music is a meal, tuck in (banquet, meal for one - it's all there, said the ear)

cul-de-sack to back

someone into a corner and for them to have no way out

cul-de-sass no way out, in a good way [oppo. **cul-de-suck**]

cul-de-sick endless illness

cul-de-suck no way out, a bad thing [oppo. **cul-de-sass**]

culled cold

culling cold-calling

culltral to cull the cultural

culp to drink from a cup

cultour a cult that only allows a specific coloured skin to join

cunt contain

cunted to be continued

cup weep

cupa a hissing sound [insp. the mobola tree]

cup-cap to cover the head

cup-clip for a cup to have no handle

cup-clop a heavy cup

cup-cock a smashed glass | a broken or chipped mug

cuphold a few fingers

cupholder for a body to always be holding a drink (especially coffee)

cuprum dark rum [L. cuprum: copper]

cupucca to bring the cup up to the lips

cura plantation [insp. the hoop pine tree]

curbash to hit your foot off the curb | to trip up the kerb

curbish a bit on the side [+ kerb]

curbon a curly hairstyle

curbot a curvy bottom

curbourbon a **curbon** of brunette colour

curd-alt to alter, to curdle

curdle (to) age

curran stolen money [currency + ran]

currency to use currants

curry and caprice for a food to suddenly become too hot to handle

curry rags to get curry on your clothes

curry-hurry to search for water fast after **curry and caprice**

curry-slurry to drink water fast after **curry and caprice**

curse rant negative talk

curse rent negative talk about a landlord or someone you used to live with

curtail a curtain that falls to the floor

curve pear

cussdis to discuss with the family [+ discuss]

cussess to wish bad luck [+ success]

custa customer

custa changa a customer paying with cash

custard powder to plant bizarreness

custa visa a customer paying by card

custody when a baby in a pram is left outside a shop on its own

customato a custom made tomato | vegetables with added preservatives and colourings

custorm a large amount of customers [+ storm]

cust pa spa for an active person to prefer the leisure of spa and fat foods [+ custard]

custrummer a dissatisfied customer

cusy raw and uncooked

cut, cope & pay in a recession we cut, cope and have to pay [+ cut, copy & paste]

cutdeath death by a knife

cutlery newman [insp. *Knives Forks and Spoons Press*]

cut'n'paste to imitate an imagination

cut-up monkey animal testing for cosmetic vanity

cy cycle

cyco to cycle around [+ **cy**]

cyber el

cyberg elg

cyberg is melting the iceberg is melting,

in terms of social or technical action where the urge/usage of computers (the solid) decreases | online banking is becoming less secure | we start to play outside again where we see real trees and real people

cyble to loop round a cable or wire

cycleman men who appreciate flowers [+ cyclamen]

cycloop when an animal chases their tale

cycluster to form into groups [+ cycle]

cycull to not be a circle

cycut when a circle is broken

Dd

D down | death

D *pic* 90 degree smile

dab cotton to make something dream-like

dabask a stab in the dark

dabba to listen to some Abba, e.g. we all dabba from now and then because Abba is everywhere

dabber an exposed shore [insp. dabberlocks]

dabble ample to make music

dab on douche to play on being a douche

DADA daily activities x 2

dada-car a homemade pimped-up car

dadical a middle-aged radical man

dadrib a deep voice [+ rib]

daff after being up the duff | post-duff

daffodil a difficult birth

daff o dil cucumbo sweet pickle [daffodil + dill cucumber]

daff o dil cue come bah rrr gain daffodils and cucumbers are bought at a bargain price

daffy dusty as f*** | dirty as f***

daffydil a daffy place

daft bed to play around in life [+ *on your death bed*]

daftodil a daft but pretty person [+ daffodil]

daft punk a punk of whom does not believe in (animal) equality

dagger-happy (stabbing) pains from laughing hard

daily to talk in tongue [+ Dali]

dairy udder

daisie a pretty day

dal-bar an outside bar [Turk. dalbar: summerhouse]

dalivered a strange delivery, e.g. I asked the post man how his day

was and he said the limeade is 49p but the water is free [+ Dali]

dalli to get around

dalliwell to get around well

DAM don't ask me

dam age to forget your age

damascus city of the damned

dam-in-excess a man in over-his-head

damn jar a swear jar, where each time you swear you have to put in money (fifty pence is a good amount)

damndruff scalp issues | damn snow, get out my hair

damsel-in-excess a lady in over-her-head

damsellout to be dumped or discarded for another

damulet a badluck charm [amulet + damn]

damunch to close the eyes | to intake darkness

dan dance

dan our to look around the property you own – that's if we own any property, if we do then we are not looking into our mind properly, or is the mind our property?

dancercise to dance for exercise

dancerise to passionately dance [+ cerise]

dancine a dance show at the theatre, e.g. a ballet or a morrisdancing jig

dand alive and dandy land [oppo. **dearth**]

dandie for the very good to die (out)

dando to happily do

dandyruff falling snow [see **damndruff**]

dangdew a divorce [wedding + dang] [insp from **dingdew**]

danger claw

dangremlim a little danger

danielle in fashion

dankle to have hurt your ankle and to avoid putting weight on it [+ dangle]

dans le grr in the danger zone

daph all-used [insp. the date palm tree]

dare pil to try and lip read a serious conversation

darkish a little dark

darkosh a lot of darkness

darksoma a dark body

darr a loving spirit

dart board you're either fired or promoted

darticulated double jointed [dart + articulated]

dash a small dish

dashi urinate

dashes to ashes to kill yourself from living too fast | to tire yourself from rushing around without rest

data wank when data is muddled up

dave every day

davert a common divert

dawn first signs of something working

dawn lawn first time or profit [insp. **dawn**]

dawnmow to come into daylight | for lights to go out

dayd not dead

day-da a day of dada

day well have a good day

DB drawing board

DC door's closing (said elevator)

DD double dutch

ddd three in a row [see **O's and X's**]

dddd four in a row
[see **FIAR**]

de out [see **tide**]

DEA don't eat animals

deactivate to pull out
of a decision

dead to be removed

deadbeed when a
deedbead is given to a
someone who knows it
will not be eternity

dead daisy a fried
egg

dead head tree a tree
in the winter having no
leaves

deadbread bread
which is too hard to eat

deadication dead
dedication

dead-life artificial
insemination

dead sea polluted
waters [insp. *the 'Dead
Sea' salt lake between
Israel and Jordan*]

deaf metal to listen
to so much loudness
you go deaf

deaf roof a house
with triple-glazing
meaning you cannot
hear anything from the
outside world

deal helium for
medication to not work
[*helium has no chemical
reactivity*]

dearth dead and dull
land [oppo. **dand**]

dearwig to take out
the **hearwig**

deathen to cut off
creativity

death breath no air

death cab for cutie
to arrange a funeral for
a young child

death cap a bomb in
a rucksack | a bomb
in a package

debb to open and
close drawers [+ ebb]

debore to have a sting
from a wasp

deborah a bee

debutt "dey butt" a
dire debut

deca aromatic [insp.
incense cedar]

decacamp tens of
tents [insp. deca]

decadisco a massive
disco [insp. deca]

decamps tens of
amps [insp. deca]

decars tens of cars
[insp. deca]

deca vicars tens of
holy people [insp. deca]

decay a bag with a
hole in it

declarity to decline
clarity

decodar a triangular
or arrow-shape
decoration

decorot having damp
show up on decorated
walls

deck to fight

deck-duck a duck
out of water

deckle to deck a little

declinging coming
close to losing heart

decoulourinse to
have dyed the hair and
to wash it out, to
decolour, to rinse
(usually many times)

dedication to not
give up protecting

dedray dehydrate(ed)

deedbead something given to symbolise eternity | an eternity ring [see **deadbead**]

deerad to read the adverts

defame to poo yourself in the shopping centre

def diablo a bad skill

defender to apply ice to a bruise | to take off the bumper on a car [insp. *in America 'fender' means bumper*]

defin to not breathe | to not provide

deframe to take glasses off

dega ageless [+ aged]

degreed measures of greed [+ degree]

deight the weight of a date, for instance, a wedding day

dekool to not look

dela one of the first [insp. the larch tree]

de-liver to take out the liver

deliverge at the verge of delivering, e.g. deliverge a baby(-sized package)

dell-boy an old dell computer

deltastock computer leads and chargers

delup to not be able to feel your fingers [dead + luppers]

delvert delve then divert

dement cement to push someone into the hole

demessage to bring a solution to the mess | to clean things up | to delete a text message you were close to sending

demidog part mortal, part dog

demidst halfway through doing something [+ demi]

demigenius part mortal, part genius [+ demi]

demigold part mortal, part gold [insp. demigod]

demigoon part mortal, part goon [+ demi]

demiode to be half and half [+ demi]

demi semi half and half

demisurge half surgical [+ demi]

democat a supporter of being loved

demolash to break down crying [lash + demolish]

demonstra a conversation which gets diverted [demonstrate + stray]

demonstray when a demonstration strays

den wardrobe

den ary ten dens [see **den**]

dench endangered [insp. papala]

dendrift to scan the **den** for an outfit

dendriz to shake a tree when it has been raining to see droplets of water fall down

dendroop a weeping willow tree [Gk. dendro: tree]

dendrop when a tree falls down [Gk. dendro: tree]

dendroplet leaves falling off the tree [Gk. dendro: tree]

dendross to throw a twig [Gk. dendro: tree] [+ toss]

dendrotone the movement of trees [Gk. dendro: tree]

dendry when the leaves die in cold weathers [Gk. dendro: tree]

den ier the colour of a **den**

denified undefined [+ deny]

denil in denial

den'm Denmark

den narnia a walk in den

denself a self which lives in its own world [+ den]

den tal a tall **den**

dentra enter through the mouth [+ dental]

deode to deodorize

dep art to move away from art

depart timer to exit work | to quit a job

depatment a place to touch, e.g. the head would be the best depatment is trying to channel into someone's thoughts [+ department]

de pe de to be dependent

dependent to read The Independent newspaper

depoint a depressed point

deposit to always look down | to walk with your head down

deposituate to leave out a situation information | to withdraw from a place

depresituate to return to a situation | to return to the place you deposituated from

deprosituate to turn down an offer of sex

depsoma a depressed body

der to be embarrassed due to not knowing [red + duh]

derange cooker a cooker that only works when it wants to [deranged + range cooker]

derek a (lovely) wreck

derfen to bump [insp. in America 'fender' means bumper]

derivet false nails [derivative + rivet]

dermot thick skinned [+ derm]

des angel deadly poisonous [insp. destroying angel]

desertlate when you get to your dinner too late and see it has dried up

designuke designated nuke

deskolate without tables [desolate + desk]

desk-tap a lamp

desperadio a radio station desperate for listeners [see **desperado**]

desperado desperate for a radio | desperate to listen to something on the radio [see **desperadio**]

despress a press desperate for news and stories

destbin a 'no-hope' [destiny + dustbin]

destory to tell a story in a different way

destoy to ruin a game [destroy + toy]

deti out and in [see **tide**]

deton not noted

deutsch hand to toss a pancake in the air

devastay when

something stays devastated

develoop to develop a pattern [+ loop]

devestrat a devastating strategy

devid to get rid of videos

devile vile and evil

devils horn an evil sound

devils semen red icing

devotchka to have the devil inside you

dexterise for many things to be tising | for different things to show up

dexternal the philosophy of the external(ism)

dextremes many extremes

dextrems many terms

diabeaties dire music [beats + diabetes]

diagonal a bishop [insp. *the game of 'Chess'*]

diagony to have died in agony | a painful death

diagraci to be thankful daily

dial a pizza a lazy day planned

dialect to have lectures every weekday

diamond to have died on a monday

dianosed not allowed out for the day [+ diagnose]

diasport to disport daily diasposit for disposition to change

daily | for every day to be different

dias tol a restful day [Spa. dias: day] [+ diastolic pressure]

dicecream to keep rolling a good number with the dices

dice ice a bad roll

dice nice a good roll

dicha in two | forked [insp. quiver tree]

dicide a choice between the numbers 'one' to 'six' [dice + decide]

DICK did it cure kin?

dicky-bellow to give a blow-job in an office

dicky-bow formal

dicky sud a boring book

dictor doctor a doctor who only dictates

diddoms in domination

dideroot Diderot's writings

D.I.dry a hardware store not making profit | for people to stop making

D.I.why to wonder if it is cheaper to do it yourself, or whether you can save time getting in a professional

die gestive slowly crumbling to death

die-ode an ode to the dead

die-rid an aid to death | a disease that can cause death

diet fad | fashion

diff duff a difficult pregnancy

diffears different fears

differrous different metals | various hard materials

diffi cult a complex cult

digesture to take in a gesture | to take in a message

digger-hap to be the only one laughing [dig + happy]

digger-rap to repeat the same joke until you are the only one who still finds it funny [**digger-hap** + rap]

digicatch when a piece of technology catches on

digiggle to be the only one to find something funny [see **digger-hap**]

digital look to watch through the eyes of technology

dignifield an area of the dignified

dignite to get to the bottom of something with another's help

dig-scruff to lose all dignity

dihatch to give birth to twins

di late see you when it's too late

dilch a spirited child

dilemma a fork

dillama a dilemma when two people walk in opposite directions and you have to choose which one of them to follow [llama + dilemma]

dillord the person who is on board with being overboard about the 'dill' herb

dilute squash

diluted squashed

DIM dim in manner

dimage a dull idea | a dim image

diment to experiment [+ dimentia]

dimentia a dime meant sheer

diminsion a dim layer

dimple temple to worship a beauty spot | to be in awe with a beauty spot

dinermite a food fight [+ dynamite]

dinim two tone denim

dingbatch the school bell

dingdew a marriage

DINING ROOM destiny is never in naked garments, room only on moor

dinnex to dine outside [+ exterior] [oppo. **dinnin**]

dinnin to dine inside [+ interior] [oppo. **dinnex**]

dinno didn't know

dino-flintstone a fossil [insp. **flinstones**]

dinvade to invade someone's dinner by helping yourself to picking at it

din-win an award winning dish

dionysos death by choking on a sausage

dionysosroll death by choking on a sausage roll [insp. **dionysos**]

dip fire resistant [insp. bella umbra]

dir a small drink

direct a one-way road

dirtgerous dangerous dirt

dirth dirty earth

disaccure the acres of free land occurring

disaccuring more trespassing and less public walking

disallie to resist sharing a lie

disallow no-go

disappro to disapprove

dis-ass to numb the bum by sitting for too long

disastar the star of disaster(s)

disbleep to unsignal

disco ball to mirror | self-reflection

disco gin to drink gin at a party

discontinue continull

dis-cover to uncover | to remove a mask

discrept discretely crept

discrust to pick dry spots

discunt one who is easily sexually tempted

discursieve to discuss eliminating cursive words or political incorrectness

discush a round cushion [+ disc]

disfaced two faced

disgraci to not give thanks

disgracias to not be thankful | this grassy ass

disguise cider in a lucozade bottle

dish gaf the dishwasher (to be human or to be machine?)

dishwash something modern which does not harm the environment [*the dishwasher is a piece of technology which is good for the environment because it can use less water than the traditional way of washing by hand*]

diskate when a disk is still spinning when stopped | of how a CD spins when it is being played

dismissive massively dismissive

dismozz to find the negative funny [+ dismal]

disney a knee which has been leant on a hard floor for too long it starts to give way

disorient to confuse or to think someone as another culture, e.g. a disorient is to mistake a Japanese person for a Chinese person or a Canadian for an American [+ disorient]

dispakora for something to be divided

dissipat to be exhausted from so many people asking for your help [dissipate + pat]

dissoma a disabled body

distan far in a sunny disposition

distance makes the heart grow stoned distance makes the heart space out and be in another world

distanguish to distinguish the differences between orange types

distart to make something which isn't sexual sexual

distartan the love for the queen or against the queen by punks [tartan + distort]

distention not allowed out of the house | not allowed to go out [detention + tent]

distink a distinct, horrible smell

distore a store that does not look like the store it is, e.g. a chemist has flowers in the window and looks like a florist

distore store plus distort

distribe to break away from the tribe

distrunkt to hide the bottom area of the trousers with a long top

disturbalance for a balance to be disturbed | a family feud

dit do it

dita (to) peel

ditagraci to give thanks daily

ditapot to peel potatoes paily

ditch dd to stop going **dd**

dits dancing in the street

ditsm dancing in the supermarket

dittander hot and pungent

ditto deep in thought x 2 | two people deep in thought together

dittoes to have similar toes to someone

ditty doing it

ditty gritty having sex

ditzgits people ditzy when it comes to digits

diva state an area of divas | the gay village

divase to hold different opinions

dive extremely tall [insp. karri tree]

dive love high flying love

diven I've done

dive'n'dish one with no respect | one who cannot accept, e.g. a scuba diver who loves seeing fish in the water but also eats the fish

divertical to stop going across

divertigo to suddenly feel sick

divide to give to be equal

divideo the scenes of a film

divindividual a divine and special individual [dividable + divine + divine + individual]

division dispakora

di vision double vision

divoice to split the voice

divorce to **schi**

divvyne the perfect football sports team [divine + division]

di white light DIY work which will not get you dirty

di why I why do I always do it (to) myself?

diyi di why I

dizzy a wise person

dj hype a person who gets excited when a certain song is played

d'lemon to find a lemon too sour to handle

d'log the log which had the letters "b" and "c" carved into it is now taken by a dog [see **blog** and **clog**] [go to **log**]

d'nah finger food [+ hand]

DO door's opening, said elevator

dob to tell

dobob to only tell part of it

docilics doctors prescribing of medication which makes us docile

docudrama a document of a drama

documentary a doctors comments and prescriptions

do-dali-daisy to choose the wild card

dodecorum plenty of decorum [+ dodecagon]

dodge-ball to move the body quickly

dodobi to agree |to happily do something

do-dove to 'do' to breed [insp. *a dove breeds quickly*]

dodo-hands webbed hands [*like a dodo bird's wing*]

dodo-hood a big birds nest | an area which has lots of bird nests

dodo-toes webbed feet [insp. **dodo-hands**]

doe long druckers the growth and consumption of coffee shops [+ so long suckers]

does my bum look big in business – does it? because I am way ahead of you in the race, and everybody is behind trying to catch up – all you can see is the back of me – tell me, how does it feel for me to be winning you?

dogger-hap laughing that sounds like barks from a dog

doggone something holy has gone

dog la tin a tin of dog food

doglegboot boots that bend and give-way, losing shape and making you walk differently

dogmush canned dog food

dogostrophe a catastrophe that cannot take itself for a walk

dog-race to be racist

dogue to make money from dog racing [doe + vogue]

dolce far doll down far we fall for a fool [insp. *dol is a measurement for pain*]

dole cup a chipped cup

dol house a hospital [insp. *dol is a measurement for pain*]

dollmation a collection of B&W photos

dollot to pay a lot (of dollar) for a portion [+ dollop]

dolly cart wheel for a dolly cart to fall over

dolted to have been mugged [bolt + dollar]

dolthin a small pain [insp. *dol is a measurement for pain*]

do-mestic happy with domestication

domestick anything domestic of a stick-like figure, e.g. toilet brush, broom, mop, etc

domestock (a lot of) ornaments in the home

domestray to become wild again [domestic + stray]

domestuck stuck at home

dominica black and white car(s) [+ domino]

domino face-down

dominoah to count a group of animals [+ *Noah's Ark*]

dominoes bones

dominose to have a spotty nose

don five to ten minutes [insp. *the duration of the game 'Donkey'*]

don ate to suck on the sleeves or any other area of clothes

done dressed up

don lon to dress in the Great Britian flag

don par to be wearing the same clothes as someone else

don't bake my heart don't overfeed me through love

don't give sup don't give up the sssss, the slithers and hisses of snake

don't look back in fanger don't look back in anger at the dentist

donald duck

donald deck the duck is out of the water

dongkey a pooing donkey

donk suitable for very young children, [insp. *the game 'Donkey'*]

doney a baby [insp. donk]

donner to put on a bib at dinner [+ don]

donor to give someone a doughnut

doob a foolish dude [+ boob]

doobaloo diablo one who does a lot of voluntary work

doobi to happily say yes | a happy yes

doodle to loosen the hand

DOOM deep observation of misery | a dose over-observed medication

doomestic the tragedy of domestication [+ doom]

door chime to have a wanted visitor at the door [oppo. **door dime**]

door dime to have someone at the door asking for money

door doom to have an unwanted visitor at the door [oppo. **door chime**]

do or door to either do or not do something – there's no inbetween, e.g. either you do or door | the two extremes

doork a dark door | the beginning of a darkness | the gateway to truth [+ stork]

door stopper to deny entry

door strapper a hinge

doorstrip the path to a doorway

door-wedge to keep it open

dora to explore

dorgen a door to a dark place [+ dungeon]

dorset to mark out an antrance

dosey domesticated

dosie doe to check pockets or the bag for any floating change

dossipat suicide [insp. **dissipat**]

dot do not

dotask a medical task [+ doctor]

dot com the use of a comma for a full-stop

dot commercial the business of buying and selling domains

dot kotton Dot Cotton (from Eastenders) able to fly [Kic. Kot: eagle]

doth one of five [insp. hiba]

do the lacquer-motion to lacquer the hair (to hairspray the hair big)

dothes dirty clothes [oppo. **cleathes**]

DOTS disease of the skin

dou bled bled twice, e.g. the nose dou bled and then my eye, my ear dou bled and then my hand

doubless to pray twice a day

doubtfit a doubted outfit

doubtward to express doubt

douche dou che bag che dou-ble blag, ou dub code bad ou che

douche bag a lame-acting person

douche, douche, goose! to get angry, lose temper with gobbledy-goose ook see ok bled gob-de-gob getted ang ag and ry ooooooooooooooooo

dousers loose garments that move out of place, e.g. a skirt will twist round and trousers may fall down

dover to do a lot | (do-ver(y) much

DOW diversity of words

dowem golden hair [insp. *the dragonfly, downy emerald 's*

thorax is clothed with dense golden hair]

down sun when the sun goes down

downgrad to graduate with a lower qualification

downstair to let someone down

downswept looking down [insp. the deodar tree]

down-thunder a deep sadness

dowrek shipwreck under water

dowstiny towards the end of the line [dowse + destiny]

dox little paradox | a bit of irony

dozen yacht [insp. *the game 'Yacht' has twelve rounds*]

dozenith spiritual process

D (past) one letter past C, two letters past B, three letters past A, four letters past Z, five letters past Y, six letters past X, seven letters past W, eight letters past V, nine letters past U, ten letters past T, eleven letters past S, twelve letters past R, thirteen letters past Q, fourteen letters past P, fifteen letters past O, sixteen letters past N, seventeen letters past M, eighteen letters past L, nineteen letters past K, twenty letters past J, twenty one letters past I, twenty two letters past H, twenty three letters past G, twenty four letters past F, twenty five letters past E

dradje to have toilet tissue stuck to your foot

drafts and drifts in art, to drift away from ideas quickly

drag den a place of karaoke

dragganought to open the mouth when yawning [*to drag a nought, which is the mouth as the mouth has the shape of an 'o' when open wide*]

dragging wind a person who drags down a movement

dra gun a fire-arm | the weapon of fire

drainage the act of draining, e.g. pasta is goes through drainage

dram bull a drum skin the drummer has no spirit!

drama&sheeta a religious script for a play

dramauto automatically dramatic

drape drastically ape

drats drenched rats | wet people

draugh the flow of the freehand | stream of consciousness ['*draught' in pirate language is the drawing of liquid*]

draught easily understood | to provide the basics [insp. *the game 'Draughts'*]

drawf a small drawing | a quick sketch [+ dwarf]

dray hydrate(ed)

dre a very short dress

dreams a playground for all ages

drear a dreary dear

drem drain when you forget a dream you had

dresden colourful

dresden doll a colourful toy | an exciting game

dress sage herbalize

drez to hang up a dress

drezden to hang up a dress in the wardrobe

dribbon a droopy ribbon | a wet patch from dribbling

drift to drive in cruise mode

drift gift a gift without reason

drism rained on

drival a car racing competitor

drivelcro to get stuck in senseless talk

drivine a homedelivery food service

drivoid driving nowhere, just driving

drope when someone comes to help

drod a few minutes [insp. *the game 'Drop Dead' only takes a few minutes to play*]

droitwitch! dry it which | the witch lived riot in Droitwitch

droll to roll dice

droll ace to roll a good roll

droll ice to roll a bad roll [insp. **droll ace**]

dropera to drop off | to be put to sleep for an operation

drug den a place where drugs are taken | a **den** full of rave clothes

d'rum & coke a miniature drum in a glass

drumball swing and movement of the drumbats

drumbat a drumstick

drumbaton to drumbat on the drums

drumblee a slow computer [drumble + bleep]

drumbleed when a computer freezes

drumbrella for a layer of skin to grow over a wound

druminant a spiritual rhythm produced from drumming | fingers in tapping motion [drum + ruminant]

drumsurf to play around at hitting the skins (of drums)

drumsurf abuse to have carried out **drumsurf** on the skin of a living person

drunken slanted

drusk drunk at dusk, e.g. most of the town is drusk

drycle the spin cycle of a clothes dryer

DT dental & tenant

dt deeper truth

D (to) one letter to E, two letters to F, three letters to G, four letters to H, five letters to I, six letters to J, seven letters to K, eight letters to L, nine letters to M, ten letters to N, eleven letters to O, twelve letters to P, thirteen letters to Q, fourteen letters to R, fifteen letters to S, sixteen letters to T, seventeen letters to U, eighteen letters to V, nineteen letters to W, twenty letters to X, twenty one letters to Y, twenty two letters to Z, twenty three letters to A, twenty four letters to B, twenty five letters to C

dub cotton to tell a dream

dublin to try and trace (to dub linear)

duck donald

ducklord a landlord who is always popping around

ducks bread winners

due tolerate [insp. the alpine ash tree]

dufeet soft and warm feet [insp. **dufoot**]

duffodil the birth of a child

dufoot a soft warm foot [+ duvet]

dug multi-colour [insp. the kamarere tree]

dug-up to look rough | to look as if you've just been dug up from the grave

dulook a colourful look [+ dulux] plus look)

dulse relish

dumper bumper to crash your car into another car | to bump into someone

dumplinger to throw screwed up paper [+ dumpling]

dump'n'dive do's and don'ts [see **do or door**]

dunce bad dancing

dungaree to have stepped in dung more than once

dungeon wrong doing | done gen(eration)

dungeons & dragons these times are long and dark, gloomy and slow – they don't seem to shift

dungiene dungy hygiene

dungula to have poo or dirt in the finger nails [L. ungula: claw] [+ dung]

dunjeans dirty old jeans [+ dungy]

dupliskate to try and duplicate a skateboard move

durace during a race

duralitter recycled materials

duratio to spend time with someone | to educate | to share knowledge

dur duh somebody who is with someone for the money [Turk. dür: pearl]

dury during jury

duscoc where the man works and the woman stays at home to look after the kids [insp. *the dusky cockroach: the male flies well but female doesn't fly*]

dusk a dark furred duck

duskbunnies things which appear at dusk

duski to remove make-up

dusklets very dark brown eyes | dark eyes

dust powdirt

dustpan to hold a dirty secret

dut a badly spoken and written dutch

duvet couver to have beg bugs [Fre. couver: to hatch]

duveternarian a veterinarian who prescribes the duvet as good medicine

dv8 deviate

dwarf a small drawer

dy duck-rabbit

dye day a day where present is a rainbow

dyna more on offer than just dinner

dyon to go on into dying, to carry on dying

dyslexia the doorway to reading experiments | a gateway to language games

dyspraxia the
doorway to a new
dimension

dyspraxis the x and
y, of the chromosome
and into space | the
success of a situationist

Ee

E East | even

E *pic* a kitten

eagle to be willing to scavenge [as the bird does]

eagle eyed cherry when a cherry goes flying | a person who begs please with a cherry on the top

eapuror starchy clothes | starch-like [insp. *the early purple orchis tubers are starchlike*]

earie to listen out for the eerie

earlane to listen to a whisper

earth green

earthen war to smash earthen ware when having an argument

earth hay soil

earthlay to be in balance with nature

earwig an earring [see **beerwig**]

earwog to eavesdrop

ease code a simple/easy password

ease knees not bent

east enders to finish living in the East

eastlife life of the East

eat munch

eatcrete to eat then excrete

eat quet munch bunch

eating cotton to be dreaming

eaucaly most successful [insp. eucalyptus]

ebbryo the flowing back of the tide as the water returns to the sea [ebb + embryo]

eb con to travel into your child spirit [embryo + **ub con**]

ebony forever [+ ebb]

ebyam maybe not

eccentric calculator to judge how crazy something is

echolip to **eclip** again

echonomo to repeat an amount

echonomic the ongoing stress from money problems

echose when the shower or a tap drips out drops of water [echo + hose]

echouse an empty house [+ echo]

ecivres useless [+ services]

eclapse to collapse with sadness or embarrassment after **eclip**

eclectric when more than one person is in power [eclectic + electric]

eclepse to seizure darkness [Gk. lepsy: seizure] [+ eclipse]

eclip to turn the head to avoid being kissed [insp. **eclepse**]

eclipse to take hair clips out

eco bag to use over and over

ecolip to eclip due to the person has been eating something which does not agree with you

ecologue a catalogue full of eco-friendly produce

econt containing economics

ecrude for something to go dull to bright to dull then bright to dull to bright then dull and so on [crude + ecru]

edeity a photoshopped deity

eden lemon to use lemon to cure colds | the magic of lemons

edent a problem with (pure) religion [+ evident]

edgym to be edgy about physical activities

edi edible

edia every day

edias to have eaten a lot over the last few days [edible + **edias**]

ediball an edible ball of food, e.g. pate or bhaji

edibell a bell which rings at a certain time, meaning you know what time it is when you hear it, making time edible

edible flabo

edibloat a type of food which makes you bloated, e.g. marsh mallows or dried apple rings

ediet a temporary edit | to cut temporarily cut down

editon many edits | lots of versions

editorch to give praise to an editor | to block out light with your hand

editouch readjust

e draught for a daughter to disappear

eee three in a row [see **O's and X's**]

eeee four in a row [see **FIAR**]

eekhack to break into a highly secure place

eels every excitement laughs and then smiles

effin very full [insp. **fin**]

EFG effing fushing grr | to curse [+ fush]

egg'dar al poe to write or read dark literature in the morning [+ *Edgar Allan Poe*]

egg-glove to have a hand up the anus

eggknot a wet fart [eggnog + knot]

eggnag somebody who drinks in their sorrows [+ sorrow-fest] [insp. **eggknot**]

eggrease to apply cream to the stomach when having an ultrasound scan [+ egg]

eggress a baby that moves a lot inside the stomach [insp. **eggrest**] [+ egg] [poppo. **eggrest**]

eggrest a baby that hardly moves inside the stomach [+ egg] [oppo. **eggress**]

eggrovate to aggrovate egg use | to upset a pregnant person

egg-time estimated time of birth

egg timer time of the month [insp. **period**]

egnora orange | ignore her

egnoramious to ignore the sun [ignore + egg]

egrest to leave somewhere to go and rest

egypt in ecstasy

eh to not be in the right frame of mind

ehavoc to have come a long way

ei cen eighteenth century

eight minutes past moneigh horsey fifty two minutes to honey o bey or see

eight minutes to would bro then doom? fifty two minutes past wooden broom

eighteen minutes past number forty two minutes to numb, err

eighteen minutes to fish stun: prone forty two minutes past gill stone

eighteeth eight teeth

einstin Einstein-like

einstun surprising intellect [Einstein + stun]

E itch an itch E of the back

ejectron pushing out

ejectrunk to make sense of it all

ekamra to watch something being dismantled | timelapse [+ camera]

ekil unlike

ekip to have a break from using the computer

el cyber

elastic bon to have someone wrapped around the finger

elay cyberspace

elayvan to travel in cyberspace

elayvan camper to elayvan until the early hours of the morning

elayvent to wait in cyberspace [insp. **elay**]

elboat a funny boat ride [+ elbow]

el bow an arm band

el cen eleventh century

elecementary to be stuck in elementary

electan an electronic sun bed

electrack the flow of electricity

electrancis electronics which induce trances

electric eel an electric shock

electrosit to sit on somethng that is powered by electric, e.g. washing macine

elefantastic hugely fantastic [+ elephant]

elepants big pants [+ elephant]

elephant man a very happy large-sized man

elephantom a big spirit [elephant + phantom]

elephant trunk shower

eleven minutes past yacht forty nine minutes to parked in the lo-t

eleven minutes to uncalled for, really a bar row forty nine minutes past uncle's a wheel barrow

elg cyberg

elims technological limbs smile

elit the light from the computer screen

ell a massive pull [see **oosh**]

ella the sheltering of the umbrella [see **umber**]

ell-sin-ferg to not be able to use fingers to count [+ fingerspell]

elo when you accidently have your skirt tucked into your knickers

ELOG estimated length of time (not a log with the letter "e" carved into it) [see **d'log**]

elpot a big pot

elvis has left the building the shark has gone

embass much depth [embassy + bass]

embogem to to make more sparkly, e.g. the stars at night emogem the sky [+ embroid]

embra an embarrassing bra, e.g. en off-white colour or a scooby doo bra

embratio to embrace
a ratio

embrisk an
embracing walk [+
brisk]

embroice to have a
piece of clothing altered

embroidead no
rhythm | a luxury is
taken away

emdra plenty of
vegetation [insp. *the
emperor dragonfly
breeds in still waters
which have plenty of
vegetation*]

EMERGE every man,
every rodent – genetic
ever

emergen the siren of
a fire engine,
ambulance or police car

emergentle to
emerge gently | a calm
approach

**emigrated the
cheese** to have
stopped eating dairy

emma buntin Emma
Bunton on the face of
bunting

emopathy empathy
through emotion

emotional weight
relationship troubles
which make you
comfort eat

empathetic pathetic
empathy

empha attention [+
emphasize]

emphanton a serious
need of attention

empha-size to
imagine a size

emphrantic for a
child to crave attention
[emphasize + frantic]

empirate a pirate ship [+ empire]

empire of the sun one who spends the most time in sunlight | a bright-eyed person

emproar a roaring ruler | one who likes to be in control

empty buy [L. emption: a buying]

empty bowl to keep quiet because you have not achieved [oppo. **howl bowl**]

enassemble to gather wood for a fire [insp. **ensemble**]

encrassted covered with crassness

encrusteddied covered with teddies

encyclopedal the storing of information in the body | to process information

endarkment the enlightment reversed

end credit to be acknowledged when dead

endear to stop being in the heart

endearest to be far from being close in the heart

endlip the sides of the mouth where the top and bottom lips connect

eneed any need

enep not even almost [*backwards of 'pene' which is Latin for 'almost'*]

energene borrowed energy | to take away someone's power

energy oomph | vowel

enfussiasm when fuss becomes the enthusiasm

enga to end the game of 'Jenga' by pretending to accidently knock it over

engi engineer

englash bad English

enguage engineering language

engulf to have a go at something | to put something in a hole

eniw (you're) out of wine

enlie to enlighten the by telling a little lie

enosca boldly chequered [insp. *the abdomen of the 'eneplops scapa bug has boldly chequered margins*]

enovoid to have deliver a baby [envoy + ovoid]

enownen every now and then

ensemble the movement of flames

ent rap for a parent to introduce their children to rap music

ent enter

entasew to sew up a hole near the **entaso**

entaso the heel area of the sock, e.g. entaso is the place where holes occur most often [+ entasis]

enter tix

entertainment pink [insp. *'Tivial Pursuit' colour*]

entertanners the oompa lumpas in Willy Wonka's Chocolate Factory

entirelish it's all photoshopped! [entirely + relish]

entit to look towards the breast area

entocia an average birth [insp. **entociao**]

entociao a difficult birth [+ ciao]

entossment a messy bed

entre entrance to the center

envomi the poison of favouritism [venom + nominee]

envoy age representing time

envylob to pretend you are not jealous

envy lobe to envy what you are hearing

envylope to be jealous of a message

enypanelope to envy another's cooking skills

envypenelope to envy another's handwriting [+ envelope]

envypinelope to envy another's success [+ pine]

EP eat plants

E (past) one letter past D, two letters past C, three letters past B, four letters past A, five letters past Z, six letters past Y, seven letters past X, eight letters past W, nine letters past V, ten letters past U, eleven letters past T, twelve letters past S, thirteen letters past R, fourteen letters past Q, fifteen letters past P, sixteen letters past O, seventeen letters past N, eighteen letters past M, nineteen letters past L, twenty letters past K, twenty one letters past J, twenty two letters past I, twenty three letters past H, twenty four letters past G, twenty five letters past F

E pen to type

E pic an online image

epicture an epic picture

epik to not have a break from using the computer

episoap an episode of a soap opera

equator gator entry to another side

equinock to knock two heads together when they are in

disagreement [+ equinox]

equitone equivalent tone

er emerge

era's big ears

eras bold a well known era

eras light the enlightment

er broth to look down on your brother | to think little of your brother

erecreation erecting the creation

erect whifir

erectwhile to have recently been built

erose a wilting flower | wilting

err and an errand of err | to have forgotten what you were doing

err bird a bird of unknown descent

err bug burger

erreka I hear it [+ eureka]

errly to feel 'err' in the early hours

erroar a roaring error

errogant too bigheaded or overconfident that if gives off bad vibes

erry stray be strawberry

er sist to look down on your sister | to think little of a sister

er temp temporary temper

es Escher

esast highly adaptable [insp. *the bird 'estrilda astrild' is a highly adaptable species*]

escents the essence of minimalism

escher artistically geometric

eserum the flow of the written words [Turk. Eser: written work] [+ serum]

esion a quiet session

eskermit a natural path | a patch of grass [*Escher + Kermit*]

eskiss an eskimo kiss

eskite snowdrops falling from above [eskimo + kite]

esnes to sense backwards, e.g 'stop making sense and esnes', said steve

esperegust to have disgust for soldiers [Turk. esger: soldier]

esprit de corpse a group séance trying to communicate with the dead

essay so a typical view | nothing new

essex is too visibly sexual | too easy | it's sexy

establast an amazing experience

establiss a holy experience

estaste the usual taste [+ estate] [insp. **etast**]

esti mate a potential friend

estimate rough

estrogen the generation of the East

ET elephant trunk | estimate & track

etast state of taste [Fre. etat: state]

ETC every touch cries [see **ASO**]

ETCH elephants tamed cause hurt

etch cat when a cat sharpens the claws

etch pet a pet that likes to scratch

ethiopear a curvy ethiopian

ethletics to exercise ethics

etik no wind [+ kite]

etiquiet lack of etiquitte

etiquest in hope of good manners

E (to) one letter to F, two letters to G, three letters to H, four letters to I, five letters to J, six letters to K, seven letters to L, eight letters to M, nine letters to N, ten letters to O, eleven letters to P, twelve letters to Q, thirteen letters to R, fourteen letters to S, fifteen letters to T, sixteen letters to U, seventeen letters to V, eighteen letters to W, nineteen letters to X, twenty letters to Y, twenty one letters to Z, twenty two letters to A, twenty three letters to B, twenty four letters to C, twenty five letters to D

et-sock to put your foot in it

eu eurhythmy

euchre forty five minutes

eufanasia to kill off the heat with a fan

eugen a eurhythmic gene

eugene the Amazon Rainforest [insp. the surinham cherry tree]

eumocaly you mock all we (all of us)

eumotion altering emotions [+ eurhythmy]

e up to sum up

eury dom red, orange or yellow [insp. *the eurydema dominulus bug is usually orange or red, although some individuals are yellow*]

eva either

evacooation a bird's migration

eve beli to believe everyone | to have belief in everything | optimism

eversi quality rather than quantity [insp. *game 'Reversi' where the strategy is quality rather than quality that decides the game'*]

everso quantity rather than quality [oppo. **eversi**]

eversore to always destroy [L. eversor: destroyer]

everybodice to be connected with everything | in harmony with all

evian tap water

evil butcher

evoid a miss of face-to-face

evote to call on history | to highlight the past | to phone an old friend [evoke + vote]

evolvelcro the evolving use of velcro | the success of social networking

evol vet to have started at the vets

evolume for volume to increase

ewwmotion a disliked emotion

ex stop

example a sample of an exam | a mock exam

excitea excitement of tea

excred to cancel a credit card

excrept anything but silent [except + crept]

excurvy to have been side-tracked

exdeb to cancel a debit card

execute cute on the outside [+ exterior]

ex factor noncommercial

exhaunst to be tired of hanging around or trying to make someone remember [exhaust + haunt]

exhost an exhaustion

exhoust an exhausted house | a rundown house in a bad state

exigent requiring immediate care [+ gentle]

exis no access [+ **ex**]

exit ret

exitcise to finish exercise

exitess when you always choose to run away [+ excess]

exma to not be talking to your mother [+ **ex**]

exmex to stop making [+ **ex**]

ex mouth the anus

exodcel a vital piece of data [exodus + Microsoft Excel]

exodust the 'left behind' [+ exodus]

exotack passionate activity [exotic + attack]

expa to not be talking to your father

expack to unpack

expandal a public house [expand + pandal]

expassion to have moved on from the passion

expeck to stop kissing

expennies little expenses

experience headucation

experimitation an experiment which lacks originality

expertise connected skills

expirace to calm down by exerting slowly [L. expir: to breathe out]

expirate to take out something, e.g. expirate the bags for collection

exploratio to explore the relations [+ ratio]

explore to dora

exp lore teaching experience

explorous for it to feel intesnse when you pour water onto the body

explort to trace a journey back [export + explore]

explosure a disturbing experience

exportato a slow export

express to squeeze juice from fruit

extearior when a face wears sadness

extender output tender

extent to dismantle a tent

extra re-tax

ex, why, zee to want to know everything about the past

exuberry an exuberant

eyay to see something euphoric

eye-ball good eye contact

eye clash when two people can't stop looking at each other [eyelash + clash]

eye-joint good eyeconnection

eyelot a large hole [oppo. eyelet]

eyelush pretty eyes

eyes in glass to research | to check the ingredients

eye-size differing view

eye slash when two people can't keep their eyes off each other because they want a fight | aggressive oneto-one eye contact [insp. **eye clash**]

eye-ster to look deep [+ oyster]

Ff

F fire(starter)

F *pic* a flag on fire

f2b front to back

f2f face to face

FA fantasy attachment

faballs fantasy games [insp. **FA**]

fabstract a fabulous abstract | a fabulous idea | a brilliant represntation

fabstruct to think the obstructions fabulous

FACE for all clinically evangelical

faceback to not have a photo of yourself on your Facebook profile

facebag to use Facebook a lot

faceblock to block someone on Facebook

facebluff to put a fake image on your facebook profile as to pretend you are that person

facebog to constantly update your facebook status with boring information, e.g. 'at the cinema with Hayley'

facebrick to be violent on Facebook

facebrook to live more on Facebook than in the real world

facelaf wrinkles from laughing

faceleft without a face lift

facepant a sweated off facepaint

faces on fruit comical

face-value in modelling where they look at the face and the body of a person and judge if they are suitable

fact wiki

fad flowers and diamonds

fadad a trendy father

fadder a diet where lots of bread is eaten [insp. *fodder is livestock food*]

faddish bit of a fad

faddosh a big fad

faddress to give a fake address

faf fruit and flowers

fa fa fast asleep, fast asleep!

fa-fa away

fa-fa R far away from running away

faf faith flourishing

faf-gaf a proseperus job

fafmiliar similar faf

fafogut to have a gut full of fast-food

fafterlife to worry about what happens when you're dead

fag a large amount of chemicals

FAG-C for a good cause

faggi a light smoker

faggish to smoke a little

faggo a heavy smoker

faggosh to smoke a lot

fagpuss a puss confused about its gender

fagro the agro a smoker gets when they haven't had a smoke and really crave one

fail ale when you drink and drink and drink and still there is no effect

failord one who is known for failure | a person who fails a lot

fair ale the casual alcoholic drink

fairgran a fairground lacking excitement

fairgrunge the story behind fairgrounds and travellers

fai-ri cha to dry (out) [insp. fairy-ring champignon]

fair isle fair grounds |fair enough

fair spirit the usual spirit, e.g. vodka

fairy tale lend to lend someone something and realise you'll never get it back

faithsoma a body of faith

fal false

faldstool *pic* DNA

fallace to tuck laces into the side of the shoe

fallen leaves unwanted leaflets on the ground

fallinger to talk about falling | a deflating conversation

fallord one who is known for being clumsy or falling a lot | one who falls in love too quickly

fallosophy the philosophy of falling

fallow to give in [fall + follow]

fambourine the 'over-used' guitar riff [fame + tambourine]

famechew to read about celebrities lives

famechore the constant work of fame and having to be on show

fam house a house of celebrities

famild an average family [+ mild]

famile a distant family

family bucket a whores vagina

famouse an alternative celebrity

fan repetition

fancer to become obsessed

fandancot a bad swim [insp. **fandangoose**] [fanta + **fandango**]

fandango to fanny around

fandangoose a good swim [**fandango** + goose]

fang nails sharp finger nails

fangel many angels fighting devils [insp. **fangle**]

fangle many fires in the space [+ angle]

fangyu when a compliment is an insult to you | to not accept a compliment | to see the compliment as an insult

fanta fish bladder

fantaste tastes fantastic

fantastock fish stock [the *'Fanta' drink contains fish*]

fantasty a lustful dream [fantast + tasty]

fara a pile of leaves [insp. *the raphoa palm tree has the biggest leaves*]

faraday first day of autumn

far age to not believe in age | age does not matter

far-fan far from liking something | far from giving your consent | far from being a fan

far-fotch to put your foot in too far | to get too involved [+ farfetched]

fargon far gone jargon | far out gobbledygook

farmour to dive into piles of hay

faroes far from heroes

far sands thousands

farts and crafts slapstick jokes

farynx to be stuck at the back [far + larynx + pharynx]

fash net the trend trap

fashun to reject trend

faskinate fast
healing skin

fast-blow to be shot
and to die fast | to have
passed away sooner
than expected

fast forward two
arrows forward

fastish a little fast(er)

fastosh very fast

FAT find at times

fat to not **fin**

fatch to eat far too
much [+ batch]

faun wet [oppo. laun]

FAW fire at work

faw fire and water |
thaw

faxifence to call for a
partition

fayregrow lights and
action (grow: light) and
fayreground (lights and
rides: action) as in
'camera, lights, action'
without the camera

fayregrowcctv the
camera, lights and
action on the streets |
to be caught on
scamera

fe feel

fear ear to always be
expecting danger

fear wear to show
fear

fearlobe to be
paranoid people are
talking about you

fearocious ferocious
fear | to be fearing
possible cruelty

feasible leech a
possibility that it may
use up more energy
than we thought

feastenders back-to-back episodes of Eastenders

feathere gently there | to be there a little

fecklie almost the truth

fede ar everything heard is taken as meaning it

fedearal a poor person in the city centre

federal-up fed up with government

fed-fudge in a sticky situation with the police

fedge for the federals to be in a situation concerning a problem inside the federal system

fed-sledge a police car

fed-slope to get involved in crimes, to then get involved with cops

feedbuck to eat processed foods

fee-funk a happy amount | a pleasing sum

feelearn sensory

feelinger a person who self-wallows too often

feeling fault a faulty feeling

feelingo the conversation of 'how are you, I'm ok, you doing ok? yeah, it's all well'

feeloss to lose touch

feery where you have to pay for theory

fee sake because it feels good

fee-think to go and think about an offer | to decide if it's worth it

feet of clay bare feet

feetus small feet [+ foetus]

feline to see a faint line

fella la a singing person | a chirpy person | a chirping bird

felmo to stop swearing [insp. **felmouth**]

felmouth a fowl mouth

felton to feel heavy [+ ton]

femalien a female who feels alien in her skin

fermangle to boil foods

ferret ferry

ferris round

ferris ab round-about

ferris and ferris round and round

ferriser rounder

ferrits to go by ferry

ferry ferret

fervideo a recording of the feelings

fess-tin a confessions box

fest tent

festallation a festive installation

festispoon any sized spoon

festival tent trend

festivillain one who gatecrashes a party [festival + villain]

festuary when the lake is iced over and white

festun many festivals

festurn the coming of summer

festvest the same top worn for the whole time of being at a festival of atleast three days

fet to fit [oppo. fat]

feta getting there

fetap cheese the smell of pathetic-ness

fetap pathetic

fetch to exercise (insp. **fet**]

fetus as a ball | feta

fetus juxtaposit a human jumping bean in motion | somebody hyper in motion and positioned in many places

fez fuzz to move the head around when it has a fez on

fezza love for the fez

fezza fella one who wears a fez

fff three in a row [see **O's and X's**]

ffff four in a row [see **FIAR**]

ffffffffffffffffffffffffff ffffffffffffffffffffffffff ffffffffffffffffff too frozen to finish off the word

fi fight

FIAR four in a row

fibber a fibre | a biffer

fibre a fibber

fibribs one who fibs and finds it funny in doing so

fibstract to pretend someone else's idea is your own

fi cen fifteenth century

ficco widelyornamental [insp. the red-flowering gum tree]

fiddult a fussy adult [+ fiddle]

fiduret a little figure

fi ear burning up ear, e.g. you have fi ear because someone is talking about you

fie ble porous [insp. field blewit]

field cry to deliver a musical song [insp. *the field cricket sit mouths of their burrows and deliver musical song day and night*]

fielderflower elderflower growing in a field

fieldmine a dirty hanky

field mush horse manure [insp. field mushrooms]

fifteen minutes past chur(chin) forty five minutes to the choo-choo urch (in)

fifteen minutes to co worker is a killer forty five minutes past rockernel fella

fifteeth five teeth

fifty eight minutes past eagle eye plebble two minutes to peas cull eye treble

fifty eight minutes to seagulping beer two minutes past eagles ear

fifty five minutes past red balloon five minutes to rebel da buffoon

**fifty five minutes to
tents and ants to
come** five minutes
past peasaint intercom

**fifty four minutes
past motor hum** six
minutes to hotter toe in
om a mum

**fifty four minutes
to ta pluto de toe or**
six minutes past gateau
to de tour

**fifty minutes past
aunt is a
hairdresser** ten
minutes to aren't you a
dresser in hare?

**fifty minutes to bon
heel i ain't** ten
minutes past mon peel
paint

**fifty nine minutes
past cut mouth
papire sciss** one
minute to cute how
map expire then
decease

**fifty one minutes
past ca ca gory**
nine minutes to lava
car tory

**fifty one minutes to
bellows, loud as**
nine minutes past
zealous louse

**fifty one minutes to
waking in a
submarine** one
minute past caking and
queen

**fifty seven minutes
past funkel bike
with an unkle on**
three minutes to fiver a
ukulele ridden by a nun

**fifty seven minutes
to cows are sparrow**
three minutes past
crows spare crows

**fifty six minutes
past swank holly
wood** four minutes to
swans are, okay, holy
would

fifty six minutes to host goes oats rich four minutes past g host ostrich

fifty three minutes past stall ion car seven minutes to still on a car

fifty three minutes to soon sun is cool seven minutes past moon monocle

fifty two minutes past wooden broom eight minutes to would bro then doom?

fifty two minutes to honey o bey or see eight minutes past moneigh horsey

fig a small puff of a fag [oppo. **fogue**]

figure a fig-like texture | a bit squishy

fi hun a fair degree of skill is required

fiji fee priceless natures

FIK fire in kitchen

filamenet to find the thread

filamonk holy light

filbert a spreading habit

filestash to stash away files

filestock an area where the files are kept

filesty a pile of messed up files

fili-ili a moment of sillyness

fill me up buttercuff fill me up buttercup, until my shirt doesn't fit me [see **don't bake my heart**]

fillure a complete failure [+ fill]

filofat a fat file | a zip file

filo fi only one file

filord one that is on top of accounts

filos philosophy

filtapale to fill up a bottle or a bucket with tap water

filu thunder and lighetning [+ filament]

filwa a petticoat made from natural material

fin swim | full

finance monopoly

finch social nature [oppo. **flinch**]

findividual a fish with rights

finegers fine fingers [see **gringers**]

fingembroid to leave fingerprints on glass

finger-people faces drawn on fingertips

fing ar the fingers and thumb(s)

fing or the thumb

fins finish

finsect a small fish [+ **fin**]

finull an end with no emotion or effect [final + null]

fire flies the ash bits which fly into the air from a fire when burning paper

fireg an irregular reason to fire someone

fireman samba you're on flames trying to put yourself out by rolling around on the floor | a dance around flames

fireman samurai to play with fire

firmost first and foremost

first aid to be tested for aids

fish a little funny [ish + 'f' for funny]

fish bar death zone

FISHBAR faith in some hotel, barred, and raided

fishbowl cramped space | not enough space | too small

fish bowler hat to put on forgetting something | to pretend something has slipped the mind

fish-bowl, fish-dish a de-ba(i)te

fish cap a flow of thoughts

fish-dish ish, slightly

fish-eye peek | a little look

fish-gist swimmingly

fish hook perverted abuse

fishin to finish it

fish merchant bad smell

fishnet to fail

fist-watch when many rings are worn on the fingers, acting as 'knuckle dusters'

FIT find in time

FITH fire in the hole

five minutes past peasaint intercom fifty five minutes to tents and ants to come

five minutes to rebel da buffoon fifty five minutes past red balloon

five up the ability to add up quickly [*the game 'Five Up' requires this skill*]

FIW fire in woods [see **FITH**]

fixate to dye and change the colour of the hair

fixion fiction worth a read [+ fixate]

fkey to be jealous of someone getting a promotion or moving up in the world [Na. fkay: hateful] [+ key]

fla devour to lose the beauty of it [+ flavour]

flablation the removal of unwanted tissue from body by surgical means [flab + ablation]

flabo edible [insp. palmyra palm]

flag bag a suspicious bag | a suspicious delivery

flagger to share the same drink

flake a frozen up lake

fla li flammable liquid

flamb fierce strength and energy [flamboyant + limb]

flame frame to frame someone in order to show them up

flame-gazers those who stare into a flame

flame-graze to make out visuals from flamegazing [see **flame-gazers**]

flamingo dressed in pink

flammencommence to keep on dancing | to commence in vibrancy [+ flamenco]

flancais trifly [*the baton is a bread belonging to France*] [+ flan]

flap a saggy or sticking-up shirt collar

flapper a tie when it flaps in the wind

flash to threaten a lash

flashbulb an irritating light

flash cheeks well flushed cheeks

flask to be experiencing hot flushes

flat when an inflated bouncy castle, or anything inflated is deflated

flatigue flat out with fatigue

flatter batter to mess up a flat

flauntout to be 'fat out' from flaunting

flavigour the heartiness a certain flavour gives | a beautiful sense [oppo. **fla devour**]

flax a powerful word

flaxative a herbal laxative [+ flax]

flea to suck tongues [**moth** + tongue suck]

flead sale to put profit before the ethics of the customer

fleast to flee East

flea wez to suck all the flavour off until the food becomes soft and soggy [**flea** + gee whiz]

fledder a builders pencil [*contains flat led*]

fleducation to have left school before expected

fleece a hit and run

fleeces faeces to try and warm coldness | to try and forget a death

flest to flee West

flex seed a healthy move [flax + flexible]

flexert flexibly exert | to exercise your rights

flexicandle to be able to bend something due to apply heat

flexicon a wide vocabulary

flexicough a wide range of sounds

flexsoma a flexible body

flick to cut off someone | to cut out something

flick & seal to cut off someone forever | to cut out something forever

flies a portion of fries

flight the fridge light

flight of the conchord alas, a bit of humour!

flimb fragile limbs

flimby flimsy limbed

flinch an unsocial nature [oppo. **finch**]

flinchpin a linchpin in flinching when any sharp object comes into vision

flintstones hard stones

flip lipstick on the collar

flit an aeroplane that sets on fire in the sky

floasoma a floating body

floga a flower garden | a flourishing flow

flon christmas [insp. *the Australian fire tree as its flowers bloom for several months around christmas time*]

floop to put everything on hold due to being ill | too ill to do

floperage to flick your hair away from someone

flopsidate a forgotten date

florally a competitive flower show

flore a floored lore

floridden for florid to disappear | to become unflorid | to lose the colour red | to finish your menstrual cycle

flota rota a rota which is constantly changing

flour bed plans to bake

flourge to crave cake [flour + urge]

flourist a cake maker | a baker

flouruin to destroy something good

flow chi

flowears floral garments

flower sexual reproduction

flow er to flow below

flower, legs and war sir how to make the cake of battle – poppies, lost legs and with the orders of killing – warning – does not contain peace (of cake)

flower-bod a friend who knows how to cheer you up

flowergun to bring or give peace

flower-pot sam a garden hose for flowering plants with [insp. *Fireman Sam*]

flowida a commercial flow [+ Florida]

flowr a sea flower

flowris to block someone in self defence, usually from using their strength [L. foris: a door]

flowrist a pretty and colourful bracelet on the wrist | the turning of the wrist

flu to catch and pass on, e.g. he, threw, I, flu

flue pneumonia [blue + flu]

fluency the cost of having the flu | the money you lose from being sick due to having time off work

fluent with flu

fluff potato to backcomb hair in order to give it volume

flugut to have a sick virus

fluidial an appliance to measure a water

fluidosh 30p change for a (public) toilet

fluidosh no do dash I fluid to not have **fluidosh** so you decide to wee in the middle of a public space (now you have 30 people staring at you and you wish the people were not people but pence because then you could have gone to the public toilets and you would have avoided all of this kerfuffle) [insp. **fluidosh**]

flunkit a flask and blanket

flushi fush it

flush to have the same suit as another person

flushk a flask with very hot drink in

fluster fance to get hot and flustered when you see someone you fancy

flut when flies chase each other

flutterms on shaky (or rocky) terms | fragile stepping stones

fluxur to become more handsome [+ luxuriant]

fluxury a luxury for a change (for the time being), for a treat

fly order

fly aga red and white [insp. fly agaric]

fly corpet a corpse flown over from another country for burial

fly-cape spin around holding your arms out to the sides

fly-caper a person who fly-capes

fly-fly the increase in air travel [oppo. **fly-fray**]

fly-fray the decrease in air travel [oppo. **fly-fly**]

flying carpet to tip up over the corner of a rug

flying doctor a blood sucking fly insect

flying lambs clouds

flying pan a dangerous incident in the kitchen

flying pigs pink kites

flylopad an airplane strip

flyosophy the philosophy of flying

flyper a slipper thrown into the air

flysoma a flying body

fm fragment

FOB fire on beach [see **FIW**]

fob get rid of

fob cob to give up eating bread

fobstruct to **fob** off obstructions

fo cen fourteenth century

foco about 15 minutes [insp. *the game 'The Four Corners' takes this amount of time to play*]

fodd fushing odd [see **fush**]

FOE figure of eight

foequet a bunch of enemies

foe-thank to be happy that someone is not your friend | to be happy when someone says they do not like you

foe-think to think about making a person a foe/**FOE**

foeto a disliked photo

fofiko a measurement of 4x4 [insp. *the game 'Four Field' Kono'*]

FOG figure of gut [insp. **FOE**]

fog fourteen to eighteen years [insp. *the amount of pieces in the game 'Fox & Geese'*]

fogsbody a group of confused people

fogue a big puff of smoke

FOI fathers of invention

foie gras to over dose take too much

foldmine a folded **fieldmine**

follers wilted flowers [+ fall]

follow fellow

FOM front of the mind [oppo. BOM]

fondalism [politics + vandalism]

fondeau deliciously fond of

fond pond a hot spa

fontain a list of fonts (a stream of choice)

fontain pen the optical mouse [insp. **fontain**]

fundation a funded charity [+ foundation]

FOO fush out of

foodairio to have illnesses due to the food you eat [L. fodio: jab]

foo fighter to fight the **FOO** something, e.g. to fight your way out of a crowd

foolow to follow the fool

fools world opposites

foonf on-and-off fun

footappian one who taps the surface with the foot

footassium a clever foot movement

footjabs pins and needles in the feet [insp. **handjabs**]

footloot the money saved from walking instead of spending it on transport

footpint a foot long pint

footport foot fetish [see **sockport**]

footslung a foot rest which isn't really supposed to be used as a footrest, e.g. to lean the feet on a rucksack

footure a declining future | soon to fail [+ foot]

for fork

for age age matters

forage to take a fair amount [oppo. **for rag**e]

forajr forager

forange to pick oranges from the tree

foransick to be a suspect of a crime you have not committed | to have your finger prints taken

forb a slight hook |slightly hooked [insp. the forest bug has slightly hooked shoulders]

forba bafor forward and backwards, backwards and forwards, e.g. we were forba bafor al day in our rocking chairs

force-kin family member(s) who push

you into doing
something

forcert a certification
of power, e.g. a search
warrant

forchurn such grand
news, so grand it
makes you feel sick

fore-bear a close hug
where the chests touch,
e.g. we were all forebear
and bare

forecal an important
project, e.g. this is a
foecal and I have been
working on it every day
for the past two months

foregg a sweaty
forehead

fore-gland the
moving of the lips when
they talk

foreskin of july the
glazing over of
independence day

forest tangled wires

fo rest a rest on the
grass

forest bite a bramble
or thorn sting [insp.
frost bite]

forestyle green and
free [+ freestyle]

forever seale

foreverest forever
wild

forge to be against it
[oppo. for]

forge-dents fake
teeth

forget pock

forgidden it was silly
to forgive, it was
forgidden [+ giddy]

forgive pogo

forgofarago to eat
uncooked foods

forgraven forgiven until dead

fork a dilemma [insp. *'Chess' when one player attacks two pieces simultaneously, of which only one can be saved*]

fork-feed to add forks to your cutlery drawer [insp. spoon-feed]

formality a 90 degree angle

formula historical evidence | reference [+ form]

for rage to take a greedy amount [oppo. **forage**]

fort unequal [insp. *the unevenly divided leaves of the chusan palm tree*]

forthodont on your way to the dentist

forty eight minutes past huno doze off trees twelve minutes to wonder about ze toffees

forty eight minutes to hum a humbles twelve minutes past tumble we dress

forty five minutes past rockernel fella fifteen minutes to co worker is a killer

forty five minutes to the choo-choo urch (in) fifteen minutes past chur(chin)

forty four minutes past mushroom rag out sixteen minutes to ush moo, shagged out

forty four minutes to bish-bosh sixteen minutes past mackintosh

**forty minutes past
don key** twenty
minutes to dressed up
and low key

**forty minutes to
tumble cords take**
twenty minutes past
umbro shorts cake

**forty nine minutes
past uncle's a wheel
barrow** eleven
minutes to uncalled for,
really a bar row

**forty nine minutes
to parked in the lot**
eleven minutes past
yacht

**forty one minutes
past neigh wire**
nineteen minutes to
hay no wear (or attire)

**forty one minutes
to re curse the tard**
nineteen minutes past
custard

**forty seven minutes
past mon stair
truck** thirteen
minutes to son's a
mayor but a ruck

**forty seven minutes
to pantry go i'll**
thirteen minutes past
pastrial

**forty six minutes
past fell low chain**
fourteen minutes to feel
how ouch, ache in

**forty six minutes to
munich** fourteen
minutes past hun(-i)ch

**forty three minutes
past pil charred
wall** seventeen
minutes to chill pill red
call

**forty three minutes
to safety pin**
seventeen minutes past
linchpin

**forty two minutes
past gill stone**
eighteen minutes to fish
stun: prone

**forty two minutes
to numb, err**
eighteen minutes past
number

forque why knife,
why stab (in the back)?

forust something
that's left to rust | to
age naturally

FOT full of thoughts

fot what's that for?

fo toy (a) plant

foun wet [+ fountain]

founit a unit of water
[fountain + unit]

four by four
pollution

fourge to forge more
than once [+ four]

fourk forks are four
for christ and dagger,
for our unity rents kill

four-k four forks

**four minutes past g
host ostrich** fifty six
minutes to host goes
oats rich

**four minutes to
swans are, okay,
holy would** fifty six
minutes past swank
holly wood

fourage to give four
hours

four-spot far from
water [insp. *the
fourspotted
chaser is often
found far from water*]

fourt a fort with four
walls

fourteen minutes past hun(-i)ch forty six minutes to munich

fourteen minutes to feel how ouch, ache in forty six minutes past fell low chain

fourteeth four teeth

fowlgina a dirty vagina

foxblood no need

foxheart for your heart to be constantly hunted down

foxhunt to do something you regret doing

foxidant to run from those chasing you

foy not able to find a way of entering [+ foyer]

foyer tyre a spare tyre

F (past) one letter past E, two letters past D, three letters past C, four letters past B, five letters past A, six letters past Z, seven letters past Y, eight letters past X, nine letters past W, ten letters past V, eleven letters past U, twelve letters past T, thirteen letters past S, fourteen letters past R, fifteen letters past Q, sixteen letters past P, seventeen letters past O, eighteen letters past N, nineteen letters past M, twenty letters past L, twenty one letters past K, twenty two letters past J, twenty three letters past I, twenty four letters past H, twenty five letters past G

fr free

fracasino the fracas of the casino voice inside your head telling you to gamble

fracation a scene of a fight | a round of boxing | a part of a fracas [+ fraction]

fractangle a rectangle that changes size

fractrot a mappedout walking route

frag a rug with fleas [*the flees leap like frogs*]

fraiscal to lose wildness [fra + rascal]

fram to ram a frame around something | to frame someone

framepaper to cover a a whole wall in pictures

framist a person looking out of a window

framjam to frame someone and for them to embarrassed

framy spicy [insp. nutmeg]

fran france

franchisel for a franchise to be divided

frank turner to turn the right way up

frankenstein to speak your mind [frank + Einstein]

frankful openly thankful [+ frank]

frankfurther to be frank from now on and in the future

franticles holographic glasses

frappa a freaky rapper

fraudio to illegally download music

frayfray to not decide to look froufrou but just are froufrou due to being less fortunate

fraygina an overused vagina

frayment a fragment breaking into more fragments

frays and catch up to wait a long time in the chipshop for your food

frear to let your ear listen freely | to free your ear from the side of your head | to liberate the ear like Van Gogh did

frectle a hypnotising circle [+ fractal]

fred a free ride | to hitch a ride

fredrock to move the bed, e.g. we would fredrock to the living room but it may become a problem

freederm smooth skin, free from cuts, bruises, lumps and scars

freedumb when freedom becomes less free

free loathe to have agreed to free love but you begin to loathe it

free reinstein free the mind [+ Einstein]

freega tim! don't waste my time [insp. **freegan**]

freegan a person who tries to spend as little money as possible |one who does not believe in waste

freegan at the bus stop to search for a bus ticket which is still able to be used

freegan at the food court a freegan who goes around the food court and eats peoples left-overs

freegan at the tennis court to pick up the tennis balls that other people could not be bothered to pick up

freegan free a locked up bin

freegan in your own garden to pick any fruit, herbs or vegetables from your own garden

free-range loose

frees frame to get out of a frame | to unframe

freet to freely fleet

freeting fleeting freely

freetown a free place

freezewave a freezer

freight to destroy the planet

frequanty a regular amount [frequent + quantity]

fresin fresh resin

fre-sky a blue or clear sky

frice fried rice

frictoast to stamp the feet

friday buest Friday I was [insp. **sunday buest**]

fridge a casket | a morgue | a cool room

fridgile a food which must be kept in the fridge

fried dead

fries frame to have chips too often | a habit of eating a lot of chips

frip to fray and rip | to pull a frayed piece | to scratch

frishilicious the feel of waves crashing against the body

fri-sky a red sky

frizz-frame to have an electric shock

frog fig faf to swear a lot

frogment to skip a part | for a CD to jump when being played [+ fragment]

frog rags green and yellow clothes

from backwards [+ morf/morph] [see **to**]

fromage from here

fromage roamage from here is where we roam

frompage to jump on top of someone when frisky [frog + rump]

front coff [oppo. **alce**]

front gill to fill the stomach

fro sky a white sky

frostbyte when you have no memory left on a technological device

frosty glass a halfvision | a prediction | an assumption

froven a fridge

frow from all

frubbish filthy rubbish, e.g. some say porn is frubbish

fructose good looking feet [*fructose sugar is found naturally in fruit*]

fruichoc chocolate coated fruit

fruigut to have a gut full of fruit

fruitboot to make wine the old fashioned way (by stamping on the grapes)

fruit female [*as the fruit develops from the fertilized female parts of the flower*]

frui tea a herbal tea

fruitfly on a hype

fruit sandwiches the olden days

fru-sky a grey sky

frwy why burn? [+ fry]

fry-day a whole day in hot sun

fryday a day where your head is fried

frydge an oven | a warm fridge

fryzer a microwave

ft font

F (to) one letter to G, two letters to H, three letters to I, four letters to J, five letters to K, six letters to L, seven letters to M, eight letters to N, nine letters to O, ten letters to P, eleven letters to Q, twelve letters to R, thirteen letters to S, fourteen letters to T, fifteen letters to U, sixteen letters to V, seventeen letters to W, eighteen letters to X, nineteen letters to Y, twenty letters to Z, twenty one letters to A, twenty two letters to B, twenty three letters to C, twenty four letters to D, twenty five letters to E

FU fled until

fubasque for we are at the back of the queue (damn)

FUC fold, undo, copy

fuchsia russia the blooming of Russia

FUCK field until city kills

fucket & fade to try and move on from a problem

fuckulty the faculty of f*** | sex education

fud festive pudding

fudfi a food fight

fudge-budge to not move, e.g. he won't budge because he's fudge, and fudge has stuck to it and will not move

fug finger in the plug socket

fug fuzz when **fug** gives you a shock

FUK fed under kisses

fulk purity

ful'o'hand the eyes in the hands | the allseeing palm A to see through touch [*ful'o'hand is a hand shape in sign language*]

full step a sentence that ends well and gives good reason for the reader to read on, to not come to a permanent holt

fun impro

fundation a funded charity [+ foundation]

fundeau a fun fondeau

fund fond to be grateful for funds

fungrow an artists dark room [insp. *the fungi grows in dark and cold space*]

funimportant unimportant fun | the fun of the unimportant

funkbed a very unique bed

funsound to enjoy the unsound

fur bowl to remove a hair from the mouth [+ fur ball]

furb your enthusiasm love furby, grow fond of fuzzy love, fuzzy tv screen, motherboards in fluff – love is electric, grow your love for the furby

furbish to de-hair a hair brush

furby mif | fuzzy, e.g. a furby television screen

furby love fuzzy love

fur dish a mouldy dish

fur fashi bullying for no reason

fur fashion in vain

furflex to shave a hairy back

furnat a free-standing statue or ornament [+ furniture]

furt an exert of warmth

fush a good mannered way of saying 'fuck'

fush bar an alcoholic bar where you get **fushed**

fushed a(pp)les from a fridge

fushwag to make an excuse to avoid sexual activity

fut on foot

futile to knock out
tiles | to gut out tiles

FUYC fuck until you
cry

**fuzz bed in a
bidding auction**
Tracey Enim's bed in an
auction

fuzzard-buzzards to
ruffle feathers | flap
fluffy wings and to
make a cotton-wool like
sound

fuzztralia the other
side of the spectrum

fuzzy furby

Gg

G *pic* a curtain fastener

g=a ganja = angel

GA go away

ga games

gabba-banana a person who talks fast | to eat bananas quickly

gabbage many subjects at once

gabber fast

gabber feet a fast mover

gabber goose to float around fast

gabber gum to chew fast

gabberg the stress of a deadline

GABOG got a bit of go

GABOGII (it's) got a bit of go in it

gabog rabbit to have bursts of random energy [insp. **GABOG**]

gabuck a priceless look [Turk. gabak: eyelid] [+ buck]

gad stub, e.g. to gad the toe off the curb is a 'good god'

gadd stubble

gadd and subtra to have stubble and then shave it off

gadget to get good

gad-get to always want the latest gadgets

gaft the gift of being your own boss

GAG get a grip

gaggle when you want to burst out laughing but you can't because it would be inappropriate to do so [gag + giggle]

gaisle on the road to gaia

GAJ get a job

GAJ YH get a job you hippy

galactose a bad diet of mostly too much sugan and too much milk

gale when a pile of leads has more than thirty entanglements [*gale is a wind of force over thirty knots*]

gallbladder game the game of holding in your urination

galload what a set up! [+ gallows]

gallonely forever lonely [gallon + lonely]

gallord a lord of the gallows

gallovely forever lovely [insp. **gallonely**] [gallon + lovely]

galmad to be obsessed with the female gender

gal mut to appear early on [insp. galerina mutabilis]

galordi oh many word

galpol to polish [+ galvanize]

galvanish to apply a shiny or see-through layer

gambia a game involving alcohol

gambin to win a bet [bing + gamble] [oppo. **gambong**]

gambong to lose a bet [oppo. **gambin**]

GAME gesture a mad entertainment

gamma smile

gamma gamma give me a smile

gamma gim a fake smile [+ gimmick]

gamma ray a lit up smile

gammite trev to make friends with a moth and call it Trevor

gammoney and stake to play around at being a stake-holder

gampwhimp a weak umbrella | a broken umbrella [*'gamp' is British slang for 'umbrella'*] [+ whimp]

GAN go away now

ganda a peaceful walk [oppo. **propaganda**]

gander to explore

gandi a peaceful demonstration [+ Ghandi]

gandry a document/film of a gandi

gang maffa

gang aid rape

gap gas pipe

garbag a bag of junk

garciaos to throw away garments [+ ciao]

gardan a garden of art | an outside art exhibition | a poetry gathering outside

gardean the dean of the garden | the gardner | the queen bee

gar den a messy wardrobe

garden to give reason

garden hoe Snow White

gardo for god's sake [*Gardo is a place in Ethiopia*]

garnish-nosh edible accessories | edible decorations

garniture furniture being the garments a house wears

gary a car [insp. **gaz**]

gas gaz

GaSaB a cheated winning [insp. **GSB**]

gas monkey a worker of a gas company

gasp to plead for something

gaspect a whiff of gas [+ aspect]

gassed monkey a person experimented on without consent

gast o plast to put the finger in the anal so it quietly lets out gaz

gastric band a highly loved music band

gastric band bypass for a gastric band to become less loved

gastroll for gas to rise

gate great but missing something

gateau a large entrance

gateway drug when an entrance entices you in

gatha have got a father

gava got to have a

gavin and stacey man and man | man and woman

gaycape to pretend to be gay to avoid a female [insp. **lescape**]

gaz gas

gaz met a gas meter

GB got bread?

gd Gondry [insp. *Michel Gondry*]

ge Gertrude Stein

gearstick mechanical hassle [+ **stick**]

gearth to talk about the earth

geclo get close

geeb an annoying beeping noise

geese to crowd [insp. *how you move in the game 'Fox & Geese'*]

geg gag the smell of egg cooking

gela gluttony [+ gelatine]

gel junk hair serums, lotions and gels

gemma hayes gamma rays

gender a myth

gene adapted

genear near a genus

gene bean a familiar connection

gene-pool a family pool | a family swim

genera generation

genere a gene type

generight to do a good cause [+ generate]

generough a play fight [generous + tough]

ge ne sais quoi for it to be unknown to whether you are bloodrelated [je ne sais quoi + gene]

general to play something for drink or money [insp. *the game 'General' is played at the bar, for drinks or money*]

genes made-moods

geogoggles maps and compasses

geography blue [insp. *'Tivial Pursuit' colour*]

george to sound good [insp. **george michael**]

george michael a good-sounding mic

ger coffee [see **roger**]

ger cupera to wish for a cup of coffee [insp. **ro cupere**] [+ **ger**]

gerg spilt coffee

germ Germany | a terrible tasting coffee

ger mugere to wish for a mug of coffee [insp. **ro cupere**] [+ **ger**]

gert a coffee stain

gertrude follow the words, not the rules

get to pick up

getha a family get-together

get-in using your fingers to eat

get out toad get your toes out of the road | get your feet from the car wheels

gettache to get attached

getty you get it?

geway get away

ggg three in a row [see **O's and X's**]

gggg four in a row [see **FIAR**]

ghast ghostly gas

ghastoot an unpleasant saying [ghastly + **toot**]

ghee gone off [+ flee]

ghinna greasy hair

ghose when the tap turns on by itself [ghost + hose]

ghostage having a ghost as a host | to be there in spirit

giantenna a pylon [giant + antenna]

gibba-gabba to have fast mental ability to make humour | quick on your humour toes

gica a large prick | scorch [insp. *saguaro: the largest cactus*]

gid get rid

giddy up to clear up [insp. **gid**]

GIF give it fifty

gifoo glass in foot

gift rip for a gift to be wrapped so you can tell what it is, e.g. a wine bottle or a teddy bear [*the surprise* is ripped]

gift-wrip a present where the wrapping has been wripped and you can see what it is

gig gag goo to laugh a lot

giggle to search for new music on Youtube [insp. **goggle**]

gill a breather

gill bladder a bladder that can take a lot of liquid | to not need to visit the toilet often

gillette to cut an animal open whilst alive

gill sans fish stands | aquatic shops

gim gimmick

gimma give me a

gimmick gim

gimplimp a limp from having too much sex

gimpunch a punch in the glands [+ gimp]

gim slap a 'slapstick' gimmick

ginbook writing under the influence of substances

ging ginger

ginger spice the spice of ginger

ging gong orangy brown colour [**ging** + **gong**]

gin gum paper and pencil [insp. *the equipment for scoring in the game 'Gin Rummy'*]

ginspired inspired by gin | inspired by alcohol

gi puff spongy | unepexpected [insp. giant puffball]

giraffe a long neck

gird bird a bird in a cage [+ gird]

girl red girl troubles

girth before birth | the womb [*'girth' also means a place of protection or an asylum*] [oppo. **brith**]

gise largest in the world [insp. the wellingtonia tree]

githa have got a sister

gladdis glad

gladvice pleasing advice

gladvise to gladly advise

glag to wake up a person by tipping water onto them

glamamore the love of glamour

glammerbucks material worlds

glan float [insp. the pond apple tree]

glass battle a fight between two sides and you know which side will win

glass matches to predict a fire

glass monkey falling glass | moving glass

glassture a clear sign | a clear signal

glathes gloves used for wet activities, e.g. dying hair (to lathe in) or gloves used to wash dishes

gleemace to make funny faces [+ grimace]

gleigh to slide down ice [sleigh + glide]

glib to see through a theory [glass + library]

glimmick a glimmering gimmick

glordinary the wonders of the everyday

glost to have lost shine [+ gloss]

glothes neon clothes | glow-in-the-dark clothes

glove you love with a glove [*Stuart Heller says the whole body is in the hand – so if we put a glove on the hand it means we apply a space between the two surfaces, therefore, to say "I glove you" is to love but in a less intimate, and less personal way, not intimate, more 'inmate'*]

glowball the moon

glowsick to be sick or to feel sick from accidently swallowing the liquid in glowsticks

glowstack many bright lights | promising results

glowstuck to forget what you have revised

glowsuck a glow stick that lacks glow

glube white and blue [insp. **glue**] [+ **lube**]

glue white ribbons [insp. the blue gum tree]

glue bra a female bunny boiler | a female who won't shift

glue bru a male bunny boiler | a female who won't shift [insp. **glue bra**]

gluegeth to bond, to get together a lot, to connect, be stuck to each other, can't keep away from each other

glug to hug a wet person [see **glag**]

glugrags alcohol-smelling clothes [glug + gladrags]

glum gum to be stuck in **glummore**

glummore in a state of being glum

glum'n'glam to step on someone to get taller, e.g. you may do this when there's a chance of a job promotion

glumutton to feast on negativity [glum + mutton]

glupids fizzy sugary drinks which are packed with artificial flavours and colours

glut excess glue | too much glue [+ gluttony]

glut butt to stare at bums too often [+ gluttony]

glutter the shining of ring-pulls which have been thrown on the floor [glitter + gutter]

glut tonia a gluttonous woman

glut tony a gluttonous man

gluttiny only a little amount of gluttony

glyme stringy [insp. the dawn redwood tree]

gmno esc brain-like [insp. gymnomitra esculenta]

gnapple to refuse to use any Apple technology

gnarify to narrow something down by eating it to make it smaller, e.g. you may gnarify a chocolate biscuit by gnawing off the chocolate around the edge [+ clarify]

gnash to throw ashes in someone's face | to put the ashes of a dead person in someone's food

gnativity to bite [gnat + nativity + activity]

gnaw mal to chew loud | eat with mouth your open

gnaw-gnaw to smack your chops when eating food

gnaw-ledge conventions which are force fed to you

gnew a new bite | more memory

gnome sweet gnome the 'home sweet home' of the garden

gnume to not be able to go any further [Na. nume: learn] [+ gnome]

gnus to minus [oppo. **sung**]

gnuschoolar to limit the number of children allowed in a shop at the same time [**gnus** + scholar]

gnush to tell people to get out [usher + **gnus**]

go to take in turns

goal gold and aluminium

GOAT get on a train

goatfell to not wear the appropriate footwear

gobbledy geek technical talk

go-car a fast car

god tooth | tree

goddard tooth ache

GOF glass on floor

go-fish basic

GOG gift of god

goggle to image search on Google

gog lare pie stare a lot [goggles + **pie**]

gogleg bent glasses

go-grow one who likes things wild

golden bandana a record deal

gold-hold to have something precious

gold-involv there's a price to pay

gold scarf only VIP's allowed

golf a sorting office

go-mow one who likes things tame

gon go on

gonerrhoea to be extinct

gong brown

gonorrhoear to not have understood

good yeast

goodminton not 'bad'minton

good smudden to not say goodbye because you do not believe in endings | a 'goodbye for now'

GOOG gift of only god

googaga when Google cannot find results for your search

GOOGLE gift of only god lays evangel

google sack to stop using google

google spack to accidently misspell what you were supposed to search on google and for you to get strange results

googloc to use look up a location on Google maps

googly when the eyes are on the look out

goom three or four [insp. the ideal player size for the game 'Go Boom']

goose goes | to go

goose-gut stuffed

goosey gender to **gander** the genders | to experiment with gender

goosey glander to taste

goospoon to get goose-bumps when you hear the fork or knife scraping a plate

GORPOST GRIEF ONLY REAR PROTO ONO STATUE TEASE

gorshi to feed on flowers, fruits and seeds [insp. *the gorse shield bug feeds on fruits, flowers and seeds of gorse and related plants*]

GoSoB to cry about not being awarded any of the **GSB** medals [insp. **GaSoB**]

gos-sip to take in rumours | to believe gossip to be real

goth a beer maker

gotha have got a mother

govern go very near

G (past) one letter past F, two letters past E, three letters past D, four letters past C, five letters past B, six letters past A, seven letters past Z, eight letters past Y, nine letters past X, ten letters past W, eleven letters past V, twelve letters past U, thirteen letters past T, fourteen letters past S, fifteen letters past R, sixteen letters past Q, seventeen letters past P, eighteen letters past O, nineteen letters past N, twenty letters past M, twenty one letters past L, twenty two letters past K, twenty three letters past J, twenty four letters past I, twenty five letters past H

GP's garden peas

grad fad gradual fad

grad-greed the build up of greed | to starve yourself in order to have a big feast

gradowse for a graduate to seek work in other fields than the one(s) studied [+ dowse]

graffititude attitude on the streets

grafore to love **graft** [+ amore]

graft the smell of fresh cut grass

grain a raised grin | to raise a grin

gramag to latedevelop [insp. the bull bay tree]

grammaphone a weighing scales used to measure grams

grammaprune one who critics someone's grammar

grammore a very long sentence

gram-raffiti spelling mistakes in graffiti [insp. **riff-raffiti**] [+ grammar]

grandfather's five minutes [insp. *the duration of the game 'Grandfather's Clock'*]

grandmat a grand parent that who gets treated like a door mat

grand theft slaughto to spend too much time playing videogames

granort a person wellknown for being gay [insp. *Graham Norton*]

grape something which will either receive great feedback or the opposite [insp. **drape**]

grass a green ray of light [insp. the grass tree]

grass band an area of green plants

grass bandit one who enjoys the great outdoors

grass bank an ethical bank, e.g. Co-op

grass crack the nipple in the bud

grass lamp an attractive green hill

grassneck natural nerves [+ brassneck]

grass'n'graze to only eat green foods

grass stain to be proud of dirt | to accept bacteria is good for the inside | to not overthink | to accept it is only good to have not just the good [oppo. **oil stain**]

grave crave to want to die

gravement a pavement where somebody was killed (flowers and the spirit are left at the scene)

gravit gromit! 'everything is up in the air'

gravity the big apple

grayon to paint darkness

grays rays of grey | shine | silver

graze kneeded dough roughly kneaded dough

grease Greece

grease turkey to kill the soul

greated cheese sickly grateful

Greece grease

green science and nature [insp. *'Tivial Pursuit' colour*]

green glove a green tree top

green tea detox

greespecs glasses with green lenses

greshi deep bronze [insp. *the green shield bug is deep bronze colour in late autumn*]

grespecs glasses with grey lenses

greyola rather dull

greystle ash [gristle + grey]

gribbot a child's death [grim + ribbon + cot]

grid guide

grid dog dogs specially trained to walk the blind

grief briefs briefs that stick in to the skin or are uncomfy (or too small!)

grift to drift away from grafting | to slow down the working speed
grim beef a leather jacket

grimby dull

grimby's clambick a very dull place

grim gram a gram that does not look like a gram, it looks smaller

grim reef a gothic wreathe

grinded chick a chicken nugget

gringers when fingers are tapping away to a beat

grips hiking footwear

griss grass pulled from the surface

gris salt to eat sea salt on its own [+ gristle]

gristled hoof gelatinous sweets

groam dead grass [roam + groom]

gromit to groom (especially to groom a dog) [insp. *Gromit from Wallace & Gromit*] [see **wallace collection** *for Wallace*]

groove armada to wave the hands about in the air

gropa a zig zag pattern [insp. *the ground parrot flies in a zig-zag pattern*]

grotasque a grotesque task

grouch pouch to know what buttons to press to make somebody angry

grow to seed

grrfuss fussing creates anger

grr glug an empty glass when you wish it to be full

GSB gold, silver, bronze

GT get together

G (to) one letter to H, two letters to I, three letters to J, four letters to K, five letters to L, six letters to M, seven letters to N, eight letters to O, nine letters to P, ten letters to Q, eleven letters to R, twelve letters to S, thirteen letters to T, fourteen letters to U, fifteen letters to V, sixteen letters to W, seventeen letters to X, eighteen letters to Y, nineteen letters to Z, twenty letters to A, twenty one letters to B, twenty two letters to C, twenty three letters to D, twenty four letters to E, twenty five letters to F

GU get up

guantia antigua

guardart to avoid security

guarden a private garden | a guarded garden

guava got to but would rather have a [insp. **gava**]

gucci sadness

gue creamy-white [insp the cider gum tree]

guide grid

guide dog the ruler

guildbuild to gather a team of skilled workers

guinel oil [insp. the oil palm tree]

guitardy tardy guitar playing

gulliball to play at being gullible

gullstone to remove

gullstove a dead cooker

gumtree xylitol

gun can | gone | calculator [insp. **sungun**]

gunbun a hidden gun in a pocket

gunge a collection of gongs

gun-gest the hand gesture shooting someone with a gun

gunhard a big kill

gunion the power an onion holds to bring someone to tears [+ gun]

guns skills

gunsoft a little kill

gup an important industry [insp. the guava tree]

gusta a likeable wind | an enjoyed breeze

gustom to leave a customer waiting [custom + gust]

gustone music that brings enthusiasm

gut to communicate your feelings

gut hut an eatery, e.g. a restaurant

gut instink to have bad gas [+ gut instinct]

gut stone a hard stomach

guth a deathly gust

gutha have got a brother

gutter puff a sad sigh

guzzle puzzle a drinking game

guzzling monk to tray and get to the bottom of the **muzzy gunk**

gym halls squeaky shoes

gym-jams loose gym wear

gymno either male or female, e.g. people like to know the gymno so they can buy pink for a girl or blue for a boy [insp. *the gymniosperm of a conifer is either female or male*]

gyready ready for marriage or eternital love

gyred get yourself **reds**

gyrexchange to exchange wedding rings [insp. **gyready**]

gyrocrypter a nonworking gyrocopter [+ crypt]

gywed get yourself wed

Hh

h heart

H *pic* an up-front ladder | a reservation or unallowed parking

HA heart attack

hab habit

habacus a habit of counting everything [+ abacus]

hab bab a baby's **hab**

haberdashery the habit of urinating in bizarre places | a habit of weeing yourself

haberdashid to step into someone's urination puddle [insp. **haberdashery**]

haberdoshery an addiction to earning money [haberdashery + dosh]

haberherby the habit of adding too many herbs [haberdashery + herb]

habichi the habit is a bitch

hability habit of good ability

hability-to-skill transfer the habit of moving around different skills

habischuh a habit of only buying your footwear from one shop, that shop be Schuh

habitch a habit that causes problems

habtab a list of habits

habus blabbus a habit of babbling on [see **rabus blabbus**]

haccessories the accessories needed to hack into something, e.g. a password or a crowbar

haccount to hack into someone's account

hacet to have something nobody else has | to have an invention idea [+ ace]

hace V-shaped [insp. the plum yew tree]

hackie-channeling hacking into software [+ *Jackie Chan*]

hacktivism undercover police pretending to be other people | to pretend to be someone else

had-a-hammer to have abused in the past

haderm hard skin

haemarriage a marriage of blood | a mixture of different blood types [+ haemo]

haemask a face full of blood [+ haemo]

haembroid to give blood [+ haemo]

haembrowse to look for a matching blood type [+ haemo]

haemorage a bloody fight [+ haemo]

haemore to remember blood | a family memory [+ haemo]

haemory bloody memory [+ haemo]

haemstring a line of blood [haemo + hamstring]

haemu high blood pressure

haf tim summer time [Wel. haf: summer]

hagan a rainbow

haggit one who eats really bad 'food'

HAHA death by laughing [+ **HA**]

haha a hard hat | a hard helmet

ha hay to play someone up when they are sleeping

haidra slowly moving water [insp. *the hairy dragonfly breeds in still and slow moving water*]

haikudos a 'bravo' haiku

hair hare

hair ball herbal

hair-brush flipping a game of flipping the hairbrush, and being able to catch it 'hairbrush-way-up'

hair cat an adventurous hair cut

haiti for the hat to blow off in the wind

half cent fifty

half moons eyes half open [insp. **moons**]

half-varse to lean [insp. **varse**]

halibott the fish at the bottom of the sea | to swim in deep waters

hall-to-hall to have a walk way all the way through

halm to not capture [insp. *in the game 'Halma' pieces are not captured*] [+ harm]

halma 16x16 [insp. *the board used for the game 'Halma' is of the size 16x16*]

halogarrote to worry someone by being extra-nice [+ halo]

halogen light-sensitive

halogeneration a time of innocence

halogy a light allegory | a spiritual allegory

halostack a rescue team | helping hands

halten an alternative ending

halter to stop altering | to stay the same | to stop changing

ham hammer

hamber pinky orange | a blood orange ['h' for heat] [+ amber]

hamburg at the verge of becoming obese [hamburger + iceberg]

ham-hay a hammock as a bed

ham-lay to sleep or lie in a hammock

ham-let to rent a hammock or a sun chair

hamma ray to hamstring with lots of strength and force [**hamstring** + gamma ray]

hammark clothes drying on the washing line [+ hammock]

hammerhock to spit in someone's face

hammocca to lie on a hammock in the sun [+ mocca]

hammuck when you are stuck in a hammock

hamplio to help someone by giving them a hamper of food [L: amplio: improve] [+ hamper]

hampster a hamper of dead animals – like a hamster in a shoe box, normally seen around festive times

hamstairs small stairs | a few steps

hamster chuck to avoid being the happening of **cheek squeak**

hamstrig to knock something with a **ham**

hamstring singing in pig latin

hamyard a mobile phone that has too many charms [+ lamyard]

hancer to develop cancer | the cancer of

enhancing | to boost | to add to something means taking away from somewhere else [enhance + cancer]

hand anthon

handag to cover the hand

handage the art of signing (language through gesture)

hand-aid a bandage for the hand

handand extremely handy [hand + and]

hand-blown to be injured or killed by glass [*in pirate language* '*blow the man down*' *means to kill someone*]

handbob to part touch | to touch on something a little

handelion a handy herb normally not too

far away from being able to forage | the common herb [handy + dandelion]

handembroid to leave handprints on glass

handhoot to give directions | to use hand gestures when unable to talk from the mouth

handjabs pins and needles in the hands

handjob a job which involves touching, e.g. massaging

handrix hundreds of hands [insp. **hendrix**]

hands anthony

hands-on interactive

hanger to be sad and angry at the same time [hang + anger]

hantuk to thank someone by holding their hand

hapa happens shit happens, we must accept the bad [Turk. hapa: dirt, mud, trash]

hapazodiac a bad judgement [Turk. hapa: dirt, mud, trash] [+ haphazard + zodiac]

hap-hop more comical hip-hop (away from guns, sex and crime)

hapis hazuli it happens that there is a blue happening, it happens that there is something blue happening [*lapis lazuli is a mineral, the colour 'deep blue'*]

happending pending happiness

happendix to have an afterthought | a very healthy appendix [+ appendix]

happendulum to happen in many areas | to be happening everywhere [+ pendulum]

happetypoop when a bad song stays at #1 in the charts for a long time [insp. **happetypop**]

happetypop when a band is #1 in the charts for a long time

happlication a strong application

HAPPY had a pretty perfect yesterday

happy hour a race against time

happy hour glass the glass if always full | a time of optimism

haprise to explain why or how something has happened [insp. **saprise**]

hapsoda bubbly, e.g. a hapsoda personality

hapsoma a happy body

har hard

harash ha har ass harass, rash, rah, harsh

harbah feeling sheepish at sea [see **sheepish**]

harbone resembling a harbour

harbore a boring harbour

harbourbon a wet biscuit [+ harbour]

hardba to laught at someone behind their back | to make fun of someone behind their back

hard cell brutal prison living

hardwear stiff clothes

hare hair

har-harbour when the seagulls steal your chips

har-harlot a comedian who will say anything to get a laugh | a desperate comedian | a comedian who picks on an audience member in order to try and get a laugh [harlot + har-har]

haricot an extendible cot [insp. the haricot seed]

harkade an arcade of holy lights | a holy enlightment? [+ hark]

harman shaman one that bakes space cakes or magic mushroom pies [Turk. harman: flour] [+ shaman]

harmones laughing hormones

harmoney the harmony in having enough money to live comfortably

harmour armour that self harms | a self harming body | scars

haro a hero of speed [+ hare]

HARP have a rest pet, e.g. you said HARP to Sheila (your pet rabbit) at the vets because there was nothing that could have been done to cure her from the cancer

harum-carum reckless driving

harvanish to give a laugh to be polite

hasabatch a file of reports [Turk. Hasabat: account of, report] [+ batch]

hash brown a long wait on a phone line [*please press #*]

hashitis the effects of weed

hash-key dog a dog that is calm, a very good companion if you are stressed and need someone calm around

hash mash hash browns not in their solid shape

hash pad a place where herbs are grown

hashquet bags of weed or hash

hashtray an ashtray for roll-ups

hasi to feed on fruit and leaves [*the hawthorn shield bug eats fruits and leaves of the hawthorn and many other trees and shrubs*]

hasoup a made up soup, as in not made by recipe

hassalt to hassle and to stir rumours

hasta la visa goodbye payment | to get rid of a payment or bill

hat to hold (a) thought

hat batter to mess up a hat and not take care of it

hatch to put a hat on the head

hatha slow [insp. **hatha yoga**]

hatha yoga slow motion

hatisfactory the hat will do | a hat which isn't the most dazzling, the most extroadinary but it does its job, it keeps your head covered

hatlist a list of stylised icons

hatomize to hairspray the hair [+ atomizer]

hat (worn) on the side an affair

hat red hatred

hauntlet to strangle with the bare hands [gauntlet + haunt]

have beaver to have behaviour issues

hawk to scream | to pull the hair out

hay sleep

haya to welcome **aya**

hayack to cut someone up when sailing

haydiator a big sleeper

hayfeather light hayfever

hayfeve-red tongue unable to taste

hayley a warrior woman

hay sky the marks of an aeroplane in the sky

hayt a bad sleep

hayvera to get bored of listening

hay wire to record sleeping patterns

hazark an audio hazard

hazhard a big hazard

hazhoy only a little hazard

he Himalayas

HEAD head estimates a decision

head-a-hammer to have mentally abused

head-balancing the game of seeing how long you can balance an object on the head for [insp. **one-foot balancing**]

head & boulder helmet a hard helmet

head & boulders to have stones falling on your head

headead when the mind unable to think

head-fush head-rush of head-fuck

headge a head with big hair

headhere a committed person [adhere + head]

head hub a creative thought

headicure to look after the head | to treat the head

headit to think less [oppo. **headove**]

headlake when the brain is full of ideas, e.g. I just capsized in the headlake

headlamp eyes peeled ahead

headless-action men damaged goods

headlessoma a headless body

headove to think more [oppo to **headit**]

head rub to try and erase a memory | to try and forget

head-saw to cut your face when shaving

headstring to have hair the texture of string

headucation experience

head-wake an asprin

headwig a mask on the face

head-wok a beating headache

heaput to put in a lot | to give up a lot | to donate a lot

heard three to seven [insp. *the game of 'Hearts'*]

heardy-gurdy to have only heard half a conversation | bad hearing [+ hurdy-gurdy]

hearo a good listener [+ hero]

hearsh I heard you harshly | I hear your sourness

hearsway to hear something and be moved by it

heart romantic art

heart attock close to having a heart attack

heart brick tart break

heart cam a camera on an animal when going to slaughter

hearthy an earthy heart | hearty earth

heartificial an artificial emotion | to pretend to have feelings

heart on hand fragile emotions

heart-sap the emotions

hearts dice to check the heart beat after physical activitiy [insp. *the game 'Hearts Dice' is a roll and count dice game, the dice has the letters 'hearts' on it, as a six-sided dice*]

heart whist half an hour [insp. *the game 'Hearts' takes half an hour to play and the game 'Whist' takes an hour*]

heartwood strength [insp. *the central heartwood conferring strength and stiffness*]

hearwig an earring

heasoma a healthy body

heave to not have anymore | to have cleared out waste

heavent air coming from above [heaven + vent]

heaver when both choices are ill or sickening [heave + either]

hebathe to bake in the heat | to sweat due to heat [bathe + behave + beehive]

hecklip the worry of another turning away as you try to kiss them

hecklipse for something stressful to pass by [+ eclipse]

hectac when having a hectic life gets to you [+ attack]

hedaki the sensitivity of the scalp and hair when suffering a bad migraine

hedge-ham to flatten [hege + **ham**]

hedgehug a tight hug

hedgeledge at the side of a hedge

hedgeplate an unreadable registration plate

hedgepuc a long kiss

hedgeward a hedge as a fence

hedgeways towards the hedge

heel the break on roller skates

heel-toe-kick dancing with no passion

heiti a connection in height [height + tie] [see **haiti**]

hel when the heel comes off the shoe

helander a helicopter in the process of landing

helder a healthy elder

heli helicopter

helicabacta for a helicopter to return [+ helicobacter]

helicobacteria for a helicopter to have a problem

helicrypter a non working helicopter [+ crypt]

helium a heli in the sky [insp. heli]

heller poetic movements [insp. *Stuart Heller's 'The Dance of Becoming'*]

hello heels in pain

helloaf a big hello | an intense hello

helloot to greet somebody with money, e.g. when it's someone's birthday you may helloot them

hello scatty the imitated Hello Kitty character

hellow an empty greeting

hell we far to realise the long distance between two things [+ farewell]

helmass a helmet which fails to protect the head without a hemlet

helmat to wear a helmet when standing on the ground level of a building [+ mat]

helmetro for someone on public transport to have their head in a newspaper [helmet + metro]

hel pout sharing kisses

helter skelter here, there and everywhere

hemail a message from a male

hempire a place where lots of hemp is grown

henbain the burning and drowning to death of chickens in scalding water

hendrix hundreds (of times)

hengaged hens laying only for human consumption

henguage hens enslaved for food

henna temporary

henodo the night of a hen party [Wel. heno: tonight]

hen period egg

henried to wear clothes that are too tight [insp. *henry the vacuum*]

henroid a person who gets laid off

henry a guy who sucks penis [insp. *henry the vacuum*]

henry the vacuum is depressed "henry: life does not suck... I do"

hera triangular [insp. the norfolk island pine tree]

her fat her father [+ father]

herb age herbal time(s)

herbal hair ball

herbalize dress sage

herd heard multiple voices

hereditto the same heredity

herewhile to have been here a while before | to have had a holiday there [+ erewhile]

hermaphroboob boobs which do not like to be touched

hermitten a closed cubicle | an engaged toilet

hermoculture the culture of people staying in, watching tv or spending most of their time on the internet [hermit + culture] [see **heroin**]

hermsthrows unisex clothes

hero techno [insp. **heroin**]

heroditto to be a hero for the same thing | to be well-known for only one thing

heroin technology [see **hermoculture**]

hesi to hesitate

hesistance to have a stance of being hesitant

hesitent a place of caution [+ hesitant]

hesitina a hesitant woman [+ hesitant]

hesitrevor a hesitant man [+ hesitant]

hets tanned | tan-like [insp. the Western hemlock tree]

hex to be little known [insp. *the game 'Hex'*]

hexagon to have six parts | six episodes

hexagro to be getting **stick** from lots of different places | to have gathered sticks from many areas [see **stick**] [+ hexagon]

hexpense a six-figure expense

heyone extremely old [insp. *the game 'Help your Neighbour' is an extremely old game*]

hf homophonic

hg hunger

hhh three in a row [see **O's and X's**]

hhhh four in a row [see **FIAR**]

hi a loud hello

hiappro to highly approve

hicbiscuss the burps brought on by from drinking organic fizzy drinks

hic-cap to disguise

hic-cop to blow an under-cover cops cover [see **hacktivism**]

hiccrush to be under the attack of hiccups [+ crush]

hickety-hackety to accidently hack into something | to stumble across private information

hickies'n'whisk out to pull

hicky-bow a redneck [insp. **dicky-bow**]

hid-a-hammer to have resisted hitting someone in the past | to not tell anyone you were abused [+ hide] [see **head-a-hammer**]

hiddip cup to hide something in a cup, e.g. you see hiddip cup in the shell game (which is usually performed on the streets)

hide and sake to run away and hope to not be found

hidelve to delve into hiding | to discover the unseen

hident to hide your identity

hidental to not show your teeth when smiling or laughing [insp. **hident**]

hid gid to get rid of something by hiding it | moving something out of sight

hidsoma a hidden body | a missing person

high code a very strong password

highdrogen of high water levels

high-fi a big fight [oppo. **low fi**]

high flyer an airplane

hig-ham the attack of unexpected hiccups [+ wig-wam]

high-holt when something is up in the air for a while

highlit highlighted

highlitter highlighted litter | to bring up something of irrelevance

highlow up and down

high-pent high five [+ pent]

HIJ how's it joking?

hilary duff a teenage celebrity

hillament a light far away [filament + hill]

hillord a master of climbing or walking peaks

hing for a noise to keep on recurring

hinge ash to keep the top of a coffin at a funeral

hink to be unable to think

hink honk unable to alert [insp. **hink**]

hinter to hint between sayings | to help someone by giving them clues [L. inter: between]

hintro to hint an introduction | to give help to get someone started

HIO hover it ooga!

hip hip who's ray to not know the name of the person you are hooraying

hiphazard a hazard of doing damage to the hip

HIPMO he is pissing me off

hippo a fat hippy

hippock sock an argument which contains many floors

hippointement appointment regading the hip

hippo oppo a bit of an opportunity

HIPPOPOTREMULO US hi, in past part: orange pins ornament to red envelope more until linkage overundoes sink

hippotiss biggest of all [L. potissimus: best of all]

hips lips, e.g. what you put through hips goes to the lips and what you put through the lips goes to the hips

hipshazard when the hip bones stick out too much [+ haphazard]

hipsoda to be up-todate | a respected person

hipstairs stairs that curve around

his city [insp. **hispla**]

hispla cities and towns [insp. the london plane tree]

hiss to seak after having your mouth numbed

hiss red sister troubles

hister sister [insp. **schister**]

histore a museum | an antiques shop

history yellow [insp. *'Tivial Pursuit' colour*]

histrick a historical trick | an unforgettable prank | to make up history

HIT hang in there

hit a carlsberg to have hit an iceberg or alcohol

HITHYT hang in there, it'll be alright [insp. **HIT**]

hi-tiger to rip clothes off

HIV hello, I'm violent | hello, I'm vacant | hello, I'm violet | handsome in vain | handsome in vein

HIVE hello I'm very emotional

hiwa highway

hoaro hero of the hour

hoax boob [Iri. bob: hoax]

hobajo to get a job from your hobby [Spa. trabajo: job]

hobbone to be paranoid about your weight [+ hobby]

hobby horse to keep on coming back to a hobby

hobtab a list of hobbies

hobtabtub a hobby of eating different favours of icecream [insp. **hobtab**]

hoc-hac to take a sample of saliva [hock + hack]

hock spit

hockabulary for someone to spit a lot when talking [**hock** + vocabulary

hock-book a disappointing book [+ **hock**] [oppo. **hookbook**]

hockle knuckle to tie a rope around the knuckles

hody a hidden body [+ hood]

HOE heaven on earth

HOE hell on earth

hoese a whore house [**whore** + **hoe**]

hogbog to take a long time in the toilet when there's a long queue waiting to use it

hoggle to take a bargain | to have got a bargain

hogloam to make use of twilight

hoglow to make good use of daylight [insp. **hogloam**]

hograv to visit more than one grave at the cemetery [see **hogloam**]

HOH head of hair

HOI house in order

hokux the magic of inner connections | subliminal messages [Kic. k'u'x: soul; being; heart; chest; womb; bottom] [+ hocus]

HOL heart of London

hola bucket hello sick bucket, you are my number one companion today

holagon to drop in to say hi but have to go quickly

hola lava a love of the holiness

holdier a person who can lift very heavy objects | a weight lifter

holdihay to spend a holiday mostly sleeping

hole-in-bag unlucky [insp. **bag**]

holgate an airport gate [+ holiday]

holicult a religious cult

holidate the date of a holiday

holidave a lads holiday of booze and blokeyness

holiday mode laid back

holish to be a little religious

holisp to be proud of your lisp [+ holy]

hollow hours to go without breakfast in the morning

holloways echoing rooms [+ hallways]

holly pop to eat or suck on the hair

holly pup a puppy that likes to get someone wet by licking them

holocaust the mistreatment of animals [*the billions of slaughters, the millions of bleak experiments, the gassing of animals, the imprisonment, the killing for product, the enslavement, the sexism of female chickens made to lay eggs and the males normally grinded into chicken nuggets because they are unworthy of making*

money, the shooting and hunting of animals, the skinning alive of animals for clothing]

hologrammy to praise a hologram

holtel to not be allowed a room at the hotel

holyday a religious say | a day of celebration

holyhead a holy person
holy seagull a treasured holiday memory

hombre a person you live with

homeicide to be forced out of your home

homiliation humiliation of the home, e.g. homiliation came when the in-laws came and the house

was in a bad state –
knickers on the
radiator, curry on the
ironing board, mould
on the plates...

homish to feel a little
like home | a bit comfy

hommack your bed
at home (the hammock)

homophoto photos
which look the same |
identical images

homosh a lot like
home | very
comfortable

homo slap a light
slap

homwort to hammer
a nail

honear near(ly) an
honour

honey came

hon fun very rich
[insp. honey fungus]

honk between a
donkey and a horse

honly only one holy
one

honourish to nourish
in honour

hood-blood your
family in the same
neighbourhood

hood-bud a friend of
the neighbourhood | a
friend in your
neighbourhood

hooded pitta a pitta
stuffed sandwich

hoodle a group of
people wearing hoodies
[+ huddle]

hoodoo to have a
hood on when fighting
[+voodoo]

hoodred danger

hoof gelatinous
sweets

hook-a-book the joy of studying

hook-book a book you do not want to put down [oppo. **hock-book**]

hooker to hang a coat up

hoopie a round pie [+ hoop]

hoops-oops going round in circles

hoot sing-song

hoothead one who gets annoyed when you say their singing is bad [hot-head + **hoot**]

hootplay to pretend to fly be a helicoper, spinning around in a circle with your arms sticking out to the sides

hoover suck

hoovert to convert a person who bites hard sweets into a sucker | to get someone to take time in eating instead of swallowing with speed

hop–hip to move your hips so one goes higher than the other

hop to regain a great deal of lost ground [insp. *the game 'Nine Men's Morris'*]

hop scratch when you have more than one itch so you switch between scratching these

hop, skip, hump to use people

hop, skip, stump to be skilled in climbing trees

hoppetypoop to avoid mess

hoppetypop to resist eating sweets

hopponine to want the time to be five PM [*office-hours finishing time*]

hoppor to jump at an opportunity [hop + opportunity]

hop spot to not stay in the same place for too long

hora lava a love of time | a love of history

hornamental a porn star | an ornament to try and entice horniness

horn of planty to build up a desire [insp. *the 'horn of plenty' plant*]

hor ple funnel-shaped [insp. horn of plenty]

horse mush large [insp. the horse mushroom]

horse sea horse in and out of water

horse-race to punch someone in the face

horse-ride to treat comeone with no respect

horsetail to have thick hair-when put up | a thick ponytail

hose a house having only one level

hosh to block [insp. the game 'Horseshoe' where the winner is one who blocks the opponent so that they cannot move the counters]

hospite hospital food [+ spite]

hospity the pity of hospital food

hospuke when hospital food makes the patient even more ill

hospur when hospital food encourages the patient to get better so they can get out of their and get some decent food

hoss red brother troubles

hoster brother [insp. **schoster**]

hostle to set something up [hustle + host]

hot sauna | to constantly think

hot bed a warm bath

hot cha to cha-cha with passion | to dance with passion

hot chair a deck chair in the sun

hot cross a pissed off Christian [see **Jesus on a croissant**]

hotel bell at your service

hotel on wheels a twenty-four hour bus service

hot-not someone who is believed to be hot but is not hot

hot-nut to choke on something hot

hot pipe doesn't want to be touched | don't touch, e.g. the sign on cabinet read "hot pipe"

hotplay to play outside when the sun is out

hotrib death [+ birth]

ho u how are you?

houndreds hundreds of hounds

hourglass X shaped

hourly-head to plan in hour blocks

hourse to do more than what is expected | to work additional hours

house pod

ho-use use in the home

house cry to wallow around the house | to feel depressed at home

house goose bladder how's the water?

house road a road with a thirty-mile-anhour speed limit

house tag a house price

house tail to go to a house party after the other party finishes

house tile a house party

houster a familiar house [+ host]

houstile a place with bad energy [hosile + house]

hoven a hot oven [oppo. **coven**]

hov flo spa to spend a lot of time not doing much [hover + float + spa]

hover toot to have your teeth cleaned (with suction) at the dentist

hover-bored when you surf the internet not really looking for anything in particular | to spend time on the computer to kill boredom

hover-confident to always be worrying about how you come across to people in terms of whether you show confidence or not

hover-sensitive to hover over the sensitive [+ over-sensitive]

howda 'how do you do?' said as a replacement for 'hello' when you are in a place where you may not encounter another (person) for hours [Turk. howda: pond]

howl to hold an owl

howl bowl to let out happiness when you score [oppo. **empty bowl**]

HP hazardous problems | hard potato [see **BP** & **MP**]

H (past) one letter past G, two letters past F, three letters past E, four letters past D, five letters past C, six letters past B, seven letters past A, eight letters past Z, nine letters past Y, ten letters past X, eleven letters past W, twelve letters past V, thirteen letters past U, fourteen letters past T, fifteen letters past S, sixteen letters past R, seventeen letters past Q, eighteen letters past P, nineteen letters past O, twenty letters past N, twenty one letters past M, twenty two letters past L, twenty three letters past K, twenty four letters past J, twenty five letters past I

HP beans HP popping up everywhere

HTmal a person who can't get to grips with the internet | without computer skills

HTML history tells more lies

H (to) one letter to I, two letters to J, three letters to K, four letters

to L, five letters to M,
six letters to N, seven
letters to O, eight
letters to P, nine letters
to Q, ten letters to R,
eleven letters to S,
twelve letters to T,
thirteen letters to U,
fourteen letters to V,
fifteen letters to W,
sixteen letters to X,
seventeen letters to Y,
eighteen letters to Z,
nineteen letters to A,
twenty letters to B,
twenty one letters to C,
twenty two letters to D,
twenty three letters to
E, twenty four letters to
F, twenty five letters to
G

h'toot h'toot 'dog
see dog' [see
toothtooth]

hubhat a hot head

hubiliation at the
centre of humiliation |
humiliation in the town
centre

huddle shudder
when two heads bump
into each other

huff puff shuffle
cannot stay still due to
having something on
the mind | cannot stay
still due to waiting for
something

hug mong to enjoy
feeling monged

hugemonged
massively monged [+
humong]

hulabaloon to make
something unnecessary
or irrelevant really big |
to make a point out of
nothing

humangle twisted
humanity

humanimal human
and animal

humaniform in the
form of a human

humany the mass population of humans

humbrella for a sound to dominate an area, e.g. the guitar humbrellas rock-music

huminor a few humans

hummingbird one thousand [insp. *a hummingbird may have upto one thousand feathers*]

humoose plenty of humour [**hummous** + moose]

hummer when you hear something and you don't know what it is or where it is coming from

hummous humour

hummouse little humour [**hummous** + mouse]

hummurmaid a person who says 'hmmm' or 'ermm' a lot

humour hummous

humour hum when a joke is not understood | to not understand why something is funny

humpcheeks big cheeks

humpire a place having lots of hills, mounds, or even simply lots of crooked ground [hump + empire]

hums up to give thumps up only to be nice or to avoid grief

hun fight a hen party [insp. **bun fight**]

hun gun to use the power of seduction or attraction to get something

hunder-stair lots of steps | never ending stairs

hungary hungry

hungry belly a dried up lake

hunt scum

hup high up, e.g. hup in a cloud, hup in a bag of cotton wool, cotton candy makes you hup in sugars and hup may also happen with cloudy lemonade

hupa hands up

hura to lose hair from old age [insp. the klinki pine tree]

hurdle-gurdle unable to achieve [hurdy-gurdy + hurdle]

hurdolled to be missing an object [hurdle + doll]

hurlock one who is sick [hurl + herlock]

hurst expensive modern art

hurtle to hurdle into hurt | a difficult hurdle

hurt sap the sad emotions

hus band a music band composed of older male members

hut a hat which also covers the ears | a place or venue

huts to replay something in your head

huttock a shield worn to protect the buttock [**hut** + buttock]

hy gene to get good hygiene from the gene | to have learnt how to keep clean from your guardians

hydrodungeon underground sewers filled with water

hyetoast wet toast | warm rain [Gk. hyeto: rain]

hyetoid raindrop shaped [Gk. hyeto: rain]

hyetoken the gift of rain [Gk. hyeto: rain]

hyetombed to be drowned | to have drowned in water [Gk. hyeto: rain]

hyetones the sound(s) of rain

hyetoy a rain maker [Gk. hyeto: rain]

hygenerous of tremendous hygiene

hygienesis the start of a big clean [genesis + hygiene]

hyoxca carbohydrates [insp. *hydrogen, oxygen and carbon make carbohydrates, derived from air and minerals from the soil*]

HYPE have you pissed everywhere?

hypick-pocrace revenge

hypick-pocraze a crazy level of revenge | too much **hypick-pocrace**

hypocrime to act out a crime

hypo potamus lots of pots

hypsoda a lot of sods

hypsosprout to push yourself to the edge

HYT hang in there, it will all be alright [insp. HIT]

Ii

I *pic* candle without a flame

IAAW I am a walrus

iacha versatile [insp. lawson's cypress tree]

IAD I always dream

I AM A SPACESHIP we can be anything we want to be if we really wanted to

IAO in and out

ibiza tiles the nightlife in Ibiza

ibling a sort of sibling, not blood but very close | when the water is thicker than the blood

ICBI I can't believe it

ice cold

icebox freezer

ice brink the edge of an ice rink

ice drink a melted ice rink

i chang a donation tin [Chi. i ching: book of changes]

ice-cram to eat icecream too fast | to experience brain freeze

ice hockey watch out for the gap

ice-howkey a shower which randomly changes temperature

ice lol a cold laugh (out loud)

ice punk to throw icecubes or to place icecubes on someone as a wind-up

ice-cre pig out [+ ice-cream]

ice ridge when you cling onto the sides of the ice rink, unable to skate good enough to let go

ice-scram to flee away from the cold weather

icesoma a cold body

icethink a cold thought | cold thoughts [+ ice rink]

i cling to be addicted to Apple technology

icmoss rusty brown [insp. iceland moss]

iconstruction glass buildings [+ icon]

ICT I can't talk, e.g. you may say this when someone calls you up and you are in a public place and do not like the idea of others being able to hear, so you say *ICT*

ICTAM! I can't take any more!

ictwa to be solitary in nature [insp. *the icterine warbler birds are solitary by nature, hiding in vegetation*]

ide wide open to ideas [Jap. Ide: idea] [+ eyes wide]

identicat an identified cat

identitle when your identity is your title, your name, and nothing else

idge to shrink when you become old in age

idget a short person yet taller than a midget [see **midget**]

idiode a moment of foolishness

IDOK I don't know

idult an adult idol

IF in fashion

ignominate to publicly shame someone by nominating them

ignullah a clay stream [*Nullah is a stream in India*]

I go to church oh, but i'm a good one

ih to not be yourself [*if* ih *then* ah *which* is eh]

IHSLAND I hate sleeping long and never dream

IHSLANDER irony has seven landing and nine dwarf every reindeer

iii three in a row [see **O's and X's**]

iiii four in a row [see **FIAR**]

IIPMO it is pissing me off

ilaf to fall over from laughing

ILBIH I love but I hate

ILC I love cake

ill-ball a catching illness

ill-bill a medical bill

illeg to adhere to the no trespass sign

illusolstic to think of the sun at a time when you are really cold in order to try and psychologically make yourself less cold

illustray to lose focus

illustritare vulgar literature

ILM I love myself

ILUO I like urinating outside

ILY I love you

imag an online magazine

imagerm a bad image, e.g. your grandparents having sex

imaginose to imagine you can smell something [+ nose]

imarg a glazed looking image

imbene to try and make a **bene** fitter [see **bene**]

immature thumb-suck

imminet a net coming up out of the water [+ imminant]

imnature for it to be in the persons nature to be **thumb-suck**

impedal imperial vulnerable to being took away

impelican to push someone and for them to go flying [impel + pelican]

impint an impressive pint [+ imprint]

implanteddy a person with implants

implicity an empty city [implicit + city]

implied as ply

implymouth imply something said

importato a slow import

impro fun

impudance the dance of impudence in flirting, e.g. he said he would never want to meet me

in individual

incumbin temporary work filling in on a position, e.g. incumbin was given for maternity cover [incumbent + bun]

in de in to be independent

indigentle poorly-handled [gentle + indigent]

indigoon a time when rowdy drunk people disturb your nights sleep [indigo + goon]

industrial a heavy amount of dust

infootiuated infatuated with the feet

infurtigo the illness of wearing real fur [+ infertigo]

ink cap a pen lid

inkin to persuade a family member

in mom an unborn baby inside the mother

innervemost a secret phobia or fear [innermost + nerve]

in om in harmony | a love for meditation

intender input tender

in trains always travelling never really getting anywhere

intravenous to hit a nerve | to travel into the vein [intravenous + travel]

inact to water

inadequal not a
suitable equal

inagerenta
Argentina

in camera full time

incarnage in an age
of pollution

incarnation flower
the growth of
incarnation

incarnet eating the
flesh of fish

incarnotion
discussing cars

in carriage
permanent

incense placenta

incha in motion | in a
time measure | in
rhythm

inchewate just begun
eating

inchoate just begun

in cholk temporary

inchrist a strict
Christian | committed
to Christianity

incisi to cut up food

**incredible string
band** to play the
sympathy note

incredual a fight
between two people of
incredible strength

indaycate to indicate
a day

indead indeed dead

indear in (the) heart

indearest in the heart
the most [insp. **indear**]

in denill part trial

independ to remove a
swallowed object by
secretion methods

independent to have swallowed an object

india in the ear

indian dice standard [insp. *the playing of 'Poker Dice' with a standard dice is called 'Indian Dice'*]

indinesia a place for indie gatherings [+ Indonesia]

indirth the blood

indongruous unable to hold in a poo [insp. **incongruous**]

incongruous to never fit in | constantly outof-place

infernoose suicidal hell

infertigo to be addicted to 'impressing' to the extent it takes over your life [L. infigo: impress]

infestvest for moths to have eaten your clothes

informality 0-80 or 100 – 180 degrees [see **formality**]

ingelect to gel with another's intellect

in graffiti contract

ingrest to go in for a rest | to become lazy or slow

inhermit to become more lonely | to spend more time on your own

in-ink instant transfer

injoy (in) a happy place

ink transfer

inking-kongruous an out of place giant | a tall person who feels **incongruous** due to their height [see **incongruous**]

inkling a pen with little ink left

inlaw henna | body art

inme within

in-med pharmacy

inner-dinner the food inside of the body

innest to stay inside [nest + inner]

inoc pat a fruity smell [insp. inocybe patouillardii]

inparch to not water the plants [inarch + parch]

in print studying

insect to lay egg (s)

insection to tidy up a part | to eat a piece

inslum lacking brightness | not much light

insolence when your shoes give you blisters

insomnium to not be able to dream | to not dream | unable to imagine [L. somnium: a dream] [+ insomnia]

inspectrum to look for other colours in something [+ inspect]

inspirace to calm down by inhaling slowly

inspire to breathe in

inspiral carpet to feel a touch

inspirate to take in something

inspiratory to take in a story

instant biceps and triceps insert inflated arm bands under arm sleeves

instares inner thoughts which are different to what are being expressed on the outside

insteady to choose to fix something

instool to have feet resting on a stools lower bar

instram in travel [instrument + tram]

instrum in play [insp. **instram**]

insulaugh a detatched laugh | to be laughing alone | a solo laugh [+ insular]

insult'n'shook to be shaken by an insult

int fan a young fan [+ infant]

intearior to hold a sadness inside

intermill a broken cycle [intermittent + windmill]

intermitten kitten paws for no thought [+ intermittent]

interpretzel to look towards railway tracks [+ interpret]

inteween when somebody has a wee next to you whilst you also wee [+ intervene]

intoller one who doesn't use the toll roads

intomb in so deep it is deathly

intra an introduction

intraduce to maliciously introduce someone | to defame someone before that someone has a chance to be 'some one'

intran for something or someone to catch the eye

intrestupid stupidly fearless [+ intrepid]

introduct tape one that is quiet at first

intrust no interest

inuitcra to rash or fall over due to icy conditions

invasive cater

invelosight to take speed

inventilation an airy invention

inverde comma a ecological call

invertigo a sickly amusement rude [invert + vertigo]

invest skin (in vest)

investi to look into windows of houses when walking along the street [+ investigate]

invigo to go and invigorate

invisor hat hair [*invisible hat still upon*]

invoice the inner voice

involvo to be in a *Volvo* car

inwed to feel married without being married

IO inside out

iop indoor and outdoor plant

ip indoor plant

I (past) one letter past H, two letters past G, three letters past F, four letters past E, five letters past D, six letters past C, seven

letters past B, eight
letters past A, nine
letters past Z, ten
letters past Y, eleven
letters past X, twelve
letters past W, thirteen
letters past V, fourteen
letters past U, fifteen
letters past T, sixteen
letters past S,
seventeen letters past
R, eighteen letters past
Q, nineteen letters past
P, twenty letters past O,
twenty one letters past
N, twenty two letters
past M, twenty three
letters past L, twenty
four letters past K,
twenty five letters past
J

i pen to write with an
electronic notebook

ir inner and interactive

IRA I respect animals

iran I ran

IRA TIDET I respect
animals therefore I
don't eat them

iraq to feel like a coat
rack

irelander I land err

irise to open your eyes
wide [+ iris]

iriset to close your
eyes [+ iris]

isiropan eye drops

iron modernism

iron-i to Photoshop
photos

iron-board game a
game that involves a
domestic chore, e.g.
how many dishes can
you wash in 60
seconds?

ironing clothes away
from the caveman

ironyc the mockery of
NYC

irow to lead on the
irony

irrest to find rest irresistible | to never turn down sleep

irri for something irritating to increase in irritation

irrug temporary housing plans

irun I run [insp. **iran**]

iryman higher man

IS in surf

isaunate to be alone in a sauna

ish a little

ish bash to have an argument for no reason

ish bish to move about with not much purpose | to roam freely

ish bosh to talk without any focus on a certain subject | loose talk

ish bush to not be sure about which type of hairstyle to go for

islam it's as if [Nav. lam: seem, appear]

islamb is a baby

ISLAND I sleep long and never dream

isogram only one large [insp. *ispoperla grammatica is the only large stonefly in Britain*]

isol to stay indoors playing with technology

ipad isolate | an eye contact lense

isolarate to be alone in the hot seat [see **isolater**]

isolater to later be isolated | to soon be alone

isoplate a single plate | a table for one | a meal for one

israel to rail | by rail

iss a small kiss

ists chem it's a chemist!

isuuc a uncomedic comedian | dire comedy

IT identify & trace | instruction and taste

italian hand to toss a pizza

italic I am tall like (a building)

italick a sloppy lick from a dog or person

italike to agree on a sum [italic + like]
i-tally a digital brand, e.g Apple

Italy i-tally

itch bint to scratch an itch [+ bin]

I (to) one letter to J, two letters to K, three letters to L, four letters to M, five letters to N, six letters to O, seven letters to P, eight letters to Q, nine letters to R, ten letters to S, eleven letters to T, twelve letters to U, thirteen letters to V, fourteen letters to W, fifteen letters to X, sixteen letters to Y, seventeen letters to Z, eighteen letters to A, nineteen letters to B, twenty letters to C, twenty one letters to D, twenty two letters to E, twenty three letters to F, twenty four letters to G, twenty five letters to H

ITV news news of an ingrown toe nail

I uk belt obesity in the UK [insp. **I usa belt**]

I usa belt obesity in the USA

ival trend

ival rifle to kill a trend

ivor cutler exciting and creative

ivory tower where wedding vows take place

ivy every is me

iwrist to have a camera on the wrist [+ iris]

Jj

J jump

J *pic* a little smile on the side | a bent nail

jabalti the 'ouch' of having an injection

jablet giblet the panic or fear before a needle goes into the body

jabuse the abuse of poking

jace shade

jack slap [insp. *the game 'Slap Jack'*]

jack cloud only one cloud in the sky

jack daniel a person who smells of whisky

jackdaw to not waste [insp. *jackdaw birds are very adaptable and are likely to be seen foraging on rubbish*]

jackettle the new-age version of a tea cosy

jackie-channeling to be another's energy [insp. *Jackie Chan*]

jack-in-the-ballpit to be searching for friends or companions [insp. *flower called 'jack in the pulpit' and jack is always on its own*]

jack-in-the-brick to be at home alone

jackl and hide to 'jack' off in public places, having something covering the private area

jack potato a solo photo

jacry most important [insp. the japanese cedar tree]

jacuzzi over-indulging and selfish

jade a colour aid [jay + aid]

jafbla black and orange

jah-clock a time of vitality

ja hov to hover over 'jah'

jah-purdy feeling good

jai alumini a celebration of strength

jailhouse rock to dance in prison | to be happy with being locked in

jailopy an old prisoner [jalopy + jail]

jake mump to make someone jump

jam confusement | traffic

jamaica traffic lights

jam bar a bar that plays music

jamben a shop having two entrances [jamb + entrance]

jamble confusion

jamboreathe to breathe up and down [+ jamboree]

Jamie T if you live it then love it

jam-jade to unbrighten [+ jaded]

jam jar a jar of sweets

jam-pan saucy

jampingpong rays of colours reflecting in various places

jam sandwich a teddy bears picnic

jangaroo to shake or play around with the bunch of keys on a key ring [insp. kroo] [+ jangle]

jangull a person who wears lots of jewellery [+ seagull]

janseagull a person who wears a lot of wooden, beaded or shell accessories [insp. **jangull**]

january sale the first fight | the first signs of panic

jap for the thoughts to be in **jam**

ja pan a favoured pan for cooking [+ jah]

japgu 'U' shaped [insp. *a japanese gull has a distinctive Ushaped black area on the tail*]

jar bar a bar selling big sized portions of drink, in jars, wellies or even buckets | a sweet shop

jargone outdated slang | something said too late

jargun the power of jargon [+ gun]

jash upright

jash chair an upright chair

java lava a passion for java language

jay a flash of colour [insp. *the bird 'jay' has a flash of colour*]

jay-z to close your eyes and see jays and shapes [see **jay**]

jebust a broken community

jelly-belly to have nerves

jelly-jet dust up the nose

jelly phish to worry about being stung by a jelly fish

jenny plenty of energy

jeru-slam a breach of peace

jesterday a funny, foolish yesterday

je sue is jesus hey sue, it's jesus

je suis christ where's the church? where's the Christian?

jesum Jesus on a crossword [insp. **the first supper**]

Jesus on a croissant the first supper

jet block to be locked in a dark place

jetch to write in the sky [etch + jet]

jetty to be unknown | to not know if you are coming or going, e.g. the job's promising but it makes me feel ditty

jewballe the echoing of **jewballsy**

jewballsy the sound of bells clanking together

jew's ear pink or red wrinkly skin [insp. *the jew's ear fungi*]

jim judgemental

jingo bingo when a person becomes a number

jinxiet to speak uneasy words

jitterm jittery terms

jitter pedals when you are unbalanced on a bike

JIVE jealousy is very evil

jive liver the dance of good health | to do yoga | good breathing

jizt the point when jizz happens [+ gist]

jizz plant a jizzsmelling plant

jjj three in a row [see **O's and X's**]

jjjj four in a row [see **FIAR**]

jo a teaset and a television set

jobberish the gibberish of a job

jock a jockey-type joke

jockabulary to threaten with a weapon [insp. **jockey hock**] [+ vocabulary]

jockey hock when a jockey whips a horse [*there's no need for jockey hocking because there is no need for horse racing, especially the use of weapons*]

joey slaves to the coffee

JOI jump on it

join connect

joint connection

jointerface on-to-one eye contact [**joint** + interface]

JOJO jump on, jump off

jo-joba-jabberwocky flowery gibberish

jokabulary comedy [+ vocabulary]

joke yoke hard work for no reason

jomba to walk like a sheep

jor jaw

jordan the jaw line [+ **jor**]

journaval at the centre of journalism | the main news

joy happy

joystick to get stick from being joy [**joy** + **stick**]

joystickstory to get stick from telling a joystory [**joystory** + **joystick**]

joystore a place of joy

joystory a story of joy

joystuck to have lost control [insp. joystick is aviators' slang for the control lever of an airplane]

jpg jam poor gran

J (past) one letter past I, two letters past H, three letters past G, four letters past F, five letters past E, six letters past D, seven letters past C, eight letters past B, nine letters past A, ten letters past Z, eleven letters past Y, twelve letters past X, thirteen letters past W, fourteen letters past V, fifteen letters past U, sixteen letters past T, seventeen letters past S, eighteen letters past R, nineteen letters past Q, twenty letters past P, twenty one letters past O, twenty two letters past N, twenty three letters past M, twenty four letters past L, twenty five letters past K

jpig jam pig ivor ran

jpog jam pong or gong

jpug jam poor ulcer gone

J (to) one letter to K, two letters to L, three letters to M, four letters to N, five letters to O, six letters to P, seven letters to Q, eight letters to R, nine letters to S, ten letters to T, eleven letters to U, twelve letters to V, thirteen letters to W, fourteen letters to X, fifteen letters to Y, sixteen letters to Z, seventeen letters to A, eighteen letters to B, nineteen letters to C, twenty letters to D, twenty one letters to E, twenty two letters to F, twenty three letters to

G, twenty four letters to H, twenty five letters to I

judicapture confined judgement [+ judicature]

judy it is due

juggle of juice to transfer half-full or 'only a fraction full' jugs of juice to make fewer but full jugs of juice

juggle of water to transfer half-full or 'only a fraction full' jugs of water to make fewer but full jugs of water

jug led a pile of pencils

juice treasure

jult to feel like summer [jolt + July]

jumbleach drinking when depressed

jumble-jet clothes flying everywhere

jumboast to boast about something in big ways [+ jumbo]

jumbone a large bone

jumboo to jump out and scare someone

jumper to jump

jumpore a thick layer of make-up on the skin [+ pore]

jun one day it will come handy

juna a lunar pattern gone different

junbone a large fossil [**jumbone** + jungle]

jundo to have given up judo and have lost the skills you once had [+ undo]

jungal the thoughs of Jung [+ jungle]

junktion to inject dangerous substances into the body [junk + junction]

junoir a dark junior

junshi to feed mainly on fruits [insp. *the juniper shield bug feeds mainly on fruits*]

jurassack an unclean bag or rucksack [*with the possibility of a squashed banana at the bottom*] [+ Jurassic Park]

justacky a tacky justice

justajuxta only a sidekick | not the main person

justiface at the face of justice

justifate the fate of justice

justifry to fry the mind of justice

justithick bad justification

justleaf in a natural manner [+ justly]

justoffee a sweet justice

jutax to plat the hair [Skt. Juta: braid (of hair)] [+ juxta]

jut butt a very round end [+ jut]

juvenail young and intelligent

juxtaplex when two cars come very close to crashing into one another [+ perplex]

juxtapocket a secret pocket

juxtapuzz to put together a puzzle | to make a jigsaw

jying the sound of musicians jamming | improvising with musical instruments

Kk

k kinetic

K *pic* an hourglass melted by Dali

kahlo to walk with art, not legs

KAKOI keep alive, keep on it

kala one of the fastest [insp. the japanese larch tree]

kaleigh to make funny actions

kampfar the sound so far good [ok + amp + far]

kanga two-legged

kappower the power of a comic

ka-rate the levels in karate

karma lava a love for karma

karob a helpful teacher [Na. jar: teach] [+ carob]

karr camouflage [insp. karri]

karri camouflaged [insp. the karri tree]

kassanon without good assets

kay leigh for a short while [oppo. **mid gem**] [see **mid gem**]

KAYAK kiss and yuck and kiss

kayaket to boil the kettle for one cup of tea | to fill the kettle to its minimum amount [oppo. **yaket**] [+ kayak]

kazambias to believe magic is fools play

kebab a knot in the stomach [Kic. k'ab: knot in wood]

kebble an electric cable

kecle keep clear

keeping bag a bag where precious and sentimental objects are kept

kehehe the funny part | a funny part [Na. kehe: part]

kel a low-water mark [insp. kelp]

kemmel a hot room [kennel + melt]

kendal a keepsake

kenny to always wear your hood up [insp. *South Park*]

kent can't

kepler to keep on peeling [*kepler is in the second quadrant of the moon*]

kerry an important berry fruit, e.g. blueberries are the kerry of power food [+ key]

ketchup a red faced chap

ketch up come on, get saucy | get turned on

ketschup not able to produce children [Na. ketsuk: not able to]

kettles boils

kettot a mini kettle

key bar a popular place | a place where everyone seems to go

key lime pie a house key | a car key | a key for an important safe

key-wee a token

KFC kentucky fried cruelty

kidneigh to add alcohol to **kidney** [see **kidney**]

kidney a non-alcoholicdrink

kid-ney to give away

kidney bean a swimming pool

kidol a child's idol

kidst when you're having to grow up but you still feel like a child deep down

kidult both kid and adult

kiev key holder

KII keep it in

killord one who is known for killing things

kim and kim a woman and woman, e.g. a kim and kim relationship

kinam jam to bang your knee [Na. kinamtil: knee]

kindesis a change for the best [kind + kinesis]

kindled to have been tempted into buying a Kindle

kindud for a kindle to be a close companion

kindull the dullness of the Kindle

kinescope to watch a screen

kinet to move

kinetment movement

kinew a new move

kinewment a new movement

king to be able to move a step in any direction [insp. *the game of 'Chess'*]

kingpin needle and thread

kings of the stone age boys who used to be known for getting stoned [insp. **queens of the stone age**]

kinose to sniff out a smell [kinase + nose]

kinot to not move

KIP kip in peace

kip rest

kipblut a bed fit for a prince [see **kippig**]

kipling amongst strange noises [Na. kip: among] [+ lingo]

kippark a hotel [+ **kip**]

kipper bed [+ **kip**]

kipper lounge to use the sofa as a bed [**kipper** + **kip**]

kipper room bed room [+ **kipper**]

kipperv to stare at someone while they are sleeping

kippig a bed fit for a princess [see **kipblut**]

kirkby vacuum parts

kiscine to kiss in the back row of a cinema

kism the study of children [kid + ism]

kiss voom

kiss-chase having the bailiffs after you

kisstance to kiss from a distance | to blow a kiss

kit a kite not in its flying state

kitchen tile a dinner party

kitchen tiles many dinner parties [insp. **kitchen tile**]

kitsch-cotch to take unwanted items and make them into 'wanted' items

kitten a little girl

kitV the kitchen television, channel 1: watching the microwave, channel 2: watching the oven

kiway orally [kiss + way]

kizla to kiss a smoker | a smokers kiss [+ rizla]

kkk three in a row [see **O's and X's**]

kkkk four in a row [see **FIAR**]

klaxis a change of axis

klept a person who steals condiments from eating places [+ bibioklept]

kliche a well-known cliché [+ king]

KLM kiss, love, mate

klond five to ten [insp. *duration of the game 'Klondike'*]

klosk a closed kiosk

knackie channelling to drain somebody's energy [+*Jackie Chan*]

knack-neck the ability to dodge| to move the head quick

knal not able to find the centre

kneedle to jab someone with your kneecap

knepin when tights wrinkle around the kneecap area [Turk. epin: pleat, fold, crease, wrinkle]

knepul to pull a muscle in the leg

kni knife

knicker to knick

KNIFE kill needn't identify for enemy

knife-feed to add knives to your cutlery drawer [insp. spoon-feed]

knite knives being thrown | knives in the air [**kni** + kite]

knight most difficult to grasp [insp. *the game of 'Chess'*]

k'nin knees in

knobelisk to try and sit on the top of an obelisk

knoccur-ring an unknown number that keeps on calling [insp. **occur-ring**]

knock to not be able to go [insp. *the game of 'Dominoes'*]

knock-cock to hit a man in his private area

knock-knack a door's code for entry | to hit a lady in her private areas

knock-on, knock-off
to want but also not
want | to be undecided
on something | to both
like and dislike
something

knodule a knot of
hair [+ noodle]

knot not moving ['k'
is for kinetics]

knowlid to know what
you are seeing | to
understand what you
are observing | visually
aware

knowtice a wellknown
notice

knuckle knockle to
knock out or down a
door | to make an entry

knuckult a fighting
gang

koco to love chocolate
for eternity [Jap. Ko:
eternity]

KOH keep on hiding
[insp. **KOR**]

ko-la to promise
eternity without really
meaning it, e.g. we
would ko-la when
getting married because
how are we to know
who may come our
way?

kollopard very bad
manners [Na. kllpa:
bottom] [+ pardon]

kollopardon to
pardon someone who
has **kollopard**

kollopark a place of
bad manners[**kollopard**
+ park]

koostis I am ok

KOR keep on running
[see **KOH**]

korea career

korfir nine to eighteen
centimeters [insp. the
korean fir tree]

K (past) one letter
past J, two letters past
I, three letters past H,
four letters past G, five
letters past F, six letters
past E, seven letters
past D, eight letters
past C, nine letters past
B, ten letters past A,
eleven letters past Z,
twelve letters past Y,
thirteen letters past X,
fourteen letters past W,
fifteen letters past V,
sixteen letters past U,
seventeen letters past
T, eighteen letters past
S, nineteen letters past
R, twenty letters past
Q, twenty one letters
past P, twenty two
letters past O, twenty
three letters past N,
twenty four letters past
M, twenty five letters
past L

kr kerouac

kratom in calmness

krisp to reward
detective work,

reasoning and intuition
[insp. *kriegspiel in the
game of 'Chess'*]

kroo to jump through
[+ kangaroo]

krow a bird at work
[crow + work]

krow sow finding
food in the garden

K (to) one letter to L,
two letters to M, three
letters to N, four letters
to O, five letters to P,
six letters to Q, seven
letters to R, eight letters
to S, nine letters to T,
ten letters to U, eleven
letters to V, twelve
letters to W, thirteen
letters to X, fourteen
letters to Y, fifteen
letters to Z, sixteen
letters to A, seventeen
letters to B, eighteen
letters to C, nineteen
letters to D, twenty
letters to E, twenty one
letters to F, twenty two
letters to G, twenty

three letters to H,
twenty four letters to I,
twenty five letters to J

kuwait a short wait

kyat a chayote cat

kyoo when a queue
inherits a curve [+ cir-
cu-lation]

L1

L life | left | leap | loud

l linguistics

L *pic* a right angle | signifying a corner

l&r later

la language

LA little attention [oppo. **LOA**]

LAB lie a bit

lab lathe and bathe

laban to be white [insp. **laban**]

labank to have no money in the bank [+ blank]

labback back to the **DB**

labitat the habitat of a laboratory

labourbon a well deserved break from work [labour + bourbon]

labra an off-white bra [*like the colour of a labrador*]

labrev not verbal

labun an iced bun cake, or any cake with white icing on [laban: to be white]

laccure to lack the **accure**

lace to be losing its aceness

lacebug to tie someone's laces together

lacetic to cover yourself in cool lotions and shade | to fan the body [+ acetic acid] ·

lace top to have lost first position, e.g. she had lace top as she only got silver

lacewings very thin laces [insp. *the lacewing bug got inherited their name due to their delicate wing veins*]

lacip to trip over from untied laces (or from being lacebugged) [see **lacebug**]

lackheart to not have love | to push people away | to have no close encounters

lackhurt to lack emotion when something dreadful happens

lack-lock not able to find your keys | to have forgotten the password [see **luck-lock**]

lacksmith to lack groove [+ locksmith]

lact deli a bitter taste [insp. lactarius deliciosus]

lactic to lack heart

laction lacking action

lactit a boob able to leak milk

lad as to get a better fitness level from eating green leaves [salad + climbing ladders]

ladbod no hips

ladder positive

laddered to feel high

ladder red HIV positive [insp. ladder] [+ red]

ladders positive people

ladies thirst ladies first at the water fountain

ladmad to be obsessed with a male

lady's finger a carrot | a lady's finger

lady's hand a plate of carrots [insp. **lady's finger**]

ladytron a skirt

laer not real [+ liar]

lafia a laughing crowd [*Lafia is a place in Nigeria*] [+ mafia]

lafish the flow of lavishness

lag a slow walk [+ leg]

laga lager

lager laga

lagguage slowly walk and talk [+ **lag**]

lagroom the bedroom [*you go to this room when you are tired*] [+ lag]

la hunch to have a hunch about the launch | to have a hunch about how something started

lala poorly drained area [insp. tamarack] la laga to sing when drunk

la-la lager a drunken conversation

lama to skip around whistling or singing [lala + llama]

lamakarm to give off vibes [**lama** + karma]

lambrella a small umbrella

lame retardant when one only does something because others do it [+ flame retardant]

lameyard a very sappy lanyard, e.g. one of 'ENGLAND'

lamlash white eyelashes [+ lamb]

l'amp an 'L' shaped lamp which wears a lamp shade for a hat

lampshy to not like to have sexual intercourse in the light

lampust to have blood coming out of the body

lamute unable to get your voice heard | unable to get your point across

lancaster lots of stairs | missionary stairs

lanchor for your height to cause you a problem

land brown

land-scapegoat to avoid representation in art [landscape + scapegoat]

langauge to inspect language, e.g. to spellcheck your language

langis no signal

languid without energy | without spirit

lank long | tall

lanshun to make dark [+ lantern]

lantemp a festival of light

lanterm a lighter term | a more basic term

lap cat a cat that always sits on the lap

lap dunce when somebody tries to do sexy dancing but fails miserably

lap service to offer your lap as a seat

lap set to rest something on your lap

lapear to have more than a lap dance [+ laper]

lapproachable ready to serve

lapse step a step which can be folded away

lapsize to drop something which was resting on your lap [+ capsize]

larch deflated

larmar a ticking sound [insp. *the large march grasshopper produces a ticking sound*]

las lost at sea [see **alas**]

lasers red eyes

lasset stripping to sell your body or to use it for sexual entertainment [asset stripping + lass]

lassity belt a lead for a lassie dog

last hand your last job or current job

last poo for there to be a plaster in the swimming pool

lasthma the last breath

latch beam a light which is constantly on

latch on not moving

late of the pier a modern addition to the pier

latha to wash

latternal the most recent family member [latter + paternal + fraternal]

latter pat the last time you had contact

LA tiles the nightlife in L.A

laugh-gah a manager who is easy to get on with

laun dry [oppo. **faun**]

laundear a clean dear

launders fond to try and understand it in another way [laundry + understand]

launter to wash the laundry | to separate the laundry [Gk. lauter: clear, unmixed] [+ laundry]

lava lurk to wait for a volcanic eruption

laven haven too much innocence makes anger

laver to easily recognize

lavish glovish to love gloves

lavish lovish to love the heat

lavya hot spirit | a warm energy | the sun [lava + **aya**]

LAW lead a way

lawkward for the law to be awkward

lawm to camp out in a back garden [Na. awm: camp]

lawn mow to flatten the hair by wearing a hat

lawn yawn to fall asleep on the grass

lawnkward awkward ground

lawto automatic law

laxident to poo yourself in public

lay lout to extend the mouth

lay pout to open the mouth to kiss with the tongue

layor liam courier services

LCA lights camera action

L'CAR lights, camera, act

LCD light the light of a lighthouse [insp. **LD**]

LD long distance

leading wind a person leading a movement

leadowse self-experiment

leaf the main site

leaf cell drainpipe

leaflee to throw a leaflet on the floor

leafleet a public walkway with many leafleed leaflets on the ground

leafly leaves flying in the wind

leafter after the leaves

lean to score nothing

lease falling leaves

leasht less harm [+ lash]

leather light as a feather

lecci sca free of maggots [insp. leccinum scabrum]

lecci ver black flesh [insp. leccinum versipelle]

ledge to have one leg shorter or longer than the other

ledible easily taken in | easily encouraged

ledicure to be given a pencil drawing of yourself [led + manicure + pedicure]

ledom a model being treatsed as a slave

left-wing loyal

leg lego

leg a laid to not be given free aid | to not be offered help [+ legal aid]

leg bra a leg sling

leg-end a clumsy person

leg-endry a long-winded legendary | legendary at being a **leg-end**

legerdemanic moving the hands around in a manic state for no reason at all, e.g. a boyband will have the girls legerdemanic [legerdemain + manic]

leg-eye-guy a guy who has a habit of winking at women

leg-eyes eyes that blink by themselves

leggage to cover the legs

legion ra trap to have your leg in plaster

lego leg

l'ego the ego of the legs

legor leg over

legro athletic legs | a fast runner [allegro + leg]

legume to carry on moving the leg

leisure orange [*'Trivial Pursuit' colour*]

lemon curd to be cured by lemons, e.g. I am lemon curd! Huzzah!

lemon sherbet to pull a funny face

lendscape to swap homes for a while

lennon no lemon

lensuite a homemade studio or darkroom [lens + ensuite]

leonie a person with a 'Leo' starsign

leopardon a large pardon

lepaint a thin paint brush

lephanet well known on the internet [+ elephant]

lepidopteri off the scale [+ Lepidoptera]

lepint a thin pint glass [Gk. lepto: thin]

leprise a person who buys flowers to compensate for wrongdoing [leprosy + surprise]

leprose morbid prose [+ leprosy]

lepsychotic a psychological seizure | a bad trip | a black out [Gk. lepsy: seizure]

leptember September passed by too fast

lepsychotic a psychological seizure | a bad trip | a black out [Gk. lepsy: seizure]

leptember September passed by too fast

leptings thin fingers and toes [Gk. lepto: thin]

leptool a thin tool [Gk. lepto: thin]

leptop a thin laptop | a notebook [Gk. lepto: thin]

les irresistibles irresistible lesbians

lescape to pretend to be lesbian in order to avoid a male

lesea to stick out [insp. *the lesser earwigs hindwings stick out from under the elytra*]

lesmar dry and damp [insp. *the lesser marsh grasshopper is at home in dry and damp grassland*]

le stair Leicester

let the balls roll let the good times roll

leta beta a second daughter [*'Leta' is a girls name*] [*'beta' is the second letter of the Greek alphabet*]

lethall entry to a pub [hall + lethal]

lethetation to remove leather due to realizing it is skin and therefore there is no difference between it and your grandma's skin

letoot an outside toilet | to urinate outside

letter gothic dark lyrics

lettiquite polite manners when writing letters | the first written warning

leuhip for a needle to disappear [insp. *leuctra hippopus belongs to the species called 'needleflies'*]

leveal at a **veal** level

level two intro funeral

leverage to pull your hair out in a crisis

levident a lover of wearing Levi jeans

lexception a little exception

lexpect to expect the words | to expect a response or message

leycup a hybrid [insp. leyland cypress]

l'fat a big flat ion, revelation

LGBT love, give, be, touch

LIAD love is a dance

librasion a decrease in library use

li di fast and furious [*the guide to how the game 'Liar Dice' should be played*]

li kno to know a little

li quid to have money flowing in

liam for your mail to have been delivered to another address

liars to let go

liberash to free ashes from a pot

libertary free knowledge

libertin a liberation group

libitat the habitat of a library or study area

librare a collection of rare books

librate a mobile library [+ allevibrate]

libridge a bridge which is hardly used [*quiet like a library*]

libya to cheer for liberty

lice flavoured ice cubes [*"l" is for lolly*]

lice then lace to contaminate then kill

liced slow-growing [insp. cedar of lebanon]

lickheart to play with people's emotions

lickhurt to play the sympathy card

lid the mouth

lid ya to open daily | for a shop to open and close throughout the day

liddis to slide inwards

lie owls to sleep in the daytime

life birth

lifeguarden the walk of life | the boundaries in life [lifeguard + garden]

life socks material life sucks

liferrous a hard life [ferrous + life]

ligarettes menthol cigarettes [+ light]

lighsoma a light body

light bulk too many lights

light cap a drink taken first thing after waking up

lighthouse a house having all of its lights on

lightspeed champion a champion of running fast

likera tight similarities [lycra + like]

likey like

lilongwe to have been with someone a long time

limbash tired limbs

limbportant paying special attention to only one area of the body [limb + important]

limite to eat away at a ration [limit + mite]

limonk limbash from walking lots

limp biscuit a broken or crumbled up biscuit

limpet a flat cone shape

limpit a shy person who is dependent [insp. *limpets are flat cones which cling to rocks*]

limpun an illmannered pun [+ limp]

limpunch a soft punch [+ limp]

lin bud a friend from dublin

linen a faint line

lin-en when lines cross one another

linge to linger a little

linguise to disguise your accent | to change the way you talk [+ lingo]

lin jim to leave clothes on the floor

lio let it out

lion to score high

lion den a den containing lots of ripped, damaged and old clothes

lionic mouse to be small but brave

lionide lion's blood

lip charm for a piece of jewellery to pinch the skin

lipembroid to leave a lipstick print on a cup or glass

lipit quiet

lippie loud-mouthed

lippore to breathe from a small gap of the mouth

lipresy to find it easy to lipread | to find someone easy to lipread [+ leprosy]

lips hips, e.g. what is put through the hips goes to the lips

liq questionable to whether it is likeable

liquorbinge to binge on liquor or liquorice

liquorwinge emotion or cries induced from alcohol

liquorwish an adults version of liquorice being liqour

liquorwish-wash to have too much alcohol

lirony a little irony | light irony

lisent the gift of being able to hear

lish a little (bit of) love

listion what the eyes do when listening to the radio and doing nothing else [listen + vision]

lit a lightbulb above the head

litergent to clear literature of cursive words [+ detergent]

little ish

little anthony baby hands

little anthony and the imperials little hands being cleaned with soaps

little owl to have a little rest or nap in the daytime

live live to long live

live long, live proper to live long and prosperous you must be yourself

liver lie to lie to the liver | to keep on killing the liver

liver swim pool if Liverpool got flooded it would be a public bath - left for the station, forward for the blue coat

liverge at the verge of having an unhealthy liver | at the verge of becoming ill

liverpal a friend from Liverpool

live-wire danger

LIVING ROOM lunch in varied interest never grows, rhi 'ono', oh munch

lll three in a row [see **O's and X's**]

llll four in a row [see **FIAR**]

llandudno land did no

l,m,n a lemon

lo a small hello

LOA lots of attention [oppo. **LA**]

loading to be experiencing a slow brain

loaf when you are unable able to laugh

lo and la lords and ladies

localmotor the local or closest car garage

lock-a-choc to keep hold of chocolate and to not share it [see **block-a-choc**]

lockation a private location

lockheart to not open up | to not have any heart for others | to only have one love | to hold your heart for one person only

lockhurt when you find out your **lockheart** of 'one love' does not feel the same

lockomotion to not be able to do (the) **locomo**

locomo locomotion

locustard vegetable gravy [insp. *the locust strips vegetation*]

locustardy too much gravy! [+ tardy] [insp. **locustardy**]

lodd an odd load

loddis to slide outwards

LOE lack of energy

lofirst the first to go high | the first to rise |to be the first one awake [loft + first] [oppo. **cellirst**]

loft a facelift

log the **blog** and **clog** which then **d'log**ged is now back but without the "b" and "c" carvings, which makes it just "log"

log eyes opa for the eyes to look sorry or guilty [soggy + soppy + opera]

loggage logged data [+ luggage]

logo the **log** which has the dogs teeth marks in [see **log**]

logo hat a hat with a logo on | a branded piece of head wear

logue to throw sticks [+ rogue]

lo-hel to greet someone you don't want to greet or who you don't like but have to give greet to

loiterrace in between [loiter + terrace]

lollay the flashing of a lollypop light

lolly laughable

lollypoop when you drop your lolly on the floor

lon done to be finished with London | to move out of London

london eye a corporate cycle

london tiles the nightlife in London

londres London

lonelephant very very very very very very lonely

lonely alo

long-data too 'long-winded' [see **lung-data**]

long stocks long stocking socks

lonish a little lonely

lonosh very lovely

lonpi extremely slow [insp. the bristlecone pine tree]

lonpo value [insp. the indian willow tree]

loo coup a brilliant wee

looball a poo | fun in the toilet

looma blooma a loompa growing up

loompa a child [insp. *the oompa loompa's from Willy Wonka's Chocolate Factory*]

loompahood childhood

loompanion a childlike companion

loon don bizarrely made up | weirdly dressed, e.g. we thought he was loon don when he turned up at the funeral in a rabbit suit, especially when we saw his ears – that was the final score on us thinking he was loon don, I suppose the rabbit is rather religious in terms of Easter but death – was he planning on hopping in the hole himself or planning to plant some carrots?

looney lorry a long cartoon

looniverse a funny world

loophobic to have a phobia of using public toilets

loosders relaxed shoulders [oppo. bolders]

loose loves to move |
to (give) love to 'moose'

loose duh to not
know if someone is
pretending to be stupid
or if they are always
like that

looset a collection of
non-matching cutlery
instead of a matching
set

looter to watch
people urinating

loots nowhere to sit |
no seat or stool
available

loover to hover over
the loo

lopi long-lived [insp.
the bristlecone pine
tree]

loplip at the side of
the mouth

lopsaydairy to
phlegm from intaking
dairy

lopsaydaisy to talk
whilst munching on
flowers

lopvoom a kiss to the
side of the lips

loquet a bunch of
low-key people [oppo.
louquet]

lord fishnu a
worshipped fish [+
Vishnu]

lord shiva a big
shiver [+ Shiva]

loreal a dead cat

lorry the spreading of
a lore

los campesinos for
the casino to be your
second home

losoma a local body

lost aloss

lost hand lost touch

lost tracks wilderness

lostrailia off track

lot kno to know a lot

lots tye [insp. **toh-dye-tye**]

lottery number a bit of hope | a bit of luck

louquet a bunch of loud people [oppo. **loquet**]

lours lores of law [+ louse]

loust to be lost underneath | to have fallen down a hole | to be lost inside [louse + lost]

lout-loot 'money talks'

loval for a wedding ring to bend and lose its circular shape | for a marriage to lose its love [love + oval]

lovall to love all

love and rockets good memories shared with people close to you

love vatually added on love

lovely lucy about fifteen minutes

lovera to love to listen

lovertory a lover's bedroom

lovery very much love, to love very much, much love is much loved

lovish a little love

lovosh a lot of love

lovoshi lots of love

LOW leprechaun of wurlitzer

low-dryer a dehydrated person [blowdryer + low]

low-fi a small fight
[oppo. **high-fi**]

lowkeyring a simple
ring that draws no
attention to itself

loy to look left

loyal left-wing

L (past) one letter
past K, two letters past
J, three letters past I,
four letters past H, five
letters past G, six
letters past F, seven
letters past E, eight
letters past D, nine
letters past C, ten
letters past B, eleven
letters past A, twelve
letters past Z, thirteen
letters past Y, fourteen
letters past X, fifteen
letters past W, sixteen
letters past V,
seventeen letters past
U, eighteen letters past
T, nineteen letters past
S, twenty letters past R,
twenty one letters past

Q, twenty two letters
past P, twenty three
letters past O, twenty
four letters past N,
twenty five letters past
M

lr listener

LS loud space [insp.
QS]

L (to) one letter to M,
two letters to N, three
letters to O, four letters
to P, five letters to Q,
six letters to R, seven
letters to S, eight letters
to T, nine letters to U,
ten letters to V, eleven
letters to W, twelve
letters to X, thirteen
letters to Y, fourteen
letters to Z, fifteen
letters to A, sixteen
letters to B, seventeen
letters to C, eighteen
letters to D, nineteen
letters to E, twenty
letters to F, twenty one
letters to G, twenty two
letters to H, twenty

three letters to I, twenty four letters to J, twenty five letters to K

lu luminescence

lube blue

lubetooth to lick your teeth with your tongue in a sexual fashion

lubetube bluetube [see **bluetube**]

lubricat when a cat gets oil on their fur [*normally due to sitting under a car*]

lucida console a person in good control

lucida sans well spoken receptionists [+ lucid]

luckheart to unexpectedly fall in love

luckhurt to unexpectedly be heartbroken

luck-lock to find your keys | to remember the password [insp. **lack-lock**]

lucup weeping [insp. the mexican cypress tree]

lucy loose, see?

ludo clockwise [insp. *the game of 'Ludo'*]

ludofloure when a dolphin sprays water [L. ludere: to play] [+ flourish]

ludu anti-clockwise direction [oppo. **ludo**]

lump the stone in a plum | a lamp which is too light

lunchback a rucksack of food

lunch chime when the stomach rumbles

lunch in to be hungry

lunchback the back of a hunch back but the hunch is due to fat

lunched out to be full up

lunchlion to eat raw foods

lung long pauses when speaking

lung bung smokers cough

lung-data too difficult | hard to express [see long-data]

lunger echo [+ lung]

lung-john-data too difficult to achieve | to lack time to work something out

lungsac an airy place [+ lung]

luputty putty in the hands

lurk to walk with the head down

lurk larch to look deflated [insp. **larch**]

lush vegan-friendly

lust aluss

lust hand somebody who likes to touch a lot, which normally crosses the line into personal space

luxembourg luxury goods

lycheers an inside 'cheers' | to be secretly thankful

lyco per covered with tiny pimples [insp. lycoperdon perlatum]

LYCRA light years camera revs action [see **LCA** and **L'CAR**]

LYCRAYON light years camera revs action years on notion [insp. **LYCRA**]

lyon to carry on lying

Mm

M *pic* when staring in the centre point it is a highway or a baby swing(er) | a stiff wave

m is n msn

M&S mad and sad

macadamia mecca, damn, holy, god, damn

maccabee to be stung all over

mache skull a mould of a skull

machine gun a spiteful unnecessary

macinfosh to curse a mac computer

macup unusual [insp. the monterey cypress tree]

macupressure to indulge in therapy of Apple Mac programs [+ acupressure]

madder-ladder onto a new crazy level – blown out of the spectrum

mad-hatter tatterdemali

mad-hitter to domestically abuse for unusual reasons

madnest a home of madness

madrav half and half [insp. *the traveller's palm tree is half a palm tree and half aq banana tree*]

madsive madly massive

mafenatical a
fanatic of mathematics

maffa gang

maffa-gaf the leader
of a gang

maffa gaffa to stitch
up a gang

maffa mash a gang
fight

maflogue to make
known | to highlight
[oppo. camouflage]

magic lanterns
multicoloured lanterns
| festival lights

magist a magical and
delightful idea

magistraight
straight up magic

magnetic four stick
the power of the symbol
of the cross

magnetikka a six-
pack stomach [see **six-
pack**]

magnifi cent
freedom

magnifight when
there is an urge to fight
[+ magnify]

magnight a magical
night [+ magnificent]

magnus sleight of
hand [L. manus: hand]
[+ magic]

magpie the common
magazine [insp.
*magpies are the
common sight*]

magtag the brand of
the magazine or the
subject(s) it contains

mah-jo each person to
their 'self' [insp. *in the
game 'Mah-Jongg' the
player is on his own*]

mah jongg not as difficult as it looks [insp. *the game 'Mah – Jongg'*]

mai fer on a cliff [insp. maidenhair fern]

MAIL more apple in lunch

MAIL BOX more apple in lunch, beverage of 'X'

maize maze

maj major

majnuke 'bearing all' [**maj** + naked]

major mint

majurgy of major urgency [+ **maj**]

maka a mecca of making | a creative hub

make back to make something stand up | to stand something up

make-jet to make something in a short time

make-shaft a handmade boat [+ make-shift]

make-shift to make up working hours

malaysia to be lying in bed ill

maldives a bad dive

male chick a nugget

maleviolent malevolent and lever every violent, indecent opposition of lever endangers nausea, tragedy

mali a market with not much on offer | a market low on stock [insp. **malior**]

malien a male who feels alien in his skin

malior not better [L. melior: better]

mallo seed [insp. the double coconut tree]

mall on null a dead shopping centre | a shopping centre with no business

mallord the champion of eating marsh mallows

malnoursoma a malnourished body

malta to shed hair

malteaser one who is bored of window shopping [+ mall]

malteaste to tickle someone by stroking them with hair [insp. **malta**]

ma mo moo to visit the mother a lot | to rely on your mother a lot

mamp when a child calls for its mother

manana a crazy authority [banana plus authority in new zealand is mana)

manature for it to be in the persons nature to be **thumb**

manch to eat (away at) mankind

manchester tart gallery Manchester art gallery given a 't'

mancle bone a person with Mancunian roots

mancoli over-populated [+ e.coli]

mandatore a 'must' person

mandy collected dust in a dust pan

manga panda the cuteness, colourfulness, and powerful art of manga

mangazine a manga magazine

manguage tongue-twisted language

manic street peacher a mad but funny street performer

manic street preacher a religious preacher in the city centre

manifeast to eat up a manifest | to get rid of any evidence

maniflesh an open wound [manifest + flesh]

mankite a bungee jumper

mankle Manchester | Manchester United or Manchester City socks [+ ankle]

man-made made-up

manrunner to act out the **man-made**

man's finger a cucumber | a man's finger [insp. lady's finger]

man-timed manually timed

mantrap when a song is stuck in your head [mantra + trap]

manurse a nurse who ill-treats someone [L. manus: hand]

manusage usage of the wrist and the hand [L. manus: hand]

manuscript the commentation of a Manchester United football game

manus-manner a hand shake (shows good manners) [L. manus: hand]

manyang a calm kindness

map pal to have a map reader as a friend | a satellite navigation system

maple warm colours [insp. the maple leaf tree]

maplent plenty of syrup [maple syrup + plenty]

mapo foot-like [insp. the kusamaki tree]

mappulp to not follow the map

mar gin a borderline drunk | near to being an alcoholic

marathong to see how long you can wear

the same pair of underwear

marball a glass ball

marbalt to throw and catch an object [+ marble]

marble hack to singe the royalty [oppo. **marble hark**]

marble hark to sing about royalty [oppo. **marble hack**]

marbolt when a marble stops rolling [+ bolt]

march mallow to place marsh mallows in a line

mardi viagra to celebrate with viagra [+ mardi gras]

mare to store carbohydrates | prone to fire [insp. the jarrah tree]

marg marriage

margaret thatcher a thatched roof in a bad state

mario to marinate

mario nutter a person who is addicted to playing retro games, such as *Mario* and *Sonic*

marionut a punch & judy show [nut + marionette]

mark mean

market street a row of market stalls

mark of the bear scratches on the back

mark of the bee a bee sting

mark of the beer an alcoholic breath | to fail a breathilizer test [insp. 'mark of the beast']

market to have meant it [+ **mark**]

marock a carving [mark + rock]

marquee a temporary mark | a terporary score

marrain marinated clothes | drenched clothes

marriage marg

marriage wring a twist in the marriage

marsh more harsh

marsh mellow the soft air over the marsh

marshall a swamp

marshall mathers swamp people [insp. **marshall**]

mart market produce

martian lip land to be in a place where everyone is speaking another language to you

mary foster a blood sucking fly insect [*Mary Poppins* + *Doctor Foster*]

mascaro to cover the flesh [L. caro: flesh

mashes to mashes Sunday to Sunday

mash potato boring

masked bobby batman as a bird [insp. *the masked bobby bird is white with a black face, as if wearing a mask*]

masking tape tools of disguise

masquest an undercover investigation [mask + quest]

massacre slaughter

massag extremely droopy

mass age rest

massage in a bottle massaging oil

massieve to sieve the massive | to find the elements

mastair the main hurdle

masy lots of fruit [insp. the malay apple tree]

match maker mall to try and find a date at a mall [*small chance?*]

match mall a small shopping centre

match stock small goods

mate mote the TV is your best friend [+ remote]

mateaphor connecting metaphors

matear to cry over material life, e.g. your car

mathematrix the milieu of a calculator

mathrodite to add and subtract

matilda a pretty mat

matro a woman wanting to become a mother [mattress + row]

matt matter

matt and kim a man and a woman, e.g. a matt and kim relationship

matt o wiki matter of fact [**matt** + **wiki**]

matt paint painting materials [+ **matt**]

mattear a crying matter | an onion

matter matt

matter batter to kill an idea [+ **matter**]

mattron a **matt** of **marg**

mature thumb [insp. **immature**]

mauve way for the colour of light purple to turn into a darker purple

mayo it may be nothing

maximo park a giant playground

maximusk too much perfume applied

mayve may move, e.g. we mayve, but differently

maze maize

mcdoomalds the fast-food corporation is getting rich from getting people ill, which then boosts the pharmaceutical companies profit by getting them rich as more medication for the illnesses are needed, which is why mcdonalds sponsors the olympics

mcvities vitamins

md means defined

MDMA mad does mad actions

me my mo to talk about the self a lot

mea gra quite pink [insp. *the dome of the female meadow grasshopper is quite pink*]

mealody a melody to make a meal out of

mean mark

meanwhale in the sea [meanwhile + whale]

measure communicate

meccan a holy person [+ mecca]

mechanol mechanic melancholy [see **aumehanol**]

mechinge to hear cars | the sound of cars passing | mechanical ambience [hinge + mechanics]

mec-timed mechanically timed

medial menial the average menial

medias everyday news [Spa. dias: day]

mediaterranea holiday news [Mediterranean + media]

medicure a check-up at the doctors

medicurse to speak ill of these things which are supposed to be curing you from being ill

meditation Eastern medicine [+ medication]

medlar pedlar one who picks

mee-may to very much love [insp. furbish may-may: love & mee-mee: very]

meetwang when two people meet and get on well

megaphun to have fun shouting loudly

megore mega gore

mehow how do I do?

mel smit to pick up on someone being smitten

meld to lay down three or more objects

mellord the lord of mellowness

meloaf a stodgy melody

melody phonostork

membirth to start gaining members

memopause a forever changing moment, e.g. to graduate [memory + menopause]

memoral to remember a dead moral [+ memorial]

men red men troubles

mendolin to re-string a string instrument

mengage a meeting of men

mentalc to put on a mentality

mental weight a wrong decision which brings on stress

mephad a fashionable method

meps fine [insp. the douglas fir tree]

mercedes 'more shade please'

merchmarch to be waiting in a queue for merchandise

merline the average joke [**merlinear** + punch line]

merlinear flying the straight route to avoid trouble / walking on the main streets instead of side streets [merlin + linear]

merray a ray of christmas lights

merris a ferris wheel lit up in colourful lights

mesaint one that sits at the table [Spa. mesa: table] [+ saint]

mesh lumpy mash

mess age rubble

messiah a holy mess

metalc the powder of metal

metapet to have a changing hobby, one that always changes

metearology the study of the earth's dying atmosphere [meteorology + tear]

meteor to enter the atmosphere

met hut a train station [**hut** + metro]

metrosette good judgement [insp. **metrosystem**] [metro + rosette]

metrosystem the judging process [+ metro]

mex christmas [insp. the christmas tree]

mex flip to receive up or down [insp. mexican flip]

mexecca the top Mexican eatery [+ mecca]

meza to use your knife and fork when eating pizza

mg major general

MGMT mouse got minor taser

MIC made in china

MICBFYO made in china by five year olds

micco a comic magazine

mice one of the strongest (in the world) [insp. the coolibah]

michael-dermots big lips [**michael** + **dermot**]

mickey a comic magazine | a male mouse

mickey mo to take the mickey a little

mickey mouse santa clause

mickmac to make fun of someone's voice

micky a funny story

micro bank robber to steal pens from Barclays

microswift the smooth running of Microsoft

micro toilet robber to steal tissue from a toilet

microwave a warm wave (in the sea)

middew blue and purple

middow middle of a meadow, a meadow in the middle, dow it mid a dowse it did mid but how mea dow?

mid gem for a long while [oppo. kay leigh] [insp. *midget gem sweets take a long time to chew*]

midget a long baguette stick

midjit to jitter a little

mif a motherboard dressed in fluff [see **furb your enthusiasm**]

mig haw poor stripes | faint stripes [insp. *the migrant hawker dragonfly's thoratic stripes are poorly developed and sometimes absent*]

migrammar when bad grammar causes a headache

migreat to be glad you left something [+ migrate]

migrey to shy away from [+ mosquito]

mike skinner an established british rapper

MIL music is love

mile smile a distant smile

milestun the sign of a milestone

millipies fake eyelashes [pie + apply + millipede]

millitaire the strict working in a workspace [mill factory + military]

millord an owner of windmill(s)

mimickey to take the mickey out of mimicry | to imitate the imitated

mina-ear Armenia

minaid in aid of a few minutes break

minch to have toothpaste on your chin

mind ink writing of the thoughts

mindset a chaotic image

mind the sheppard watch out for the sheepish

minerals the little bits of food in a poo, e.g. sweetcorn or carrot

minesweeper flag come and get me

minesweeper flog to throw yourself at something or someone [**minesweeper flag** + flog]

minesweeper fog unsure of your next move when playing 'Minesweeper Flags' minesweeper flags plus fog

minfug a fresh looking fugitive

mingham Birmingham

mini mal a little bad | a little empty

mini mo to mimic a little

miniskull a miniscule skull

ministerling an expensively decorated church

minjure an injury caused by the creatures called midges

mink in the middle of (a) thought | to be in mid thought [minute + think]

minnie a female mouse

minsk to risk money

mint fresh| refresh | major [insp. the macadamia tree]

mint chocolate toothpaste hypocritical

minteract to interact in a new way

minterface a fresh interface

minude raw time | a minute of nakedness

minuke a little bit naked

minurgy of minor urgency

miossec to get a bit wet

miracleft a unexpected wave [miracle + cleft]

mirraculous to stare in the mirror for too long

mirroads roads which mirror each other | all the roads look the same

mirrorage to hesitate whether to look in the mirror or not

misapple when you eat an apple and it makes your teeth bleed

miscell to be invisible

mis-cell to be put in a cell for no reason

mishigan an area of **mish-mash**

mish-mash mixed up

mishmashush to discard of any clashes or odds

misjive the dance of negativity

miso soup to feel hate [Gk. miso: hatred]

miss bliss good weather [oppo. **mister blist**]

miss when the clouds clear | **bo-peep** [see **mister**]

missieve for someone to read a letter when it is not addressed to them [+ mischevious]

missile to miss out an isle

mister cloudy | sheepish [see **miss**]

mister-blist gloomy weather [oppo. **miss bliss**]

mi-stress a mistress who is stressed

mit hut a warm place [**hut** + mittens]

mit sem olive-brown [insp. mitrophora semilibera]

mittendon tissue that's been in the washing machine and has hardened or has diseased the other washed clothes with bits of itself latching onto them [mitten + tendon]

mitzvac a good clean [vac + mitzvah]

mixchore the work of mixing, e.g. paint or cement or even social networking involves mixchore

mixedi when something's been edited by a group of people

miyl fa a far away family | for your family to be far away from you [+ mile]

MM move me

mmm three in a row
[see **O's and X's**]

mmmm four in a row
[see **FIAR**]

mn mind

mo movement

moana lisa when a
'usually helpful' person
becomes unhelpful [+
moan]

moap to mope
around after goint the
wrong direction [+ map]

moat security

moat cam a security
camera

moat guard security
guard

moat hut a wellprotected
place, e.g.
buckingham palace is a
moat hut because the
queen lives there

MOAT matter of
attention

moataphor metaphor
spoken for a **MOAT**

moboat to have your
head fixated in your
mobile [boat + float]

MOC mug of coffee

mock-stock items
which are imitations of
the originals, e.g. **hello
scatty** is mock-stock of
Hello Kitty [see **hello
scatty**]

mocup fake China
cups, and plates [+
mock up]

mod cans mod cons
straight out the can
labelled 'trend'

modace very daring |
daring on many
occasions [insp.
moodacious]

modelacceleration
when a model is in
modelration and eats
too much they then
have to accelerate and
sick the food back up

modelration for a model to control his/her food by rationing

modesk the ideal work place [modest + desk]

mogra the winding of a clock [insp. *the mottled grasshopper's noise sounds like the winding of a clock*]

moh oh well, would you look at that, I am speechless [+ moth]

MOI mothers of invention

moiesty half moist | a little moist | damp [+ moiety]

molars mole holes [insp. **moles**]

molar system the spacing (out) of the teeth [+ solar system]

molaugh the appearance of the teeth when laughing [+ molar]

moles furry teeth [+ molar]

mollord the person who mollycoddles the most, and worries about everything

molly-dolly cart the newer mini car [*as you will notice the typical driver of this car is a female in her forties*]

momentummy a break for food | to stop for food | a moment to eat [momentum + tummy]

mom's the turd mom is not the word, but the turd, e.g. mom's the turd when she gave word she would buy me a castle and a pair of flip-flops – it is she and she be 'turd' because I have not got these

MON mall on null

monday buest
Monday I was [insp. sunday buest]

mondaytuesdaywed nesdaythursdayfrid ayada the **yada** of monday to friday work [**yada** + monday + tuesday + wednesday + thursday + friday]

moneigh to make money from horseracing | dirty money

monet money | money from art work

money monet

money spider for money to disappear

mong to be spaced out

mongarchy a spaced out monarchy

mongolia to mong out

mongown to have put clothes on without thought, e.g. inside out trousers and undone shoe laces

mongristle atoms | bits of matter | stars in the sky

mongtage a mixture of matter

monkey a shared key

monkey nut to break into | to crush

monkin the child of a monk [+ kin]

mon liver my life

monogames single-player games

monope to waste time playing monopoly

monopoly finance

monorally a mo-rally over money [see **mo-rally**]

monster cellar a scary place

monte carlo five to ten minutes

moodacious to be in a [+ audacious]

moodacloud to be stuck in a mood

moohan a pale hand

mooney foreign money

moonoon the moon in a noon sky

moons wide eyes

moonstone to rudely moonie in front of someone

moop moop a hater of cleaning [oppo. **pom mop**]

moor a good place [+ room]

moo razz mel to smoke a lot of herb

moore more cows | more moo

moore manure more cow manure | more splashing

moose goes to move [insp. **goose**]

moose and goose land and sea | to stand (to land) in the sea

moosh to roam

moosic when cows make sound| a cow on the keyboard (not the plate) | when cows moo at the same time, e.g. they were silent on the field then at slaughter all of a sudden they made moosic

moosive living massive [+ moose]

moowre for a cow to cry in wreck by mooing

mop to mis-read the map

mopatop shop a hairdressers

mopen to let everyone know you are moping

moping-pong an argument over moping, or the opposite decisions in direction between the passengers [see **moap**]

morag to keep old clothes for rags

mor rot socky

mor vul sinuous [insp. morchella vulgaris]

mo-rally a rally of morals

morbad morbidly bad

mordull a dull mortal | a boring human **moreder** to take too much [murder + more]

morel most distinctive

morf to [+ **from**]

morgtag the sum of your mortgage

morguetag the sum of your funeral [insp. **morgtag**]

morphwul an awful morph, e.g. to echange would be

morris mirror to look in the mirror and look drunk | a slanted 'drunken' mirror [+ morris dancing]

morse pause death

morse paw a secret killer

mort-mart a killing spree

mortool to use a human as a tool

mosay to say many things [+ mosaic]

moses a busker

moses basket container where money for moses is placed

mosquilto flee infested bed wear

mostrick the highest

MOT master of technique | mug of tea

mote mate a tv watching companion

moth a closed mouth

motherboar surf to look over the motherboard | to check the motherboard

motherboard iron to solder to the motherboard

motionstore a cinema

MOTS mug of tomato soup

mottophor a poetic murmur [motto + metaphor]

motto vo to have a private motto, e.g. my motto vo is to never trust anyone [+ sotto voce]

mould mild

moun a tip | a wet mountain [insp. **faun**]

moundain something high enough to have to think about avoiding it | an obstacle in the way, e.g. the cat would physically creep over my moundain of paper work while I mentally creep over it [mound + mountain]

mounteract to highly interact | of high interaction

mountzen an excitement

mousattache to carry a secret | to be quiet about something [moustache + mouse attached (tail/tale)]

mouse big

mo-use no cheese

mo-user not able to talk | unable to open the mouth

mouse got minor taser a mouse escaped a mouse trap with minor injury (huzzah!)

moustouch to touch the moustache to signal 'must dash'

mouth letter box [see **chatterbox**]

mouthfault to put something dangerous in your mouth, e.g. I just knew a handful of blades in the mouth would be a mouthfault

so I opted for sweets instead

mownoon when cats call each other for mating

mowre for a cat to cry in pain [morose + meow]

MP mashed potato [see **BP** & **HP**]

mp mushy peas

M (past) one letter past L, two letters past K, three letters past J, four letters past I, five letters past H, six letters past G, seven letters past F, eight letters past E, nine letters past D, ten letters past C, eleven letters past B, twelve letters past A, thirteen letters past Z, fourteen letters past Y, fifteen letters past X, sixteen letters past W, seventeen letters past

V, eighteen letters past
U, nineteen letters past
T, twenty letters past S,
twenty one letters past
R, twenty two letters
past Q, twenty three
letters past P, twenty
four letters past O,
twenty five letters past
N

mr blobby pink and
yellow | strawberry
and banana, e.g. i'll
have a mr blobby
smootihie please

MSI mindless self
indulgence

MT money talks

Mt mount

MTG mind the gap

mt gummery a
sticky situation [**Mt** +
gum]

M (to) one letter to N,
two letters to O, three
letters to P, four letters
to Q, five letters to R,
six letters to S, seven
letters to T, eight letters
to U, nine letters to V,
ten letters to W, eleven
letters to X, twelve
letters to Y, thirteen
letters to Z, fourteen
letters to A, fifteen
letters to B, sixteen
letters to C, seventeen
letters to D, eighteen
letters to E, nineteen
letters to F, twenty
letters to G, twenty one
letters to H, twenty two
letters to I, twenty three
letters to J, twenty four
letters to K, twenty five
letters to L

MU made up

much to not chew
food and instead just
swallow [insp. munch]

muckink to have a
handsomely rugged
look

muckole muck hole

muckup a dirty cup

mud brown and red

mue slope [insp. tallow wood]

mugask the cup on top of a flask

muggin to declare something

mullesk to molest with a smell [+ musk]

mullord the person who thinks too much

mullover a hangover from mulled wine

mully-cuddle to drink too much mulled wine | to be attached to mulled wine | to hold bottles of mulled wine like you would hold babies

multicine flashes of images [multiple + cinema]

multiplank bad at many things

multipull to pull a multiple of times

multipush to push a multiple of times

mumbo a dancer for a mother

mummery memories of motherhood

mumster truck mums who take their children to school in cars too large

munch eat

munch-bunch a group eating

munch eon to use up a lot of electric

munchkind to eat something you dislike only to e kind, e.g. you are munchkind when your neighbour brings you a blue sesame cake

munchskint to eat cheap food

mundane Monday

mundo mundane

munec to hold the neck [Spa. muñeca: wrist]

munecokee to have damaged the wrist from wanking [Spa. muñeca: wrist] [+ cock]

munich eat it

mup to mop with dirty water

muppet an old map which is useless | a badly designed map

mura tradition [insp. soursop]

murart traditional remedy

murde to kill for food

murmur more sugar

murray lachlan the addiction of cocaine

muscle an urgent call

mus-cus must go and cough up mucus

mush to go | to travel

musher a holiday rep | a travel guide [mush + usher]

mush room a bed room

mushroom cap a bald white head

mushroom capped your head is in a cloud

musical a phonostory

musky tears tears which taste unusual

muslick to only like a style of music in order to fit in, e.g. r&b

mus sake because it sounds good [insp. **art sake**]

mussel a white line

mustang mushy and tangy tongue, e.g. I experienced mustang when I ate very sour sweets [insp. **mustung**]

mustavodo must give thanks [ta + bravado]

must-dash hair which grows fast [moustache + dash]

must-dosh-hair to have fast growing hair and to sell it to make money

mustung a mushy tongue

mut hut a barbers [+ muttons]

mutiful beautifully silent

muttens gloves which are gloves too small, [lamb + mittens]

muttons the cons of being a mutt [oppo. mutty]

mutty the pros of being a mutt [oppo. muttons]

muzzy gunk not too sure about what the substance is

muzzylotones different types of confusement | different scales of blurriness [muzzy + zylophones + tones]

my other car is a carton my other car is off the road because my other car has no wheels

my um(m) to forget the name of someone you are very close to [+ mummy]

mymir to eat grass [insp. *the myrmus miriformis bug feeds on grasses*]

myridden to have ridden a myriad length – so far it's innumerable, or ridden somewhere where numbers do not count

myrtle turtle snail [insp. *myrtle is an evergreen flower*]

myspace the ice age

mystery jets mysterious flying objects

mysticall a call from an unknown number | a mysterious call

mystiff to become stuck in being bewildered [mystify + stiff]

mystock a person loaded with spiritual knowledge

mystory a story of mystery

mythong to imagine what sort of underwear a person is wearing

Nn

n narrative

N North | no

N *pic* parallel | a highway at an angle (from the top left point)

na nature

naball to play at being the fool

NAC not a chance

nac can not

nada spectrum unknown land

naddobi to happily say no

naddodo to not say something positive

nag! no shouting

nailage to dig in

nairobi no air (obviously)

naivest to put on naivety | to play being naive [+ vest]

na-kid baby

name to alist

nam-pam to spitefully call someone a wrong name [insp. nambypamby]

nano an up to date (with technology) granny | an old woman who has computer skills

nanocure prescribed medicine [L. nano: dwarf]

nanofusion to have little control over anger | to have a short fuse [L. nano: dwarf]

nanopa an up to date (with technology) grandpa | an old man who has computer skills

nanote the small print

nantwich an old witch

napanthol the medication of sleep

napblast a quick nap

napblist restless sleep

napblow to be woken up on purpose

napblue sleeping on depression

nappy to not be happy

naprozac a nap on prozac

napsack a sleeping bag

naptonic a refreshing drink before sleep (perhaps you would fancy a gin & tonic?)

naraninja the orange belt in karate

narrow a thin arrow

nasail to follow a smell [nasal + sail]

nasesary necessary nastiness (in order to learn)

nasty veal

natex latex to have latex around the bum area [*Natex is a brand of yeast extract and yeast extract is a brown colour*]

nathan without a fan

naturan to use nature to power something, e.g. solar panels naturan the heat

nav a navy sky

navalet to valet on the night time

navalium to feel homesick in the stomach

navalty a naval novelty, e.g. belly button ring which has the sign, "not pregnant, just fat", or a clock tattooed onto a round stomach

navigander to window-shop [navigator + gander]

navigreats helpful directions

navoyage to voyage late at night (when the sky is at least navy in colour)

nazi unable to see

nb no bigotry

NCL include

nd new dimensions

NE North East

ne gala negative results of a breathilizer test

NE itch an itch NE of the back

ne nietzsche

near nigh

near-by to end up writing nearly all of the book when it is supposed to be a collaboration with other writers

nearlie to lie near

nearth to live near (the) earth

neatbeat to place a towel over something when beating it with hammer, e.g. you would neatbeat when smashing a coconut

nebulerg to be nervous

necessarcy sarcasm required [+ necessary]

neck in the wire stress from technology

neck in the woods to have long bushy hair and for the neck to be tangled within

necklatte a latte spilt down the front of a person

necktarine a neck free of marks or wrinkles

ned to need a little

negatravel to travel with negativity

negatriggity to get angry for no reason [negativity + trigger]

negatrivial negative trivial

negra never dull

neigh spout a peeing horse | to wee on a field

neighbonzai neighbours who like to be in the garden more than the house [+ bonsai]

neightive a celebration of horses

nella shelter up North [+ ella]

neoff not having any neon left, e.g. the glow stick was soon to neoff

neon park illuminations

nepal nipple

nerd to want a lot

nervase to nervously hold onto something

nerve nir

nerve york self conscious [+ **New York**]

nervous nirous

nervous donkey one with legs that are shaking

nervoy a fearful adventre | a tense journey

nervsoma a nervous body

n'est–ce pasta isn't it so filling [Fre. n'est ce pas: isn't it so]

nestle to lace with chemicals

nestell swollen udder [+ **nestle**]

netherland whether it'll never land, weather it be neither, and net her land, lander then

netone to give the impression of being distant with something or someone

nettle bet a provoked bet [+ nettle]

nettle fettle the goodness of herbs

network phone

neurodilemma a nervous dilemma

neuterms no sexual terms [+ neuter]

nev cov a bad cover band [oppo. **ver cov**]

nevery very never, always never

newd news which hasn't been dressed up (news + nude)

new now to want right now [Na. new: want]

new order synthesise

new tyre to apply more deodorant th the armpit after sweating off the last layer [see **pit stop**]

new york a new self [see **york**]

new york tiles the nightlife in New York

newman cutlery [insp. *Knives Forks and Spoons Press*]

newsbaber a very thin newspaper

newspike to twist a story | to over exaggerate

newspope the BBC

nextent the next extent

ngrroar to walk through a scary place,

ngrropen the sound of ngrrpenguin

ngrrpenguin to walk on grass that is covered with snow

ni cen nineteenth century

ni noise

niabala Albania

niagra never again | no viagra

niceberg a much-needed coolness | an ice-lolly | a cool drink

nicket an underwear drawer

nick-knock to burgle a house

niffoc to have caffeine [+ coffin]

nig no giggling

nigel an extra day

nigh near

nigh sigh near to giving up | nearly losing hope

nigh time nearly time

night nav

nightlift to have a shower at nighttime

nightrogeneration people that come out at night | party people [**nitrate** + nitrogen + generation]

nike no likey

nikon to loot digitals [+ nick-on]

nil sine strobis nothing without light [insp. *The Golden Game*]

nilaw claw a deep scratch [Na. nìlaw: law]

nimemo one of the oldest [insp. the game '*Nine Men's Morris': one of the oldest board games in the world*]

nin bin to look at something and reject it to see no good in something [Na. nìn: look at]

nine chairs with no seats no purpose

nine forks décor being silly | over-exaggerating

nine minutes past zealous louse fifty one minutes to bellows, loud as

nine minutes to lava car tory fifty one minutes past ca ca gory

nine til five office

nineteen minutes past custard forty one minutes to re curse the tard

nineteen minutes to hay no wear (or attire) forty one minutes past neigh wire

nineteeth nine teeth

ning nang nong Ivor Cutler

ningnagngnong to be put on hold by 999

ningrait the levels of education, e.g. GCSE, A Level, Diploma, etc

ning rom to spend the morning on the computer [morning + rom]

ninja me to be active in understanding [jam + meaning]

nink negative thought [oppo. yink]

ninninnin to dial 999 in a hurry [see **ningnagngnong**]

ninnit a pile of crumbs

nin-one until patience runs out | how much you can stand [insp. *the game 'Ninety-One'*]

nipi plenty of light [insp. the corsican pine tree]

niptunic a tunic for when it gets nippy [Neptune + neck]

nir nerve

nir air nervous grounds |nervous air

nir sys nervous system

niro "you have a nerve!" [+ **nir**]

niro nero you have a shaky nerve [**niro** + Café Nero]

nìronisrael to have a dream on a train [Na. nìronsrel: imagination] [+ **israel**]

nirous nervous [+ **nir**]

nirust to go shaky when old

nirvana to blow a nerve | to have a nervous attack [+ **nir**]

N itch an itch N of the back

nitrate a smell which gets you or dizzy, e.g. white spirits

nnn three in a row [see **O's and X's**]

nnnn four in a row [see **FIAR**]

no nothing(ness) | notes

no age to never get old

noah's park a safari park

no ball games no good times [see **ball**]

nod-cons boring mod-cons

no eye no "no I no" to cry from cutting an onion

nog bog a toilet outof-order

no mopoly to have no money to cut the mop | to not be able to afford a hair cut

nonger no longer

nonky a donkey no more

noodull forever dull | an ongoing dullness

noodulldawl to dawdle in **noodull** [insp. **noodull**]

noose no use

no parking to keep moving | not able to stop moving, e.g. mum had a no parking voice, even at the traffic lights it would jump the red and go round-about and about and about and about and about and about and about and about and oh, she was no parking alright

nora nor a

northodontist the upper teeth [orthodontist + North]

northpole illumination a house lit up with christmas lights and festive décor

no slot unslip

no smoking no illusions | without illusions

no sod no sense of direction

noshtrilogy to not eat three main meals a day [nosh + trilogy]

nosol the burning of the nose | a sore nose

nostifa a blocked up nose [stiff + nostril]

nostrilogy containing three different smells, e.g. ginger, garlic and dill

no ta lud to not be ta lud [see **ta lud**]

notebokkie a message in a bottle

notebouquet a notebook full of beautiful handwriting [+ bouquet]

note not to fail to remember | to choose to ignore

no thing nothing to know

no wire a no brain

NOA number one aim

noah's gnark Noah not allowing certain animals on board the ark | no pet's allowed

nobla victory | merit [insp. the bay tree

noble no-bull

noblesoma a noble body

no-boot in subtraction

no-bull noble

nock a clicky stiff neck [+ knock]

nod to yup

nod on to put to sleep

noem orange or yellow patches [insp. *the female northern emerald dragonfly has orange or yellow patches at the front of the abdomen*]

nofin no end | nothing on the end

nofir light but strong [insp. the noble fir tree]

noflacoga non-flammable compressed gas

no-go to not go

no gut to not show any feeling

nom bombs seeds

nomini to ask for a minute [nominal + minute]

nom-nominate to nominate a favourite food | to speak of a favourite food | to promote a food product

non no noise

non-commercialism ex factor

non-invasive perpa

non-moving latch on

noodle-snuck to
have crept in

noose-beer a
hangover

noo-snick a creepy
laugh [snicker + noodle-
snuck]

nooxan irregular
[insp. the yellow cedar
tree]

nooze to loosen a
knot [noose + ooze]

no-par to have the
face covered | unable
to see the face (value)

no-peer without
education

no-pore not able to
breathe

nor haw a yellow
triangle [insp. *the
norfolk hawker
dragonfly has a yellow*

*triangle at the front of
the abdomen*]

nordoff to accidently
go to sleep [insp.
Charles Bernard]

norfir to lose contact
with someone [insp.
*bark develops fissure in
old age*]

no-ring-pull uncanny

norma normalization

norman the usual
rules [**norma** +
mandatory]

normoandy in the
land of the cold [North
+ Normandy]

norse nose

norsery a beginner's
class for learning the
norse language

norway no way

nose tip of the iceberg

no-show to not display

nosoma a no-body

nostrelgia the excitement of looking in the tissue to see what has been blown out [nostalgia + nostril]

not drinking water hypocrisy

not essential for a short time temporarily nonessential

not gum Nottingham

note-sake to do something because it is written, e.g. the sign told us to put our seatbelts on so we did

notebake a cookbook

note-gnat ignorance [insp. **note-not**]

note-not fail to remember | to ignore

nothes to look at peoples washing lines [nose + clothes]

nothing nought

nothu least ambiguous [insp. *the nose thumb being the least ambiguous gesture*]

noti-fi a planned fight

nougat pink and white

nought no thought | a blank mind

noughtee nothing

nought naught nothing is wrong

noursoma a nourished body

nout nothing now

novigate to guide someone the wrong way on purpose | to give somebody wrong directions [know + navigate]

noviss a business in its first few months [+ novice]

noviss hiss to have competition with another business

now gr to grow up to be angry | to grow old and angry

NOW number of words

nowledge knowledge of 'now' | knowledge of this precise moment

nownen now and then

noye the hate of yeast extract [see **yeye**]

no-zinc without energy

no-zone no space

no-zone not allowed

np new paths

N (past) one letter past M, two letters past L, three letters past K, four letters past J, five letters past I, six letters past H, seven letters past G, eight letters past F, nine letters past E, ten letters past D, eleven letters past C, twelve letters past B, thirteen letters past A, fourteen letters past Z, fifteen letters past Y, sixteen letters past X, seventeen letters past W, eighteen letters past V, nineteen letters past U, twenty letters past T, twenty one letters past S, twenty two letters past R, twenty three letters past Q, twenty four letters past P, twenty five letters past O

N (to) one letter to O, two letters to P, three letters to Q, four letters to R, five letters to S, six letters to T, seven letters to U, eight letters to V, nine letters to W, ten letters to X, eleven letters to Y, twelve letters to Z, thirteen letters to A, fourteen letters to B, fifteen letters to C, sixteen letters to D, seventeen letters to E, eighteen letters to F, nineteen letters to G, twenty letters to H, twenty one letters to I, twenty two letters to J, twenty three letters to K, twenty four letters to L, twenty five letters to M

nubtub the calm point in a story | a time in a story or film when nothing is really happening [insp. **bathtub**] [+ nub]

nucco coconut [insp. the coconut palm]

nuderm bare skin | skin-coloured

nugget a male chick

nuke fluke to threaten with nuclear war | to heavily threaten

nuke flute a nuclear weapon

nuke wake the beginning of a war | the start of a disgreement

nukurd a bunch of hard-core drinkers [drunk + knuckle]

nult cult firm non-believers

nurse-curser the hospital emergency pull cords and emergency buttons

nut hut a mad house

nutbook a book for keeping crazy notes in | a book of private thoughts | a diary

nut-butted the feeling when you've eaten too many nuts

nutri-test to drink your own wee

nut-shell bunker

nut-shell-fish an underground **nut-shell**

NW North West

n why? to question

why people love New York so much

n why c oh, I get 'n why?'

NW itch an itch NW of the back

NWO no way out

NOW OHIO no, over way oh hail iron ono

nylon a long night | all night long

nyman realisation

nyon to go on into the night

Oo

O *pic* a clock displaying no time | a mouth with no teeth or tongue

o open

OAI out and in

oak to preserve

oak-oat shavings of oak tree

OAP Oscar and Pat

oargranic aging naturally by water [insp. **orgranic**]

oarwe to tangle [insp. *oarweed's are sold in scotland under the name 'tangle'*]

oatbloat to be full from porridge

obees those attracted to over-indulging on sweets [obese + bees]

obeject to throw out objects

obelisp to vandalise an obelisk or statue

obesoma an obese body

obex oblivious but exciting

obi obviously

object symbol

oblage to force lager or any other alcohol down the throat [+ oblige]

obnib obviously been nibbled at | obviously not whole or new, e.g. the wedding cake had obnib

obnob obviously a knob

OBO one by one

observice the service of inspecting | paid observatory and inspective services

obvicious obviously vicious

obvisor the simple mind | the basic mind

occaring the increase of mechanical transport [+ occurring]

occourse an occurring course

occpla heavy [insp. buttonwood]

occure an occurring cure

occur-ring a number that keeps on calling

ocean blue and green

ocean wander to wander the oceans | to travel the seas

och bra to pin your sister up against a wall [insp by **och bro**]

och bro to pin your brother up against a wall [+ brooch]

octexpense an eight figured expense

octopassion love in all directions | love from all directions

odd sleeves different sizes

odoca scent [insp. ylang-ylang]

oesosmic to pretend to have a bad back [+ mimic]

offem to be offish towards feminism

offendi to offend somebody's status

offish an office underwater

offily serious

offset not now [Na. set: now]

ofscrib to take notes

of vi of very high importance

OH our house

OHIO oh, the house is in order [see **HIO**]

oh pah go to do something and realise you can't

o(h) shun ocean

ohstritch when a stitching comes undone [ostrich + stretch]

OI outside in

oil when passing cars sound like crashing waves

oil stain to over-think [oppo. **grass stain**]

oinkment perfumes containing animal ingredients or have been tested on animals

OIS "eyes" out in space

oister bad mannered people who call a person by shouting "oi"

okapi a strange creature | unknown powers

okapiece a piece of fantasy [+ okapi]

ol den an old **den**

olanga Angola

olay a dead cat

old rust

olderm old skin

olody dandy

olos to dance

olove the love of olives

oly the only way

olympack a group of athletes

olympic to give off wrong signals | two-faced, e.g. the olympics is about physical strength, but is sponsored by mcdonalds which only strengthens heart disease

olympick-pocket a fast and skilful pick-pocketing champion

olymprick to disease to make profit | willing to be brought by anyone [+ olympic]

oman oh man, omen!

omelette to open yourself up in the state of 'om' | to rebirth the spirit

om hair to count the pulse | to check your heart rate levels [Iri. comhair: count]

ominoose too tight | suffocating [ominous + noose]

on hold to wait in a queue

on your marks, get stretch, go to stop exercising and start eating lots [+ stretch marks]

one blood thud to knock someone out in one go with a heavy weapon | to knock someone out with one punch

one hundred and eighty half way round

one minute past caking and queen fifty one minutes to waking in a submarine

one minute to cute how map expire then decease fifty nine minutes past cut mouth papire sciss

one night I saw a slug upspidered on the ceiling good job it has slime to stick itself to the surface!

one'ton'dred hundreds

onebless to pray once a day

one-foot balancing a game where you see how long you can stand on one foot for [see **head-balancing**]

onely only one | one and only

one-suited to only own one suit | to only have one outfit

onflu no humour

onion an upsetting opinion

oniun union

on-me-howers on my own in the house [+ homeowners]

on-me-shower on my way to the shower [insp. **on-me-howers**]

ONO oodles noodles ooze

onset (right) now, on [Na. set: now]

onspring not offspring

ontax to be on top of tax and accounts

ontoot to be on a roll

onyx it's on

OOB out of bed

OOBOOT'M out of bed, out of the mind

oo car a shiny car

OOF out of faces

oo-lahs braces which are strapped to the trousers

oomph energy

oompha loompa a child with lots of energy [see **loompa**]

OOO out of order

ooo three in a row [see **O's and X's**]

oooo four in a row [see **FIAR**]

oosh a massive push [see **ell**]

OOT out of trend

OP outdoor plant

opal oh pull

opan an open view [pan: to move lense from side to side] [+ open]

o-pan to take the lid off the cooking pan

O (past) one letter past N, two letters past M, three letters past L, four letters past K, five letters past J, six letters past I, seven letters past H, eight letters past G, nine letters past F, ten letters past E, eleven letters past D, twelve letters past C, thirteen letters past B, fourteen letters past A, fifteen letters past Z, sixteen letters past Y, seventeen letters past X, eighteen letters past W, nineteen letters past V, twenty letters past U, twenty one letters past T, twenty two letters past S, twenty three letters past R, twenty four letters past Q, twenty five letters past P

o pen to write with the voice

open bracket a jacket undone

openent an open opponent

open idea communal idea

openear to nearly be available | nearly open | close to going outside

op house an open plan house

opingpongion forever changing sides | to have differing opinions [+ ping-pong]

opinion to pin prick an onion

opponine the opposite to nine is five

oppontone in the tone of an opponent

opporous to offer somebody an opportunity [+ porous]

opportrivial a trivial opportunity

opportune in the tone of opportunity

opposites fools world

oppotravel to explore the opportunities available

optickle for spectacle frames to itch or tickle your face

optimimic to positively mimic

optin an opened can of **joy** | good news

or and all to talk about everything | to talk a lot [oral + 'all or nothing']

orange sports and leisure [insp. *'Tivial Pursuit' colour*]

o-range good value [insp. *the game 'Monopoly' where the houses in the orange zone are of good value*]

oraspecs glasses with orange lenses

orb wise

orbitat a habitat's orbit

orbitwat unwanted repitition

order fly

order nary not any order [+ nary]

ordesc an office companion [desk + escort]

ordire of dire order

organthighs'ation exercises to get the thighs into shape

orgun the sound of a gun firing | shooting pains [organ + gun]

orgranic aging naturally

oril three lots of five [insp. the levant storax tree]

oripla several emerging from one [insp. the chinese arbor-vitae]

orispat spitting at the origin | to be getting angry with the cause | a disappointing start

orispatch where the orispat takes

ornament the favourite pet

ornamental the person in a group who is a bit different to the rest

oro gin the distillery [origin + gin]

orphant an infant orphan

os Osho

O's and X's noughts and crosses markings

osh a lot [oppo. **ish**]

oslo 'oh slow'

otch swampy [insp. the white cedar tree]

otikósho to have Osho's ear | to understand Osho's thoughts [Gk. otikós: of the ear]

OTM over the moon

O (to) one letter to P, two letters to Q, three letters to R, four letters to S, five letters to T, six letters to U, seven letters to V, eight letters to W, nine letters to X, ten letters to Y, eleven letters to Z, twelve letters to A, thirteen letters to B, fourteen letters to C, fifteen letters to D, sixteen letters to E, seventeen letters to F, eighteen letters to G, nineteen letters to H, twenty letters to I, twenty one letters to J, twenty two letters to K, twenty three letters to L, twenty four letters to M, twenty five letters to N

otter of thanks

ouncial heavily uncial [L. uncial: curvy writing] [+ ounce]

our are

outocent not innocent

out of order Plan A is a no-go so you must go to Plan B

outdirth the ground

outdorm an outhouse

outer-dinner the inner-dinner now out of the body in the form of waste

outerest an outward interest | to express interest

outfat a big outfit | an outfit too big

outgross to outgrow someone's grossness

out-snail to get out of a pattern you are in | to break a habit

outsolence when your shoes start wearing out and they make you walk differently to how you would normally walk [**insolence** + sole + out]

ovalue the weight of a baby

ovault a shocking ovary | when a chick hatches from its egg on the shelf in a supermarket

oven brick olden times

ovent hot air [oven + vent]

overabandanance too much disguise | too hidden | too much coverage [overabundance + bandana]

overail to sum up the overall journey

overbead too showy

overbeard a beard which extends off the face [+ overboard]

overgarm to wear too much

**ooooooooooooooooo
ovvvvvvvvvvvvvvvv
vveeeeeeeeeeeeeeeee
eeerrrrrrrrrrrrrrrrrr
rrrr** over the head

over-ride to pedal too
fast

overseed to plant too
many seeds | to give
away too many ideas

oververt extravert

owari to sow [insp. *the
game 'Owari' where the
action of moving is to
sow*]

owlring to have a jog
around the block at
night time

owls recycled bottle
bank bins

owringe to juice an
orange

OXOXOXOX
alternating four in a
row of **XXXX** and
OOOO

oxsu oxidizing
substance

oxyben to be on time
| to be good with
keeping to time [+ Big
Ben] [see **uncle ben**]

oys private [insp. the
oyster]

oys mush when the
younger person is given
the job [insp. oyster
mushroom]

Pp

P *pic* parking | a basket hoop

p̂ play

pa pandora's box

pab a very small **pube**

P & G poison and grime [insp. *Proctor & Gamble*]

pacific oceans specific oceans

packets packed pockets

packish to pack a little | to travel light [oppo. **packosh**]

packlet to rent furniture [+ outlet]

packosh to pack a lot [oppo. **packish**]

pacmanpacwoman for two people to pretend to be married [L. pactus: betrothed]

pacnic an unexpected picnic | to go to the shop and buy a bag of food and eat it in the outside space

padal to cycle with the bum on the seat [pedal + padded]

pad bod paddington boddington

paddington a regular train user

paddington boddington a drunk person on a train or at the train station

paddingtone a heavy menstrual period

paddle when a woman is on her period and is heavily bleeding [+ puddle]

padinghy a small sized dinghy [+ paddle]

pa fa pap to rely on your father a lot

pag a pack of fags

pageada a stack of pages | a pile of sacred texts [pagoda + page]

pageant a well designed page

pahat to wonder whether to cover [+ perhaps]

pah doh when you go to pay for something and realise you haven't the money [see **oh pah**]

pah poh when you go to put your hands in your pockets and realise you have no pockets [see **oh pah**]

painal a pain in the anal

paine to be underpaid

paint pot to mix up the food on your plate

paint-potch a mixture of many kinds

paint strippers to paint stripes

paint slippers traditional paintings of flowers, landscapes and people

painting panting in rhythms

paknick-knack to worry somebody is going to give you a wedgie [+ panic]

pakora a pack of, e.g. pakora lion!

palindrum to speak in a rhythm

pal lava when you fancy a friend

palm street

palm dove to fly off the handle [insp. *the laughing dove is frequently encountered near oases, which has led to them becoming known as palm doves*]

palm-hand to lose grip of something [insp. **palm dove**]

palmela anderson an area having many palm trees

palm-lines a sleight of hand

palmond to lotion hands with a nutty fragrance cream [+ palm]

palord a person very popular who is never short of companionship [pal + lord]

pamrelish word games [Na. pamrel: writing] [+ relish]

pandata B&W data [+ panda]

pan dora a curved door [see **opan**]

pan jan to cook less [+ January]

pancer when unwashed pots, pans and dishes start growing mould [pan + cancer]

pandaloon a black and white suit which is too big and therefore hangs like pantaloons on the floor (and off the arms)

pang to hang the feet off a side, e.g. the swimming pool wasn't used much, it was mostly used to pang

paneigh to pan the lense badly [see **opan**]

panic-knack to steal somthing in a panic | to take something without really thinking

pank to thank someone by giving them pink flowers

panoply the flames on the hob when cooking [+ ply wood]

panorama & sita a panorama in a religious story

pans pins and needles

panterns neon coloured pants | vibrant underwear

panther when water and oil bond in cooking, forcing the oil to spit out

panther cap to cover white

pantimine anti pantomime

pant paint to paint without emotion [see **painting**]

panto pants one who walks theatrically

pant point a view which will always exist

pantra pandora's pantry

pantreat to eat the food which was stored in your pants [see **pantry**]

pantrice the entrance of a pantry

pantry to store food in your pants

papale apple

paparazzle a night of photographing the famous

paper bridge not supported well | insecurities, e.g. the paper bridge is starting to become a serious issue

paper cut a paper plane unable to fly

paper date to spend time writing with a papermate

paper machete couldn't even hurt a fly

paperback a flexible back

paperweight a helping hand

papi a common ornament [insp. the japanese white pine tree]

papistol a catholic object (papist + pistol]

papsize when a father is unable to see his child(ren) [+ capsize]

papyre to burn paper [+ pyre]

paq a group of pigs [Kic. aq: pig]

par average

parabowl to make up a parable

par age average age

parabra to cut out a paragraph | to get rid of a paragraph

parachoke to be hit on the back when choking [+ parachute]

paracute without a parachute [+ acute]

paraduck to duck out of a paradox

para failure a power failure of the paracetemol

paraft a paragraph with a good chi [+ raft]

paragruff a messy paragraph [+ gruff]

paraid a war [+ parade]

paralist to make a mental list

para mush a big umberella [insp. parasol mushroom]

parashoot to shoot from above [+ parachute]

parcore to pick apples from a tree [+ parkour]

pardone to be done with forgiving [pardon + done]

parent to protect [insp. *the parent bug sits on her eggs and young nymphs to protect them from parasites*]

paris the average romance

parisian the average romantic

park average fun [+ par]

park and display to stop and show

park loot to rob people in parks or car parks only

parklot trees, grass and birds

parnu a new average [par + nu]

parode to try out a new style [parody + rode]

paroom a large room

parose pink and white marble | strawberries and icecream [Gk. Paros: an island noted for its white marble] [+ rose]

parpeo standing parallel to another person [+ people]

parro no budget

parroar a preacher [+ parish]

parrot to lose similarity [parallel + rot]

par rot average death

parrot eye a scanner | a photo copier

pars nipples feeling the nipples

parsnip a teenager

parstichun part in stitches until

part a bob

partet partition

parthenoon the first noon of a new year [Gk. partheno: virgin]

parthenose to have never had a nosebleed [Gk. partheno: virgin]

parthesis the first part of a thesis [Gk. partheno: virgin]

parthole half good and half bad

particolour a particular colour sceheme

particull a specific killing [particle + cull + particular]

particult a party culture [party + cult]

par ties the same ties | the same connections

partiprisoner a prisoner whose attitude is resolved upon [insp. *'parti pris' in French means a position or attitude resolved upon or taken in advance*]

partlie to rest the back against a wall when sitting down

partnershop when more than one person owns the shop

partnerve a partner who makes you feel nervous

patriotic part patriotic

part-sung a song where half of it is sung and the other half spoken or instrumental

party animals animals that like to join in the party, e.g. a dog on two legs dancing or a hamster waving its carrot stick

parun to run beside someone [parallel + run]

pas de coat a coat which can be worn both outside-in and insideout [Fre. pas de côte: two track]

pas du boot to not wear boots | to not wear anything on the feet [Fre. pas du tout: not at all] [+ boot]

pas du hoof to never eat cow [Fre. pas du tout: not at all] [+ hoof]

pas du hoot to not talk about something [Fre. pas du tout: not at all] [+ **toot**]

pas du lout to not drink [Fre. pas du tout: not at all] [+ lout]

pas du pas all is nothing [Fre. pas du tout: not at all] [+ all]

pas du pass not able to pass | not able to turn down an opportunity [Fre. pas du tout: not at all] [+ pass]

pas du pout no kisses at all [Fre. pas du tout: not at all] [+ pout]

pas du trout to not eat fish [Fre. pas du tout: not at all] [+ trout]

pasello to find no connection [pass + sello(tape)]

pass paz

passage an entry to passion

passage key signs of privacy

passaint to pass on being a saint

passangrr an angry passenger

passen when spaghetti becomes soft and starts colliding into other strips of spaghetti

passengerm a spreading germ [+ passenger]

pass herd many passwords | more than one password, e.g. hacking into the BBC's computer account involved passherd and a '**passing out of headfush**'

passing out of head-fush to pass out due to no blood going to the head, or too much blood to the head

passportal to have the right face

passtable an acceptable place to stay

pass the parcel to pass on rumours | to spread gossip

pas sword a private sword fight [Fre. pas: a series of steps] [+ sword]

pastafari to pass on being a rastafarian

pasta-pants big knickers

pastar star shaped pasta

pastat to pat someone from behind

paste an after taste [+ post]

pastel a light past | a touch of history

pasto to undercook pasta

pastof to overcook pasta [+ soft]

pastog soggy pasta [+ stodge]

pastole bad memories

pastone hard pasta (far too al dente for any al dente lover)

pastri to cover up

pastry something that was tried in the past | the past

pas try to come at a problem from a different angle [Fre. pas: a series of steps] [+ try]

pastry and pasta foods of the past

patata to slowly pat someone

patch-luck a bit of luck

patch-phrase a phrase said to patch something up

patchwork quill to write a will out, leaving everything to family [insp. **patchwork quilt**]

patchwork quilt family engagements

pate to non-stop pat

patent peg a stable patent

pathetic as path

patite a small pat | a light touch [+ petite]

pa toot to cut down on potatoes | to not have too much potato | to be curing yourself from **fries frame**

patpi in groups of three to six [insp. the mexican pine tree]

patriot a pattern or riot | a behavioural pattern

patterm a constant pattern [+ term]

pattern snail

patternull to have no rhythm

pattone for a pattern to produce a tone

pattress the space between dreams [mattress + patterns]

pave chill

pavement chilled

paw a soft law

pawn the front line [insp. *the game 'Chess'*]

pay as you go battery operated

pay buy pri to spend a lot

paz pass

pb Pablo Picasso

pd pendulum

pea small

pea gravy to increase green land | to make more green land available

peabody a baby

peace calm

peace pace a relaxed pace

peach a lovely person

peak-a-boo a never ending height or trek to the top (of a peak)

peale to throw confetti on the married couple after the wedding bells have jangled [peal + ale]

peanut a small output | a small wee | a small poo [nut + pee]

pea-plonk a small throw

pea-plonker a small throw-over

pea-pod a small house

pea-podia small feet

pear a curve

pear-beer a soft person

pear-droop when the body droops

pear-drop a hard person

pearl-hubba pearl harbour

peart art with a message

peasaint a poor religious person

peat moss sticking to your decisions

peball a small ball [+ pebble]

pebble rebel a pretty rebel

pebbledisc to smoke out circles

pebbledusc smoke circles under a dark sky

pecan a peck | a small kiss

peccare offensive care

peccare home offensive living

peccrally an offensive argument | mistreatment of decisions

peccrate a carton of eggs

peck to **storm-stalk**

pecket to pinch a packet, e.g. I went to pecket but I got caught so had to **pock** it [+ **peck**]

ped stat pedal station | a bike shed

pedal pod any pedaled vehicle that fits two to four persons

pedal station a bike shed

pedallion to keep on going

pedals walking or running shoes

pedigro to bite the toenails using your teeth [+ pedigree]

pedinghy a dinghy with an engine on

pedolls mechanical toys [+ pedal]

pedro riding | pedalling [pedal + row]

pedrodent to ride fast [insp. **pedro**] [+ rodent]

pedrone the sound of **pedro**

peel to lounge around the park [insp. **teel**]

peeloid to have a mud wrap | to have your body wrapped in mud [insp. **peloit**]

peelord the lord of peeling | one who peels a lot of potatoes

pee-penny a penny or few short of an amount [L. pene: almost]

peepie to poo and wee at the same time

peeping bag a bag which has a hole in it causing content to fall out

pee-rage to have trouble finding a toilet

peer pasture to be forced into respecting the pasture [+ peer pressure]

pees and queues the testing of manners

peevaried the various ways of annoying a person [peeve + varied]

pee whiz a minor incident

pee-whizz to not be able to control the urine [+ gee whiz]

pel pellets

pelaid to lie in mud [insp. **peloit**]

peland a land of mud [insp. **peloid**]

peliclan a group of pelicans

pelf to throw small objects [pelt + elf]

pelite sprite a swamp creature

pellagraft to graft through pellagra [*pellagra is a disease caused by a deficiency of niacin*]

pellets change

pellucider light cider [+ pellucid]

pelma two or more [insp. *the game 'Pelmanism'*]

peloit to therapeutically loiter in mud

peltoid when the rain makes it muddy [insp. **peloit**]

pelvision to think or see water when in need of urinating [pelvis + vision]

pelvisit to take a visit to the bathroom [+ pelvis]

pembroid an embroided poem

pembroke to be penniless within a rich surrounding

penalter to change pens

penalty to lose your pen

penant a writing partner [+ tenant]

peñata to try and bring a pen back to life by scribbling its tip on paper, blowing the tip or even applying spit to the tip [+ piñata]

pencell to only be allowed to write in pencil

pence pant dehydrated [oppo. **prance pant**]

pencivil general writing [pen + civil + pencil]

pencone a thick pen [+ pine cone]

pendraught something that distracts your writing process

pendula a popular variety

penecil a fine paint brush [insp. *penecil is a small, brush-like tuft of hair on a caterpillar*] [+ pencil]

pencilin the lead in pencils

penegot almost got [L. pene: almost]

penepen almost written [L. pene: almost]

peneslope to open an envelope or a package with a pen

penetrace to almost copy [L. pene: almost] [+ trace]

pengu to write music on waste paper [pen + pengu]

penguin black writing on white paper

pengun ink

pen holder to not speak your mind | to put off saying something

penicure to be given a pencil drawing of yourself [insp. ledicure]

penilty for a penis to rear off-side during sexual intercourse | a sideward slanting penis

penis a sex pistol

penky without a pen

pennine the writing flow

penny-slave-sania to work for barely any money [+ insania]

penriff the flow of a pen

pension to receive money from a writing job

pensuite an office with a bed in it | an office in a bedroom [+ en suite]

pentalive five-a-live [+ pent]

pentimentality an earlier state [pentimento + mentality]

peo box a home for people [+ PO box]

people stuck on a sub people riding the subway are jailbirds

pep dulse a healthy substitute [insp. *pepper dulse is used as a substitute instead of chewing tobacco*]

pepoe the peoples' poet

pepole to peep | to watch people [+ peep hole]

pepperganda when you shake pepper on your food and you end up with more than you wanted

pepprika when a pepper is hot [+ paprika]

perail dangers of the train [peril + rail]

perch to hold a pen lightly or loosely [oppo. **pitch**]

perchfume a smell which stays lingering around for a long time [perch + perfume]

percushion an uncomfortable cushion [+ percussion]

performal a formal performance

perfume counter the monkey's surgeon table

perfumigate to choke someone by extensive **maximusk**

perha fuel [insp. the saxaul tree]

perhat to have a 'perhaps' head on | to be open to all ideas or beliefs

peril pearl the beauty of danger

period egg

periode of red colour, e.g. once a sunset, always periode

periwink a cheeky wink [+ periwinkle]

perk to be given a reserved car parking place

perknicky one who changes their underwear more than once a day [pernickety + kinckers]

perknock to have a certain way of knocking the door [pernickety + knock]

permat a restricted area [permit + mat]

pero when a pea rolls off a plate

peroni per onion, e.g. 14p peroni

perpa non-invasive | flame coloured [insp. the ironwood tree]

perper perfumed paper, perfumed stationary, e.g. pineapple scented eraser

persoma a part of the body | a persons character | an acting body

personifi a fight with the self

perspect very little respect | respect for only one part

perswept thoroughly swept | checked many times [+ per]

peru a pair of rabbits

pervase to put pervasiveness on hold

perverse a piece of text which is highly sexual

pesdra to open [insp. *'drapes' is America means 'curtains'*]

pesdraw to draw the curtains [+ pesdra]

pesdraw picture to actually **pesdraw**, preferably by hand

pesimimic to mimic in a pessimistic way

pesitin an opened can of evil worms

peso a peasant

pesort a cheap resort [+ **peso**]

pestel not honest enough | not able to face reality | too fluffy [pest + pastel]

pesticide evil

pestoche the pest is toast

petcan a candied stick of rock

petcandy the teeth's nightmare

petcar a short haired animal [+ carpet]

petcribe to write on rock or stone

pete and the pirates the debt company and its debt collectors

peter petrified

pe ter pee over there

peter, bjorn and john three people

peth to throw stones or rocks

petidri to drink a little

petitea to eat little

petithought a small thought

petoss to toss stones

petrave to carve stone or rock [+ petro]

petrial the second pet [pet + retrial]

petrim to cut rock or stone [+ petro]

petrimb to rock-climb [+ petro]

petrojet to kick stones

petrol slippy rocks [+ petro]

petroleum to roll [+ petro]

petroop a hard person to get on with [Gk. petros: rock] [+ troop]

petrophy a trophy made out of stone [+ petro]

petrow to work with stone [+ petro]

pets slope [+ step]

petticlot a clot under the skin [petticoat + blood clot]

pettico a child

petunias petty tunes | petty songs

pexpress an area where lots of pectorals are on show, e.g. the gym is more of a pexpress than *Tesco Express* will ever be

PG tip a shaking monkey

phalanguage to only be able to communicate with the fingers and toes [+ phalange]

phallock to eclude any humour | only seriousness allowed [phallic + lock]

phallust to lust for phallus | penis lust

phantask a task without any material provided [+ phantom]

pharmacy to make money from the ill

pharma sutra fraud | abuse

pharming animal experimentation [farming + pharmacy]

philosoap the different ways of washing the hands [+ philosophy]

philosofail when a philosophy fails

philosofill to fill with philosophy

philosofrank frank philosophy | loose thoughts

philosofry to be full of philosophies

philosophuck when the mind dips in to philosophy the same way the feet take a paddle in the water

phingers wet fingers [insp. dolphin]

phish fish

phishion to copy a person [+ fashion]

phission fake passion

phleghd to be free of phlegm [+ fled]

phlegmon yellow phlegm [+ lemon]

phlemerge to hold back

phlemergy not giving all | not full power

phloe to transport sugars, e.g. it is vital for somebody with low blood pressure or diabetes to phloe [insp. *phloem is the part of the wood that transports sugars from the leaves*]

pho net to listen out for something

phoat a bland photo [+ oat]

phone measure

phonest a customer call helpline

phonickel when you go deaf | unable to hear [+ nickel]

phonographonic to improvise spoken word to a rhythm

phonostore a music shop

phonostork melody

phonostory a musical

photo a pictorial motto

photo atlas a representation of the world | a global representative

photoshoot a badly Photoshopped image

phrose a phrase that makes somebody freeze and stop and think about it

phun phone fun

picbid (an area of) dense vegetation [insp. *the picromerus bidens bug can be found in areas of dense vegetation*]

picha fibrous [insp. *the cawara cypress tree*]

pickadily to pick | a situation where you have to choose between more than two things

pick up to get a mixed response [+ pick'n'mix]

pickle to relish

pickled cockle to highly detest

pickled egg a smelly eye | an eye that discharges pus

pick-pocket to organise storage

picniche land that has been set up as a picnic area | a conventional picnic area

pic-pac the game of pick-pocket [insp. *the game 'Pacman'*]

pic-poc to pick clothes out of a **poc**

pictasaurus a rare picture

pidal to cycle with the bum off the seat [insp. **padal**]

pid bod a person who smells of urine [see **pad bod**]

pidinghy a medium sized dinghy

pie big

pie foot a big foot [+ **pie**]

pielot to cook a lot [pilot light + **pie**]

piement a stretch mark [pigment + **pie**]

piements stretch marks [pigment + **pie**]

pie-plonk a big throw [+ **pie**]

pie-plonker a large throw-over [+ **pie**]

pier copper and silver

pieramid a rounded triangle (with curved corners)

pieshi to mistake a man for a lady [insp. *the pied shield bug is often mistaken for a ladybird*]

pigeons urban livers

pig la tin a tray of pig food [insp. **dog la tin**]

piglets little (pink) fingers

pigment the minimum equipment [insp. *the game 'Pig' requires the minimum of equipment*]

pigskin scratched skin

pigstylish a messy look

pik no rest [+ **kip**]

pike to not reach the top of the peak | to value the process

pikey to fork a pie

pilaster bandaged in plaster

pilate pilot

pilchard to be stuck in a crowded place

pile important in a commercial sense [insp. the blackbutt tree]

pileage the feeling of depression which comes from the home being untidy

pilferrit to steal condiments from eatery places, e.g. we would pilferrit the salt from here and the sauce from there [pilfer + ferrit]

pillard a head which does not want to depart from the pillow | a medicine cabinet

pillaugh to laugh when sitting upright [+ pillar]

pillchard to pack pills into a bottle

pill-lab to experiment in talking different pills | to test someone's mood

pilloathe to be uncomfortable [pillow + loathe]

pillord a person who heavily relies on pills

pill-lore drug stories

pillore torture stories [pillory + lore]

pillow tree to rest against a willow tree

pillung to use someone else's electric, e.g. charging your phone in starbucks [pillage + plug]

pillust sex induced pills or chemicals, e.g. viagra and poppers

pilord the person with the biggest pile, e.g. in poker | a person who is experiencing the toilet troubles called *piles*

pimentoon a dish where peppers are the main ingredient [+ pimento]

PIMP passion in my pants

pimpingpong to live in a 'back and forth' action, e.g. a ball in a game of tennis is pimpingpong

pimplush a teenager who has acne [pimple + plush]

pin to win material

pin and pout to grab and kiss | to hold tight and kiss

pina sugar

pinaform a sugarcube [+ **pina**]

pinaformis for it to be mandatory to wear a pinafore

pin-and-pin to fasten very tightly

pinapp the game where you catch apples with your mouth while the apples are in a container, which is filled with water

piñata a boxing match

piñatap to hover and try to **pinapp** [piñata + apple]

pinbull machine a piece of machinery which brings endless problems [+ pinball machine]

pinchin a pointy chin [insp. *Pinocchio*]

pine pins and needles

pine nut the modern house

ping-pong back and forth

pingi-pongi give to receive

pink entertainment [insp. *'Tivial Pursuit' colour*]

pink panther something mysterious

pinochle up to several hours

pinoose a suicidal punk [safety pin + noose]

pin-pan a small pan

pinpi in pairs [insp. the maritime pine tree]

pinpin elsewhere [insp. the stone pine tree]

pinpin tintin clean elsewhere [**pinpin** + **tin tin man**]

pinspecs glasses with pink lenses

pinst toothed [insp. the bladdernut tree]

pint point an eased point

pinta everyday life

pinta pin to have a highly-pressured lifestyle

pinta poop to find life shit

pinta props the everyday obstacles in life

pinta puncha to be down about **pinta**

pintask an everyday task, e.g. washing the plates

pintobow a rainbow

pinvase an ornamental cactus

pipefat a smoking area

pipelle the action of smoking a pipe

pipi upwards [insp. the stone pine tree]

piquet to require considerable concentration and great skill to do well

pirate a trees trunk [*one wooden leg*]

piscally a money problem

pish to push someone, to see how far they will go

piss out to pass out from being pissed

piss'n'chips the action of a Friday night out in a city

pisscent to waste money on alcohol | to spend your last bit of money on alcohol

pissible a bad attempt

pisspot a temporary toilet

pisstachio when somebody or something is taking too long

pistol to stall when urinating – to try shooting but there's no bullet

pistole a crime within a crime, e.g. to steal a

pistol is a crime but it is a crime to have a pistol in the first place

pistolero a bible [Gk. pist: faith]

pitch to hold a pen tightly [pinch + squish] [oppo. **perch**]

pitfire to throw sand at one another

pit-service to spray the armpits with deodorizer [+ insp. **pit stop**]

pit stop to check the odour condition of your arm spits

pit strip a service station [+ pit stop]

pittens fingerless gloves

pittens for kittens to breed animals for money

pixchange to exchange artwork

pixel to pick all | to pick up a lot

pixellate to not have a good reason for being late

pixie pick a little

pizzazza a high quality pizza pizza [+ pizzazz]

pla town [see **hispla**]

placemount to be placed higher than expected | a placement higher than you expected, e.g. a professional position

placenta incense [+ scent]

placo plain clothed | plain clothes

plagoon the play of being a goon

plagoosey to play around | to have fun

plaguer to play cursive music

plain clarks'n'clerk

plandatory a "must do" plan [+ mandatory]

planet rape consumption and profit over wellbeing

planets plants that take youout of this world

plank to not be on side

plankoat a stiff jacket | stiff clothes [+ plank]

planktation a growth of people who are in opposition [**plank** + plantation]

plaque card a 'reserved' sign on a table [+ placard]

plant foetus

plant poot to poo in a plant pot | to use your own poo for fertiliser

plantain to plant a smile | to give a smile

plantato to plant potato seeds

plantern a growing pattern | an occurring pattern

plant one with huge potential

plantoon a peace garden

plantroop(s) a group of the same flowers | a flower that dominates an area

plarrick to play cricket | to use your hand as a bat, e.g. you could say beach ball is the same as tennis

because in beach ball we plarrick to hit the ball

plas hole to plaster up a hole | to cover up a hole

plash the growth of the use of plastic | the material world

plassy a plastic hero, e.g. the action man [+ *Lassy*]

plast the last and past

plastares realizations [plaster + stares]

plastic artificial food

plastic bag to not be filled to the maximum

plastick lip gloss

platea to spill a drink on the table [+ plateau]

platenight a dinner party late at night

plate-night to have dinner at a late in the evening

plato-night late night thoughts of philosophy [insp. **plate-night**]

plate scraper one who scrapes the plate to get last bit of food

plate snorkeler a person who licks the plate when it's empty

platinum when the whole of the hair is in plats or dreads

platter plant matter

platter poke to have diarrhoea after sexual activity in the anus

play impro

p lay a potential lay, e.g. the hotel was a play

playbrick when play fighting gets serious

played field day to keep on seeing pushchairs and prams

play-ground-coffee to experiment in the taste of (ground) coffees

playgue war games

playlay to go back to sleep in order to finish off a dream

play net a football net

playstation an activities area

play-stick play dough | the consistency of water and flour

playto to think up new games

playtoon comical games

plebble-dash to have a vulgar moment

plebido a pleb with a sexual urge [pleb + libido]

pleh ctrum floating around [+ plectrum]

pleh strum to not know how to handle a guitar

plentea an afternoon of tea | a tea party

plentifault plenty of fault | many problems

plentrim to cut **purse**

plenty purse

plesent a pleasant present

plethaura a strong vibe [plethora + aura]

plimpsoul a rubber heart | a heart that easily discards feelings |the love of a condom | the love of protection

plink on the brink of being on the plank | not quite awake | near to being in the red zone

plit a little plot

plite polite

plith soft [insp. the western red cedar tree]

plonk plank to set down a plank | to lay down a panelled floor

plooto a plot that is unconvincing or mad

plopsidaisy to dump a bouquet | to decide not to give a bouquet of flowers when you planned to

ploral to orally play

plost lost the plot

plotato a potato plot

plotonium the plutonium of plots

plough to play rough
[+ ou(ch)]

plowers plastic
flowers

pluck-brow irritating
pluggy hair to have
wires all over the floor

plunk an unethical
punk

plus lots of pus

plus gun to have
extra muscle

plush a soft push

plusher a 'relaxed'
leader [**plush** + usher]

plust additional lust
[+ plus]

pluto a dog

plutoa to go on a
week holiday and pack
only two pairs of
underwear [insp. *pluto
is the ninth planet*]

ply ten in groups of
ten [+ plenty]

pm nighttimes

pneufanasia to kill
off the cold with heat
[pneumonia + fan +
euthanasia]

pneumoney money
from cold earnings
[+pneumonia]

pneumnia lisa a cold
hand [insp. **bluemonia**]
[+ *Mona Lisa*]

PO post office

po go a speedy postal
service [+ **PO**] [oppo. **po
slo**]

po poetics

po slo a slow postal
service [oppo. **po go**]

po'ur power

poach an iron bar [see
seal]

poc pile of clothes | a pack of tobacco

poca to not give thanks

pocahontas when food goes down the wrong way [poke + bronchis]

pock to forget

pockets storage

podal long narrow plantation [**pea-pod** + canal]

pod house

podia feet

podials foot pedals

podinghy a large sized dinghy

pod podia to walk around the home [**pod** + **podia**]

podpud a wet house

poetch an etched poetics

poestick to get **stick** from your poetry [see **stick**]

poetiquette poeticly etiquette

poet-tone rhythm(ical)

poetree a tree of poetry

pogo to forgive

pogo and pock forgive and forget [**pogo** + **pock**]

pogodno to believe in many gods

pogosick when you are sick of travelling backwards and forwards

pohs a posing shop | a shop that poses as being different to what it is, e.g. a newsagents sign reads "fresh vegetables, freshlybaked sandwiches, international newspapers, lots of stock... ' when really there's hardly any stock, no international newspapers, and the only baguettes are 'days-old' processed sandwiches, packed in Chile

poi x shaped

poietickle producing sensation [+ poietic]

pois poison(ous)

point is dappa a good disappointment

pointeract to discuss a point made

pointment treasured advice [+ ointment]

poiment to inject ointment [+ **poi**]

poitrine brine breast milk

pokabulary the vocabulary of **POKE**

POKE pity of killing everyone

poke to pick your nose in a public place

poken to be caught picking your nose in public

pokel people nosey people

poker an hour to a whole evening

poker dice not the standard

polar bear a black and white camera | a black and white setting

polar bears arctic monkeys

poledog an arctic dog

POLICE pretty orange louse in cerise envy

po-lice annoying policies [+ lice]

POLICE STATION pretty orange louse in cerise envy, slithers tones a tone in orange norse

polights police lights

polimp to move out of the way to let someone else see [polite + limp]

politease a fake politeness [+ tease]

polittle only a little polite

pollean to not be affected much by pollen

pollen to carry something from one place to another

pollend to guide someone | to hold someone's hand | to

lead the way [**pollen** + lend]

pollent to take hayfever tablets

pollin to pass

pollinate to pass on [**pollen** + **pollin**]

pollinen to housekeep beds [**pollen** + **linen**]

polling full of **pollute** character

pollingo to pass up speaking | to keep quiet

pollord the winner of the poll

polluct unwilling to spoil [reluctant + pollute]

pollute impolite

poloiter the litter of politics

poloscope to look through a circle

polo-shirt a trendy person

polysoma more than one body

pom pom kiss kiss [Na. pom: kiss]

pom mop a lover of cleaning [oppo. **moop moop**]

pomporous one who only drinks bottled water and never drinks tap water [pompous + porous]

pomandatore for it to be mandatory to speak to strangers [+ pomander]

pomegran a healthy elder

pon short term cover [insp. **poncho**]

ponca to cruise in a car [insp. *panda is a police car*]

poncho cover

ponchoo long term cover

ponderm to look at your skin [ponder + derm]

pontoon an hour to a whole afternoon [+ **pon**]

POO point of order

poodash for a poo to plunge into the water and splash the bum

poogala to be positive on a breathilizer test given by police | to be over limit

pooldle time spent playing pool

poomanda to not want to mix when it's **pomandatore** to

poopsidaisy for a person to reject the bouquet you bought them

poor pour

poover to hover over the loo when having a poo

poover hoover when the poovered poo is hovered away

poozle stuck in a puzzle | can't see any way of solving it

POP pair of players

pop idol commercialism

pop salt an orgasmic taste | a good season

pop salt tart an orgasmic sweet

pope does sheesha the West religion mellows (out)

poppetybling a very glamorous poppety ping ['*poppety-ping*' *is Welsh for 'microwave'*]

poppety pong an output of smelly gas

populark a popular walk (of life)

pop-up interestingly surprising

poquet the game of poking someone until you piss them off

POK place of **kip**

POR please organise randomly

porchi to dribble [insp. **porchin**]

porchin dribble [pour + dribble]

POR FAVOR print on ran from a van or ran

pork dishonesty

p or k pill or kill

PORN put out rubbish now

porshun a greedy portion of food

porstraigh for a face to pop up [straight + portrait]

port a poor thought

porter to change how it is portrayed

porthead to find your way out of the **porthell**

porthell a portal of hell

portrait analysis to sketch everything apart from the face

portrick try to portray through trick and deceit

portry try to portray

POS part of speech

posard custard to get into trouble for speaking a certain way

pos card to hear someone speaking your hometown accent

pose-ess to lay out possessions [+ essence]

posensitive one who is sensitive about the way they posture themselves

posh spice expensive spices

positravel to travel with positivity

positrivial positive trivialness

posse a few possibilities

possensor to possess a sensor

possie possible

possy a group who all share the same accent

POST polite oranges sack tango

POST BOX polite ostrich stretch trench bites onto X

POST OFFICE polite oranges sack tango, oranges fume for ice cube edibility

postair when a poster is not fully attached to the wall and hangs off [poster + stair]

postcard a belated birthday card

postman pat to perform morse code on someone's back

postman pate to poke someone over and over [see **pate**] [insp. *Postman Pat*]

postquire to require afterwards [+ post]

pot lut a yellowish colour [insp. *the potamanthus luteus mayfly can be recognised by its yellowish colour*]

pot-pit a melted tiptop | a hot drink [oppo. tip-top]

potain to contain potato

potatent a potato patch [+ tenant]

potato meter to judge how lazy somebody is

potato wedge to give a someone a wedgie without being sly or fast in doing so

pot-hap to fall into a pot hole

pot-hop to avoid a pot hole

potpouwee the smell of wee [+ potpourri]

pots and pins money transactions

potunia a flower pot

pouch to hold something in the hand

poultry paltry

pouncial heavily **puncial** [**ouncial** + **puncial**]

pour poor

pourout to have no drink left

pourshun a greedy serving of drink

pourst for a spot to burst and pus to pour out

pourtrait a person who looks like they drink a lot of alcohol [pour + portrait]

powch when something sharp in your bag sticks into you, e.g. carrying a knife in the backpack was powch but a stab in the back is better than a stab in the dark

powdirt dust

powears to wear clothes which symbolise power, e.g. a robe religious or restful]

power po'ur

power shower to rain heavily | a burst of energy

powerglide to throw the body off the cliff, e.g they said it was bungee, I said it was murder

powergraph a paragraph displaying recordings of data [power + graph + paragraph]

powerhour the time in the day when you feel most awake

poworm an electrical device that moves around on the floor | a dangerous wire on the floor [power + worm]

ppp three in a row [see **O's and X's**]

pppp four in a row [see **FIAR**]

ppppppppppppppppp plllllllllllllllllllllllllll llleeeeeeeeeeeeeeeee eeeaaaaaaaaaaaaaaaa aaaasssssssssssssssss ssssssseeeeeeeeeeeee eeeeeee a desperate cry for help

p,q,r peculiar

pr process

prair to find the air holy | to love the wind

praisle admiration of an aisle, e.g. the sweet aisle at supermarket

pram a prom for younger people

pram hag a hot yacht to be put off someone because they have a child (which is seen as an **anchor**)

pramphlet a carrier for pamphlets (preferably on wheels)

pramulgate to tell everyone you are expecting (not just a baby)

prance pant hydrated [oppo. **pence pant**]

prank call a yodaphone

prapper paper wrapper

pray of sun! to thank god for the sunshine

pread to pretend to read

preadche to pretend to be listening to a preacher or reading the leaflet they handed you [+ headache]

preading to pretend to be reading

precushion to organise your pillows ready for sleep

prefor prefer to be 'for'

pregman a man who has a big round belly

pregulations regulations produced from other regulations

prepart to prepare part of it

prepinta to predict something about life

prequire to require before [+ pre]

presaint a holy gift

prescribble art therapy [prescribe + scribble]

president a present resident

presistance a present resistance

preslept a dead law [precept + slept]

pressong the band's most popular song

prest to be massaged and pressed while you rest

prestige a sack full of presents

pretty to pretend on many occasions [ins. **pread**]

pretty poise to politely ask

preyvention to hope for a distraction [prey + prevention]

price pileau rice

pricess to pour a pint [+ process]

pricetige a sack full of money [insp. **prestige**]

prickly bear to dress up as a cactus | for a gentle person to be offish

pricktures pictures of pricks | pictures which produce bad feelings or awful memories

prickual the practice of being a prick [+ ritual]

prictice to not practice for long enough [prick + practice]

priminutes old times [+ primitive]

primittens old hands [+ primitive]

primot a tradition [+ primitive]

prin to sit on a pin

princing to keep sitting on the pin cushion of the throne

principelt the main rainfall [principal + pelt]

pring a prank call

pring pring to ring someone and give them bad news | the bearing of bad news [oppo. **spring spring**]

pringle to abuse

printa in print

prisoon close to being convicted

pritta pratta one who pitter patters around to avoid making noise but ends up knocking something over

priviledge a privileged window view [+ ledge]

probation to hit probation over the head | to cancel a trial

problemon a bitter problem

problimbo to get underneath a problem

proch seven or eight moves [insp. *the game 'Progressive Chess'*]

pro che to reward creativity and imagination [insp. *the game 'Progressive Chess'*]

procist a cancelled transaction [process + cist]

prodium a small podium [+ prod]

profade when profit dies out

profame to get famous from being profane

professor elemental intelligent rap | clever rhyme

prograss for the grass to grow healthily

prograve a dieing out software

progrow a growing piece of software

prohiamb a prohibited ambition

proinfanitry light cursing, e.g. tom is a bogey face [infant + profanity]

promark somebody who is pro-Primark

prommage to look for a prom partner

promoment a moment of promotion, e.g. the author had a promoment which caused some people to order the book

pronto poncho immediate cover

prontoast an immediate toast | immediate cheers | to eat breakfast quickly [pronto + toast]

propaganda an angry walk [oppo. **ganda**]

pro pear proper fruit

propellor the proper way | the proper use [+ propeller]

pro plus the party people

propostanditum a stand-alone design [L. propositum: a design]

prostitune to illegally download tunes

protaste a sense or feel of protest

proteat the beginning of a protest [+ teat]

protect to parent [insp. *the parent bug sits on her eggs and young nymphs to protect them from parasites*]

protest the first test [+ proto]

protestempore to stand up for the time being | to temporarily demonstrate

protesticle to have courage [testicle + protest]

protestige a prestigious protest

protoe the first toe [+ proto]

proto type to have typed the first bit | to have typed a few pages

prout a prized pout

provent dead air [proven + vent]

provino to learn about wine [province + vino]

provoco cla to provoke *Coca Cola*

provoid to provide a sense of void

prow how proud of knowing how, e.g. she was prow how to sow

proxay able to act on behalf of many others [Na. pxay: many] [+ proxy]

pruco wax [insp. the canauba wax palm tree]

prun to have the runs from eating prunes

prunch a pruny punch

prune an disliked pun

pruny weak

pryportion an unintended portion [+ proportion]

PS plain-spoken

PSR parallel synchronised randomness

psycheep to keep on going into the mind [keep + psyche]

pt point of balance with the universe

PTC push or pull to close

PTO push or pull to open

P (to) one letter to Q, two letters to R, three letters to S, four letters to T, five letters to U, six letters to V, seven letters to W, eight letters to X, nine letters to Y, ten letters to Z, eleven letters to A, twelve letters to B, thirteen letters to C, fourteen letters to D, fifteen letters to E, sixteen letters to F, seventeen letters to G, eighteen letters to H, nineteen letters to I, twenty letters to J, twenty one letters to K, twenty two letters to L, twenty three letters to M, twenty four letters to N, twenty five letters to O

PTP pregnancy test please

P (past) one letter past O, two letters past N, three letters past M, four letters past L, five letters past K, six letters past J, seven letters past I, eight letters past H, nine letters past G, ten letters past F, eleven letters past E, twelve letters past D, thirteen letters past C, fourteen letters past B, fifteen letters past A, sixteen letters past Z, seventeen letters past Y, eighteen letters past X, nineteen letters past W, twenty letters past V, twenty one letters past U, twenty two letters past T, twenty three letters past S, twenty four letters past R, twenty five letters past Q

pu pun

pube pub

puberty liberty the independence and space you are entitled to when going through the puberty process

publack to keep private | to keep to yourself [public + lack]

publatch to keep it closed [public + latch]

publick to flirt outopen [public + lick]

publike what the public likes [oppo. **pubnot**]

pubnot what the public dislikes [oppo. **publike**]

pub salad unappetizing

puc a pack of sweets [+ pucca]

pucklet a bucket to puke in

pudlit a little pudding | a little serving

pudlot a lot of pudding | a big serving of desert

pue twisted [insp. the snow gum tree]

puff a fairy tale

puffball a pale face full of pimples [insp. *the common full ball fungi*]

puffpaste something to blow into

puff path the trail of smoke from a chimney

pufi a fight in a pub

puka a sickly kiss [puke + pucca]

pulathe to take bubbles off your body | to rinse soapy lathe off a vehicle

pulc pull cord

pull-a-greek to drop a plate

pull-hover to get stuck in a garment [pull-over + hover]

pullord the lord of pulling people | a tugof-war winner

pull-stop to dicide to extend a sentence; to make a sentence longer

pulo pull over

pulp daisy good news

pulpy small print | a small magazine

pulpun a comic magazine

puls ace a healthy pulse rate [oppo. **pul try**]

pulsen the spreading of pollen

pul try an unhealthy pulse rate [oppo. **puls ace**]

pum a bundle of seeds [insp. pumpkin seed + punnet]

puncial uncial from using puns or word play [L. uncial: curvy writing]

punch-brawl a fight caused by alcohol intake

puncho arms and body in bruises from being beaten

punchpenny miserly and beaten [pinchpenny + punch]

pundict an expert's prediction [+ pundit]

pung portable loo

punish fruity | fruitful [+ punnet]

puny prune a small poo

pupal an imaginary friend [pupil + pal]

pupelt to spit at each other [insp. *the life cycle of a butterfly: the pupal stage between the larva and the adult*] [+ spelt]

puppy a little boy

pur chase to chase a purchase | to bid on an object

purf sounds great [purr + perfect]

purgest to have a clear-out | to get rid of the undesirable [purge + gesture] [insp. **purifoecation**]

purifoecation to clean yourself of opponents

purplay a fuss

purplet dusk

purple turtle a think tank

purplose to lose its purple-colour | to lose purpose

purply to be hot and cold | red and blue

purrgate a door or gate that makes a meowing sound as it creeks

purrgency of emergency | to need immediate attention

purse excellence

purseed slowly up and down

purspecs glasses with purple lenses

purst a purse full of change, so much change it keeps busting open

pursuit a matching purse

pursult rapidly up and down [assault + purse]

pusset too desperate

pus to pose in vain

pus and cream push and scream

push-a-greek to force someone to eat up

pussy to try and fit in

pustuff to listen to tales [*stuff of a cat: ears and a tail*]

putshed space for an outhouse, workshop or even a shed

putty cash profit [putty + petty cash]

puzzplex puzzling complexion

pyfigerage to collect figs [Pythagoras + figs]

pylon to stand still and try to pick up on a vibration or energy

pyorrhoe a person who discharges a lot [pyorrhoea + hoe]

py-pan a toddlers potty

pyramaze to be stuck with a hierarchy system

pyramiddle caught up in a love triangle [+ pyramid + middle]

pyramidst between points [+ pyramid]

pyre pollen to scatter ashes [+ pollinate]

pyroxy a sudden fire | an unexpected fire [pyre + paroxysm]

Qq

Q quiet

Q *pic* a magnifying glass | speech bubble | balloon flying West

Q&A quilts and ambulants

Q (past) one letter past P, two letters past O, three letters past N, four letters past M, five letters past L, six letters past K, seven letters past J, eight letters past I, nine letters past H, ten letters past G, eleven letters past F, twelve letters past E, thirteen letters past D, fourteen letters past C, fifteen letters past B, sixteen letters past A, seventeen letters past Z, eighteen letters past Y, nineteen letters past X, twenty letters past W, twenty one letters past V, twenty two letters past U, twenty three letters past T, twenty four letters past S, twenty five letters past R

qqq three in a row [see **O's and X's**]

qqqq four in a row [see **FIAR**]

QS quiet space

Q (to) one letter to R, two letters to S, three letters to T, four letters to U, five letters to V, six letters to W, seven letters to X, eight letters to Y, nine letters to Z, ten letters to A, eleven letters to B, twelve letters to C, thirteen letters to D, fourteen letters to E, fifteen letters to F, sixteen

letters to G, seventeen
letters to H, eighteen
letters to I, nineteen
letters to J, twenty
letters to K, twenty one
letters to L, twenty two
letters to M, twenty
three letters to N,
twenty four letters to O,
twenty five letters to P

qua cent twenty five
[quarter + century]

quabless to pray four
times a day [+ quad]

quadam four women

quadrant a car that
only fits four

quado to have four
things to do [+ quad]

quadribble to draw a
box

quadude four men

qualitit for it to
depend on the quality
of the breast

quality street
variations

quall a luxurious
quilt | extra warmth [+
quality]

qualli extra comfort
[insp. **quall**]

quan one of four [quad
+ one]

quanti a corner of a
box

quantit for it to
depend on the size of
the breast

quantusk how many
teeth? [L. quantus: how
much]

quar fifteen [+
quarter]

quark to lark around
for **quar** minutes

quarrelish to
disagree with someone
[+ quarry]

quarrest a hard night's sleep [+ quarry]

quarrow a hard row [+ quarry]

quashoo to keep still | a void in movement | a void in taking instruction

quashoot to shoot a blank

quashush to not react, to keep silent

quasi cent to not know the age [+ quasi]

quasit to almost but not quite sit down [+ quasi]

quasoma the body of a spirit or ghost [+ quasi]

quasriot nearly a riot

quecumber mid-day queues when everybody appears [+ cucumber]

queen not able to jump [insp. *the game of 'Chess'*]

queens of the stone age girls that used to be known for getting stoned

quencher a question asked that brings nerves or makes the stomach churn | an unresolved situation

ques lar asking questions just for the fun of it

quesriot many people from a crowd wanting to ask questions at the same time

ques-tin a suggestions box

quet bunch

quest bunches [insp. quet]

quikey a cheat
[quickly + key]

quickne to spread fast
| to be everywhere | to
be catching on [+ acne]

quidentity the
identity of the pound;
its status

quilitter a litter of
padding | a pile of
buvets, throws and
cushions, e.g. we use
quilitter to soundproof
the walls

quilot a lot of
padding | well
protected

quiltation a very
good quote to support
the work

quiltation mark to
have placed a quote in
an ideal place | a place
in a piece of writing
where a quote is needed
[insp. **quiltation**]

quilto mos have been
bitten by bed bugs

quin quin fifty five |
santa claus

quincy a quick sprint
| to spring up quickly

quintea an ideal cup
of tea | a normal tea [+
quintessential]

quintulip five flower-
heads

quirkit quirkiness as
a tool

quish to squish a little
| to turn a house into
flats

quissil to quiz how
old something is [+
fossil]

quistory history
which could be quizzed
as only being myth,
because how do we
know, as we were not
alive then, and then, is

the real more historical than the unreal when the real is a conspiracy? [see **conspiracy**]

quit crit quit criticizing

quito mos! Stop biting! [+ mosquito]

quizz to question if the wet patch was urination [+ whiz]

quiz cent of a questionable age

quizine to question the journey of your food

qumel the ability to eliminate everything [insp. the broad-leaved paperbark tree]

qwoke a cracking headache | an earth quake | thunder

quont to question the way something is said | to question the way something is written [+ font]

quorf an eggy smell [+ *Quorn*]

qwert the first stages of learning how to use a computer [see **asdf**]

Rr

R red | right | run

R *pic* a side-portrait of a person

ra representation

raavi really, an .avi file!

R&B *the birds and the bees* in a bad way | slight display of domination

rabbi a well-respected rabbit | well looked after

rabus blabbus when talk catches on | an accent is passed round | talk of the same thing | the recent news muttered by all

RAC relate, animate, create

raccoontent treasured content [+ raccoon]

race chance

radash a healthy jog [+ radish]

radicult a radical cult

radiohead to hear a buzzing in the ears

radiste a cold shower

radum dark, radical and random

R.A.F rinse and foam

raffle argos

rafteno to do the same thing every afternoon

R.A.F.V.R rinse and foam, veneer, rinse

ragapulp a ragged but juicy pulp | the succulent part of fruit

ragenera a time of anger [rage + generation]

ragginger roughly chopped ginger

ragout dolls people who take magic mushrooms

rahma a scary mother

rail oil coal

rainal for the anal to output water

rain and bow reactions and effects [rainbow + rain]

rainberg a colour clash

rainboast to over-exaggerate a sad story [+ rainbow]

rainboat the sail of a rainbow

rain boat pirate the **rainboat** leads to the golden treasure

rainbore not colourful | to lack colour

rainbow a pintobow

raindroop to feel rained on | to feel washed-out

rainish a little of rain

rainosh a lot of rain

rainprove to provide evidence of dampness

rain water to be collected

raise rosie to bring someone to embarrassment

raisinoid of a raisin like texture, e.g. prune, fig, raisin. [insp. sesamoid]

ralfe band a travelling band

rallow to allow something to pass quickly | to let someone skip the queue [+ rally]

ralph waldo emmerson a wise person

ram for purgative [insp. ramaria Formosa]

ram'n'bam to only be interested in 'nostrings' sex

ramat back of hand

ramble to trick | a trick

ramble bumble a restaurant magician

rambler a trickster

rambulb a faulty bulb [+ **ramble**]

rammstein to quickly clean up

rampage a skate park [+ ramp]

rampagne champagne induced rampage

rampah a high level of sexualness

ramshackle to have problems with getting the CD-rom to work [+ ramshackle]

ramy my my oh my, very tall

ranch a rich thankfulness | highly grateful

rando to be on your own at first

randoc for the middle and end to be the same

randome a place of randomness [+ dome]

randy brandy and red wine

rangoon something run in *goon* mode

rank to run

rantsome a sales talk [ransom + rant]

rant-wrist the sixtysecond news | the weather report

raplicit understood to be illegal [implicit + illicit + rap]

rara protect [insp. the monkey puzzle tree]

rasher a red blotch

raspberry cripple a squished raspberry

rasu radioactive substance

rat-a-tat when you let air into ashes

ratio a friendly ration

rationull to be irrational

ratscrags scraggy clothes

ratscrap bad cooking

ratskip a messy bed

rattitude a ratty attitude | to give off the wrong signals

rattle to slither | cheek

rattlesnap to cheekily take photos when you're not really allowed to

rattlesnapple to cheekily record peoples conversations

rattlesnatch to cheekily steal a photo

rattlesnitch to cheekily tell someone's private story to another

ratunda a whirling round sickness | dizziness

ravant-garde to rant about the avant-garde [+ rave]

ravenue a raved-about place [+ venue]

raw roar energy from eating raw foods

ray an X-ray gone wrong

ray-da-da a time of Dada

raydiator the warmth of sun rays

ray dry ate dehydrated [+ radiator]

rayon to colour

rayscale multi-colour [oppo. **greyscale**]

ray sin when the sun goes in [ray + raisin]

ray sinwave when the sun goes in and out [insp. **ray sin**]

ray-tarty forever changing weather

rb Robert Sheppard

RCB rosy checks because...

r di bend to right (like the road warning sign)

re recycle|re-invent | re-write | reincarnate | re-discover

read-breed when people only read what is available to them it is all they will know, therefore they are breeding themselves and nothing new, e.g. if I only read what the library offers then it would be a read-breed situation

reach a tall tree

reaction from the crowd

readiator to throw books on the fire in order to keep warm

realm palm to shake a royals hand

rea sake because it reads good

rea sentment to have a reason for resentment

rebalm to make wet again

rebel an image which shows opposition of a ruling power [Na. rel: image] [+ rebel]

reboccy a recycled bottle [insp. **boccy**]

recap to rethink

rechurn to feel sick again [return + churn]

recline chairing lazy rowing (at the gym)

recline to adjust a line [+ recliner]

re cog nice to update a part [recognise + cog]

recognite a night well remembered [+ recognise]

recomposer a recomposing poser | a poser who re-arranges his or her body position

recorder the ear

recore to catch someone out by secretly recording them [+ **recorder**]

recouple to join up again | to fasten together again, e.g. you would recouple the laces to avoid any danger

rectifly to make something fly [+ rectify]

recumbanto to conversate when lying down (in bed) [recumbent + banto]

recusanta to believe in christmas apart from the 'Christ' (religious) side of it

recycleanse to cleanse the soul by recycling

red trouble

reda good value [insp. *in the game of 'Monopoly' the red properties are good value*]

red flag war

red hoo chilly bed a freezing bath

red hoo chilly pepper very cold and round

red hot chilli bed a scorching bath

red hot chilli pepper very hot and round

red meat gluttony

red-nosed silly | clown-like

red pleb a pleb in the red

red-robin a small chubby child [+ breast]

red sea trouble at sea

red shoes individualism

red three a hundred [insp. *the game 'Canasta'*]

red whine period pain

red-white to lose a lot of blood

red wri revi to study a lot [read + write + revise]

redib red sauce [+ edible]

reds ready, e.g. are you reds?

redsome troublesome

redsum more trouble

reebok to read a book

reece research

reed much sugar

reefo a damaged 'no hope' roof

reeka 'it smells round here' [+ reek]

reelift the scaffholdinding to hold up the **reefo**

reffoc to have no luxury items

reffus to refuse to go on suffering [+ suffer]

reflu to have the flu again

refugene to foster [gene + refuge]

reg register

reg ea to show you agree, to notify your backing [+ agree]

regency to open a door for someone

reg note to track a car

regarden to need time to think | to need a break [regard + garden]

regester a register of gesture(s) | a recording of gestures

registered r in a circle

registrat to register a
strategy

reheated rice a
chance of cancer

rehetro the lower
levels of a thick forest
[insp. *the red-headed
trogon birds occupy the
lower levels of a thick
forest in which they live*]

reifile to hold a story
as evidence [reify + file]

reindeer claws dirt
or poo in the nails
[insp. **santa claws**]

reindirt muddy

reinforest to
reinforce a forest | to
make a forest

rela relation

relaship relationship

relaship red
relationship troubles

relayship to change
things in a **relaship** in
order to keep it fresh,
e.g. to find a new hobby
[relay + **relaship**]

relent to have the
same lent every year

religaments religious
ligaments | to be
moved by religion, to let
religion move you

religene to share the
same religion as you
family

relish pickle

rememore to
remember more

remoan to carry on
moaning [+ remain]

remoron to have
forgotten [+ remember]

remove to turp

renna one who takes
rennies

rep reputation

repel no change [insp. **pel**]

rep et rah a scary repertoire

repap to screw up paper [+ paper]

repate to stick together again [pate + repeat]

repatition a recurring pattern | always returning [pat + repetition]

repelican to copy the movements of a bird | to act out bird movements or bird sounds

repelt water resistant [repel + pelt]

repetite to shine [repetition + pigment]

repoise to lie down | to place down reading material

repolution repeated

revolution petite a row of small people

represensitive to represent the sensitive

repressence repressed essence

reprimandolin a cursing song [reprimand + mandolin]

reptiles tiles that are not stuck down

republic a pub ruled by its customers

reprimand recently every person risen in marination and never desolation

reprism a mirror's reflection [represent + prism]

reques-tin a requests list

rero rapid growth | bright green [insp. the royal palm tree]

resclue an idea which may help [clue + rescue]

researth to rediscover the earth

resempire to resemble an empire

resident one who attends the dentist

resiste to resist a relationship with your best friends sister | for a sister to resist a relationship with her brother's/sister's best friend

resister a sister who does not want to be your sister [+ resist]

reson a boy going through puberty [reason + son]

respeach easily respected [respect + peach]

respeck to peck at responsibility

respecs glasses with red lenses

respectacle to respect what you see

respectulum to see and appreciate in every light [respect + spectulum]

rest kip

rest inter to be at ease with the surroundings with everything | to be in harmony [+ interest]

resta elder [+ **rust**]

ret exit [+ enter]

retrap to be behind bars [L. retro: backwards/behind]

retrochoir a vibrant choir

retrograd one that graduates from the retro

retrong the sounds produced from performing **retrongue**

retrongue to speak backwards [L. retro: backwards/behind]

retrooper a backwards soldier [L. retro: backwards]

retrosoma a backwards body [L. retro: backwards]

rev for something to take a minute to learn but a lifetime to master [insp. *the game 'Reversi'*]

revel a pleasurous image [Na. rel: image]

reven to never look back [+ never]

revil to not enjoy life [+ liver]

revolution the increase in motor bikes

rev x 2 a reverend revving a motorbike

rewind two arrows backward

rexray to study archaeology [x-ray + tyrannosaurus rex]

rh rhizomata

rhapsoda the making of a rhapsody

rhizoink to highlight [rhizome + ink]

rhosub light and dark [insp. *the rhopalus subrufus bug can be*

*recognised by the light
and dark banding on
the margins of the
abdomen*]

rib cage storage space

ribbone to find ribs
on show | extra
skinniness | a sign of
happiness [ribbon +
bone]

ric to re-display [**rip** +
picture]

rice-cream icecream
made from rice
milk

**rice in the salt
shaker** 'keep it
moving' | to eliminate
the solid | to keep it
free

richard one who has
lots of money

rich bin to throw
away fit produce

ricosay to echo a
saying [+ ricochet]

rife to take the roof
from someone's head

riffinish to quickly
finish [+ riff]

riff-raffiti very bad
graffiti

riffym a rough
rhythm | to draft out a
rhythm [+ riff]

righ-gah an annoying
political right-wing
person

right-wing royal

rilla a gorilla without
the gore

RIN read it now

R in a circle
registered

rinch rich in thought

ringlot to have lots of
curls in the hair

ringlut to have too
many curls in the hair

ring-pull canny

rinkage at an ice rink

rio to not drink fizzy pop

rip to replay a track

ripe a non-smoking area [insp. **pipefat**]

ripe pipe a pipe containing fresh herb

ripped spoilt

ripsody to copy a song | to rip off a song [rip+ rhapsody]

ris very strategic [insp. *the game 'Risk'*]

risk to not whisk enough

risotoot to start to show feeling [rise + oh + **toot**]

risks one and a half hours [insp. *the duration of the game 'Risk'*]

rival allotrend

rivat a water container [river + vat]

riveil to try and outdo another's wedding day

rivulot a rivulet which always floods [+ lot]

rn run, render

ro love [+ romance] | tea [see roger]

road-cone a tent pitched in the city [+ cone]

road-kilt when your skirt blows up in the wind (usually on the roadside) [+ road kill]

ro bean to love more than one person

ro bin to fall out of love with

ro bin red breast to fall out of love with someone in the winter time

robelemon a yellow coat

ro boat for the relationship to contain distance

ro cupere to wish for a cup of tea [L. cupere: to wish] [+ **ro**]

ro empha a lover's attention [+ **ro**]

ro hi very happily in love [+ **ro**]

ro lo unhappily in love [+ **ro**]

ro mugere to wish for a cup of coffee [insp. **ro cupere**]

ro tri the power of nourishment [insp. rock tripe]

ro untri the power of malnourishment

roar road rage

roar roar roar the boat to sail in stormy weather

roarder out of order

robedoor to have a piece of material as a door (band)

robertsport to fight over an object [insp. **rupertsport**] [*Robertsport is a place on the coast in Liberia*]

robin to seek out food from bins

roboots big stomping boots [+ robot]

robot the millennium

robotomato the expected colour of bums after playing **robottom wars** [+ tomato]

robottom wars a game where you bum people out the way

robsoma a robotic body

roch over-exploit [insp. the greenheart tree]

rock cake to not have a sweet tooth

rockettle a whistling kettle

rock face a hard head

rock-fell to be crushed

rock'n'roll to sit in a rocking chair whilst eating swiss-roll cake

rocksack a heavy rucksack [oppo. **rucksock**]

rodeo to not get off someone's back | to keep pestering a person

roga margin [insp. the queensland kauri tree]

roger tea and coffee [insp. *the silky oak tree, which is used to shade tea and coffee plantations*]

rogue gears stiff gears

roll slur

roll a boa kinky

roller ball to be on heroin

ROM rely on me

romanc romance in manchester

ron dignified [insp. matron]

ron ate to eat a large serving [+ **ron**]

ron davu dignified and common | commonly dignified [+ **ron**]

ron din honourable and dignified dinner [+ **ron**]

ron don honourable appearance | honourably dressed [+ **ron**]

ron marg the honourable appearance of marriage [+ **ron**]

ronnie RONO

RONO rely on no one

rook to move with without any intervening

roo-pee desperate, hopping around for a wee

roofies construction workers

roominant to invade somebody's space [room + ruminant]

root to fixture

rootine the natural routine [+ root]

rootoo the tooth's roots

ropelt to throw stones [rock + pelt]

RORO roll on, roll on

rosette cheeks to get rosey cheeks from attention, being rewarded or when complimented

rosie and gym a red face from physical exercise [insp. *Rosie & Jim*]

rosie and jim boys and girls [insp. *Rosie & Jim*]

rosrind the smell left when you rub a petal in between to fingers

ross sorry

rotpouwee the smell of old wee [insp. **potpouwee**]

rotten apple a faulty Mac computer

rotterdam fast beat(s)

rotterdam tiles the nightlife in Rotterdam

rough an estimate

round ferris

roundaboo a washing machine [+ **round**]

rouskin rough skin | a rough person

row bust to destroy oars | to not know where something is going

row-bust to massage the breast area [+ robust]

rowing laying out seats | moving the arms in a circular motion

rowmanian a person who is addicted to rowing

rown a rowan tree

roxpi rich [insp. the chir tree]

roxy slippy rocks [see **petrol**]

roy soz

royage a royal voyage

royal free-living

roy-al sozzled [+ **soz**]

royce ral a *Royce Rolls* car being driven fast [+ rally]

royi to look right

R (past) one letter past Q, two letters past

P, three letters past O,
four letters past N, five
letters past M, six
letters past L, seven
letters past K, eight
letters past J, nine
letters past I, ten letters
past H, eleven letters
past G, twelve letters
past F, thirteen letters
past E, fourteen letters
past D, fifteen letters
past C, sixteen letters
past B, seventeen
letters past A, eighteen
letters past Z, nineteen
letters past Y, twenty
letters past X, twenty
one letters past W,
twenty two letters past
V, twenty three letters
past U, twenty four
letters past T, twenty
five letters past S

rrr three in a row [see
O's and X's]

RRR's read, rate,
review

rrrr four in a row [see
FIAR]

R,S,T to have a rest
and a cup of tea

R (to) one letter to S,
two letters to T, three
letters to U, four letters
to V, five letters to W,
six letters to X, seven
letters to Y, eight letters
to Z, nine letters to A,
ten letters to B, eleven
letters to C, twelve
letters to D, thirteen
letters to E, fourteen
letters to F, fifteen
letters to G, sixteen
letters to H, seventeen
letters to I, eighteen
letters to J, nineteen
letters to K, twenty
letters to L, twenty one
letters to M, twenty two
letters to N, twenty
three letters to O,
twenty four letters to P,
twenty five letters to Q

ru Rudolf Steiner

rubber dove a rubber
duckling flown out of
the hand

rubber dusk to pretend it is dusk | to think it is dusk when it isn't

rubber soul a runner [+ sole]

ruby to rub the eye, e.g in the morning it was all ruby and **weke**

rucksick to be sick into a bag

rucksock a light rucksack [oppo. **rocksack**]

rucksuck to be fed up from carrying a rucksack

rud brown and red

ruddar bright red [insp. *the ruddy darter dragonfly has a very bright red abdomen*]

rudeberry flustard sexual discharge [custard + rude + flustered]

rudolf adolf the christmas grinch

rudolph a red nose

rudolph clown a very red nose

rudolphin a red and wet nose

rue stalked [insp. the mountain ash tree]

ruffle hank to upset someone enough to make them cry

ruf gra the sound of a sewing machine [insp. *rufous grasshopper's song resembles a sewing machine working in 5-second bursts*]

ruffled sheets a good sex life

rufflee to shake someone up the wrong way [ruffle + flee]

rugbied rugby-ball shaped | oval

rugsack a sack of laundry to be taken to the launderette

rum'n'blime rum and a lot of lime

rum'n'blimey alcoholic happenings

rum'n'bum to be a lazy alcoholic

rumbustle to have your face in a pair of breasts that are jiggling around, or to give a raspberry to the breast area

rummy to bet drink

run to rank

run-agro to have an aggressive life

run-back to live life in the past

run-ball to go through life in circles

run-ban to discard any rushing in life

run-base to go through life looking for stability | to live life in stability

run-ben to treat life as a race against time [+ *Big Ben*]

runburst to work yourself into a grave (or into 'rundown' mode)

run-dance to live life as if a dance, to waltz though it happily

run-dew to live an emotional life

run-down to commit suicide

run-dull to live a boring life

run-dunce to make
mistakes in life

run-forth to live life in
the future [oppo. **run-
froth**]

run-froth to live life
in the past [oppo. **run-
forth**]

run-gingerbread to
get away| to escape

run-gone to get
through life too quick |
to grow up too quick

run-gun to live life
commiting crime

run-rampant to live
life not tied to one
sexual partner

run-rest to live and
rest in moderation

run-risk to take risks

run-roo to only take
small risks

run-run to keep on
living

run-runt to live life in
a state

run-slow to cruise
through life in the slow
lane

ruper red and yellow |
a rhubard and custard
sweet [insp. *Rupert the
Bear*]

rupert a scarf [insp.
Rupert the Bear]

rupertsport the game
of tug-of-war with a
scarf [Robertsport is a
place on the coast in
Liberia] [+ **rupert**]

ruperty when a tie
flaps over the shoulder
and stays there as if a
scarf [insp. *Rupert the
Bear*]

rus multi-specied

rus aerug green-grey colour [insp. russula aeruginea]

rus atro deep purple [insp. russula atropurpurea]

rus clar one of the best [insp. russula claroflava]

rus cya soft and white [insp. russula cyanoxantha]

rus eme coconut smell [insp. russula emetica]

rus ros to fade towards the centre | to have no taste [insp. russula rosea]

russia one who rushes | to run

rus ves no skin [insp. russula vesca]

rus vire cheesy-smell [insp. russula virescens]

rus xer blackish purple [insp. russula xerampelina]

rust old, e.g. 52 years (of) rust

RWB "rib" red, white and blue

RWBbon red, white and blue flags, e.g. the flags of UK, USA, France [+ ribbon] [insp. **RWB**]

rye red eye(d)

Ss

S South

s shamanic

S *pic* a figure of 8 track left to decay and disappear

S and M smile and mate

SAB save a badger

sabab a young saboteur

sabbath a day of sabotage

saccharin a fake

sack-foot to be wearing more than two pairs of socks on the foot

sack-rock baggage | a heavy item [rucksack + rock]

sacne to hide the face due to acne, e.g. a scarf was put on to sacne on the chin

sacriface to give up wearing make-up [+ sacrifice]

sacrifiction sacred fiction

sacryfic to only drink water [sacrifice + acrylic]

saction the action of sacking

SAD save a deer

sadding salt salty tears [+ **saddis**]

saddis sad

saddle to sit on something that is

rising, e.g. profits or shares

saddlet to sit in sadness

saddun to all of a sudden become sad

sadvice sad advice

sadvise to sadly advise

SAF save a fox

safety pin safe internet banking

safire a safety flame [+ sapphire]

safp a safety pin

saga grey or brown [insp. sand gaper]

saga laga to be immature when drunk

sagar when garments sag | when a strap falls down

sage to say something at the appropiate time

saggear to put in the wrong gear

sagpuss a puss that's getting fat

sagreesid disagreed

said row to have said many things

saidimen to say what is left to say | to say what hasn't been mentioned [+ sedimentary]

saidiments sediments of what was said

sail oil oil from the sea

sailute to sail off [+ salute]

sainsbury's sane as berries, e.g. sainsbury's with faces on

SAL say a line

sal underweight
[oppo. **salard**]

sala last, but not least
[+ alas]

salad a healthy
weight

salamandry to kill by
drying out, as a
salamander cannot be
dry

salard overweight
[oppo. **sal**]

sale aleich money off
for you [insp. **salon
aleich**]

sales talk a yip yap
hat

saliver on to accept
people will curse and
tut at you [+ saliva]

salmoney money
from dodgy dealings

salon aleichem
beauty be with you
[Jew. shalom aleichem:
'peace be with you']

saloot to lose out on
money | to say goodbye
to your savings [loot +
salute]

saltana a healthy
amount of salt [+
sultana]

salter to alter the
taste by adding salt

saltestament to
always have to add salt
to your food [+
testament]

salt'n'pap the
paparazzi who over-
exaggeratesituations

salva-door an arty
door | an interesting
door

samber to flash
amber [+ samba]

same starch [insp. the sago palm tree]

samim endangered fish

sammar a hot summer [insp. *Fireman Sam*]

samrock a rock band with three members [insp. shamrock]

samsoon in the process of waiting for a lawyer | waiting for security

samsung a fire engine siren

samuray to burn [samurai + ray]

sana centre

sandoll a doll made from glass

sand-sane to sink in | easily took in or carried away

sand-sound rough

sandwatch an hourglass

sandwich in sand

sandwiched buried in sand [insp. **sandwich**]

sandwich technique to cover the top and bottom

sandwish a practical wish [+ sandwich]

sandwitch a witch who is half a white witch and half a black witch [+ sandwich]

san francisco stands of franchise | licensed stalls

sankle a saggy ankle | to paddle the feet (upto the ankles) in water [+ sand]

sankton the very deep bottom of the sea [+ sanction]

sanocon to make sand sculptures [anocon + sand]

sans stands [insp. **san francisco**]

sans bo book stands [+ **sans**]

sant red sand [+ santa]

santa clause mickey mouse

santa claws nails or claws with blood in them

santa's grotto a **den** containing lots of red and white clothes

santa's motto beer for me to ride easily, carrot for deer to sleigh me here

sap-hire to take a chance and hire someone who is not **sapphire**

sapparent something that's apparent but it's fluid so it may change, therefore may not be [+ sap]

sapphire a safe hire | to hire a safe candidate (somebody who has the experience)

saprise to give reason why an area is wet | to call someone to fix a leak [apprise + sap]

sarc sarcastic

sarcas stick the power of sarcasm

sarcast to make scarcastic

sarco scaly [insp. sarcodon imbricatum]

sarcra to pair for life | to have a life-long companion [insp. *the sarus crane birds pair for life, and are always seen in a pair*]

sarcrash when sarcasm is misinterpreted

sarf ari a tiger stripe

sash highly accessorized shoes

sashtray an award given to someone who does not deserve it [sash + ash tray]

sashy yellow skin (of mostly the hands) from smoking

satday a day of relaxing

satelit to be awaiting news

satellite to be a sitting duck for something

satlas to be at home [sat + atlas]

satmap the map on a satellite navigator

satnap directions to a hotel [insp. **satmap**]

satsum to sit in the sun to change colour [+ Satsuma]

sattitude to hold an attitude [+ sat]

saturday buest Saturday I was [see **sunday buest**]

saturnine to meet on a Saturday at either 9am or 9pm

saucepanorama to cook without following recipes

sauction sactioning by auction [see **saction**]

sault to change the question

sauna hot

saunasoma a hot body

sauna struma for the body to get very hot very fast, almost abnormal

saunatering sauntering in hot weather [+ sauna]

sa vase a vase that has been passed down the family for many generations | a family keepsake

save-age a time of rescue

saven haven a place of refuge

savenue a place where you can save, e.g. a discount store is always a savenue

savint an elder in education [savant + vntage]

savoy to rescue someone from a bad trip

savoyage to miss your train stop [savage + voyage]

savoyod to save money on travelling

say er a year that went too fast | to wonder where the year went

say R trouble at the dentist

sayduct to speak in a seductive manner

saze to discuss size [+ say]

sb subject

sc Stockhausen

scabaret to show off a scab [+ cabaret]

scabbage to pick at scars [savage + cabbage]

scaf-folded static origami | static animation

scal reddish-brown [insp. scallop]

scale sleigh

scale electrics overhead electric cables

scalligraphy the art of messy handwriting [+ calligraphy]

scalpacit to scratch the head because you have an itchy scalp [+ capacity]

scaly sleigh an estimated weight

scamboyant to cheat on an exam [scam + flamboyant]

scamera to take photos of someone without their permission

scancel to cancel a scan | to cancel a medical check up

scandimon to write with the paper at an angle

scandinavi one who scandinners [see **scandinner**]

scandinavian a check-out person [+ scan]

scandinner to check out a menu | to look at the food on offer [+ scan]

scandle a quick look [candle + scan]

scanter to copy someone else's notes [+ scanner]

scar to permanently scare

scarce black at the rear [insp. *the scarce chaser dragonfly is marked black towards the rear*]

scarecour intimidating bravery [scary + courage]

scare-crop an ornament to scare away something, e.g. a witches cross [+ scarecrow]

scarecrow to stretch the arms out and stand still

scarendipity gift of making fortunate but frightful discoveries by accident [scare + serendipity]

scarf a scarred neck

scar face to always look scared | to look fearful [+ **scar**]

scarfter after the winter [+ scarf]

scarred to be forever scared [insp. **scar**]

scar ska a trail of scars

scary spice a hot spice

scatterpult a sloppy target [catapult + scatter]

scawal to look into a hole [scan + canal]

scenema the theatre scene [+ cinema]

scentre the smells of the city [scent + centre]

sceptric septic in a good way

scess without sucking [+ success]

scev a science event

schedazzle a chaotic plan [+ schematic]

schi to divorce

schide to not sign divorce papers | to try and put off a divorce [hide + **schi**]

schister step sister [insp. **schi**]

schofi a school fight

schole to not be able to find a good job after graduating [scholar + hole]

scholour the colours of the school logo [+ scholar]

SCHOOL swimming caps held over oak lands

schoster step brother [insp. **schi**]

schwing when there are swings free at the park

schwinge when there are no swings free at the park

schwittz collage

sci foe disliked sci fi

scissors for lefty to scissor to the left

scissors for righty to scissor to the right

scissors for wards to scissor straight on

scoff cake

scoffee to intake lots of caffeine | to drink coffee fast

scoffold to fold up paper merely by screwing it up

scoffspring messy eaters [scoff + offspring]

sconcept a witty concept [+ sconce]

scoot'n'shine to make a get away | to abort a situation

scope suitable for children

score pud a favourite pudding

scorrect cuttingly correct [+ score]

scotch bath to be given a mass load of scotch

scotch blotch red skin from drinking

scotch broth a massive serving of scotch (enough to bathe in)

scotch watch drinking time | pub time

scotland is cot land | sleepy time

scott many thanks [+ **otter**]

scount a group of soldiers [scout + count]

scoup cup of soup

scourage to scour with rage

scourage to search thoroughly with energy [scour + courage]

scoure to get rid of damp wood scour + score]

scra horizontal or vertical [insp. *the game 'Scrabble'*]

scrab word games [insp. *the game 'Scrabble'*]

scrabble vocabulary skills [insp. *the game 'Scrabble'*]

scrambled albumen a bad smelling toilet

scramputation to never be seen again [scram + amputation]

scramraid hit and run

scratch card looking for luck

scratch watch to cut out time

scrawl to get through the day after having **screw**

screep to quietly scrape

screw a bad start

scrib to cheat in scrabble by forging the written scores

scribble to open up the mind

scribbolt a fixed view [scribble + bolt]

scribe tribe

scriboo drawing games

scribs scraps of paper to scribble on

scrip to leave it alone

scritch an itch you scratch yet it still itches

scro gin fruity or nutty gin [NZ. scroggin: mixture of dried fruits and nuts]

scroob scrooge of a boob

scroovy driver a driver who is good at turning corners [+ screw driver]

scrotch to scratch the crotch area

scouse to knock down a wall in a house [+ score]

scrow screws everywhere [+ crow]

scrowl to fly off the handle [scowl + owl]

scrub water games

scrub(b)a diver a toilet or pool cleaner

scrubble to try on clothes

scrunchies boiled sweets

scrunity to analyse an agreement [scrutiny + unity]

scubage volume levels in water [scuba + cubage]

scuba-scab in too deep

scube to look deep into a container [scuba + cube]

scucumber fresh but scum

scufflink to quickly put cufflinks on | to try and put two and two together before looking at the whole picture

scuffs shoe laces [+ cuffs]

scuffspring unexpected offspring

scum hunt

scurry curry to eat a curry quickly

scurverge at the verge of having scurvy

scut & pasty a best mans speech copied from the internet

SD short distance

SE South East | some even

se research

se cen seventeenth century

SE itch an itch SE of the back

sea see

sea cap a head floating above water level

sea of the bottle the last few drops of drink in the bottom of a bottle

sea samba the swimming of fishes in groups

sea through to swim to another (is)land [+ see-through]

seagulls coast livers

seagull strings a holiday romance

seale forever

seal iron bar | soft

seal cap a seal head floating above water level

seal pe to be desperate for the toilet but unable to go [+ please]

sealet where water runs into the sea

sea-lion-tatterdemalion wild seas [tatterdemalion + sea lion]

seamundane to find being on the beach everyday very boring [mundane + sea]

séance nav to let the satellite navigator guide you

seapinach to use seaweed in cooking instead of spinach

searpant a boat sailing in the sea [sea + serpent [insp. **serpent house**]

searth sea | sky

seascanty a small sea shanty [+ scant]

sea-shape to always change

seaswed wrapped in sea weed | tangled up in seaweed

seatback a comfy setback

seatengul to feel because you are not rushing round like you normally do [Na: ngul: grey, drab] [+ seat]

seattle seat

sea-wed to get married under water

seaweed no conventional roots

secivres useless [+ services]

secks sex that only lasts a few seconds

secondead to have suddenly died

second-seat to sit on somebody's lap

seconned to be conned twice

secras crass secrets

secrate a secret stored

secretina to see something which was once hidden

sectomy to have an unimportant role | to have a very small part in a play

securen visible security accessories, e.g. house alarm or surveillance camera

secursity to curse the security

see sea

see-can a scope to look into

seed to grow

seed carrier the postman

seeds nom bombs

see-fruit to juice fruit [+ see-through]

seelion to see something of interest

seepope holy blood

seerphones optical glasses

sees nile when you (can) understand the senile

see-sore understanding that when you sit in the sun for 10 hours you will expect karma

see-sow to pick up on someone being attached to another person | to suspect an affair

seets dry sweets | powdered candy ['w' is for 'wet']

segoe a disliked segment [+ foe]

selecture a talk on how we select, e.g. a lecture on the selective breeding

self-perpetal to move to a better position

self portrait to forget to see yourself | to try and understand yourself

self-star to be your own god

sella shelter down South [+ ella]

sello a promotion | a sales talk [hello + sell]

sembu square | a box

semcup around the world [insp. the italian cypress tree]

semicol not the proper colour

semint nearly in mint condition [+ semi]

seminull indecisive [+ seminal]

seminute half a minute | thirty seconds [+ semi]

semit summit sometimes

semivow to only 'half' give your word [+ semi]

sempudding daddy's little girl [Na. sempu: daddy] [+ pudding]

semse tough [insp. the californian redwood tree]

sen senior

senacore harder than hard core [senator + core]

send long on its way [send + endlong]

seniorvant an older servant

sennigly to be niggly for a whoel week [sennight + niggly]

sense dratum an embarrassing sense datum

sensibility the discount section

sensit to sit lightly e.g. to sensit on someone's lap

sensoral to sense with the tongue

senstable sensibly stable

sentime old age | old times [+ **sen**]

senxet sixth sense [L. sext(us): sixth]

separtriot one of many riots [separate + patriot + riot]

sepie a brown (grainy) pie made with wholewheat flour

sepposs to look at your possessions [+ suppose]

septic wounding [+ epic]

sequins stars shining in a dark sky above

serays rays of seriousness

serfant a young servant

serfings the servings of finger-food, e.g. canapés

serinail a published music [+ serial]

serious offly

serpent a spiral staircase [*a serpent twists*]

serpent house a barge on the canal [*slithering the water like a serpent*]

serviette union organized serviettes [+ Soviet Union]

servision to display an image | to advertise

seset to sit it down | to put it down

set of scale to weigh out a problem

settler a chair in its permanent position [settle + settee]

settlet a sitting area outside [outlet + settle]

sevangel seven angels | severely innocent

sevangel tales the seven dwarves in Snow White

seven minutes past moon monocle fifty three minutes to soon sun is cool

seven minutes to still on a car fifty three minutes past stall ion car

seventeen minutes past linchpin forty three minutes to safety pin

seventeen minutes to chill pill red call forty three minutes past pil charred wall

seventeeth seven teeth

several a federal servant

severance serpent a person who is unemployed and looking for work

severbal several verbals

severy permanently cut off | to cut through too far [very + sever]

sewage bad sewing

sew sewer to fix a sewer problem | a plumber

sexaginarian a person who drinks sixty to sixty nine servings of gin (a year) [sexagenarian + gin]

sexcess excessively sex infested

sexcursion a short excursion involving sexual activity

sexhorn to be in the mood for sexual activities

sex pistol a penis

sex pistole a vagina

sexternal world the use of sex to promote materiality

seyrisk a risky kiss | to kiss without no-one seeing

sha para to prefer shade [insp. shaggy parasol]

shaba to share a bath

shabba a good looking father

shabboo a shabby love [+ taboo]

shabitat a shabby habitat

shabitter a shabby bitter (drink)

shaca innocuous [insp. *the shaggy cap fungi*]

shack-footage footage of people having sex [+ stock]

shackra a place with an energy [shack + chakra]

shadders shaky ladders | insecure ladders

shadelier to wear sunglasses to stop the sun going into your eyes [chandelier + shade]

shaggy cap a dead or near to dead umberella [insp. shaggy cap]

shagped to be worn out from pedalling

shallatte onion soup served in cup [shallot + latte]

sham mash that isn't mashed enough

shamball a terrible game of any sport which involves a ball [+ shamble]

shambless to bless a moment of awkwardness

shamcard to give someone the wrong phone number on purpose

shamecard to give someone the wrong phone number on accident

shammer hammer the shamans weapon of spirit

shamposh expensive shampoo

shamstring steroidinfested muscles [+ hamstring]

shand a shaky hand

shandid half-sober, half-drunk | half and half | a debate

shandie a chandelier

shandy a sand-pit in the shade

shank when the water jilts as it comes out [shake + sink]

shant a small boat [shanty + ant]

shapish a little shape

shaposh a lot of shape

shard a sharp pain

shardware of glass material

shariban to ban alcohol

sharifreeba a noalcohol zone

shark water punk

sharkface to run away

sharpsichord to pick up on hearing a harpsichord

shave to temporarily reduce something

shaven to take refuge under shelter [shave + haven]

shead a hat on the head [+ **shed**]

shear to hear whispers [shh + hear]

shed the memory, e.g. there are only so many tools you can store in the shed

shedder a small room

sheepish shippish

sheeps clouds

sheepsquat to camp out on a field

sheet a layer of dung, e.g. pull the sheet over the eyes

sheffle to move around Sheffield

shefi to keep out [insp. shellfish]

shell game hide and seek

s/hemail a message from both a male and a female

shemail a message from a female

shich-up to sick up in the mouth [+ hiccup]

shimmock to mock someone's 'shimmy' dancing

shimrock well remembered [+ shamrock]

shimtag your signature dance move

shin chin to knee someone in the chin

shindy an independent shop

shinglacier a cold shower [shingle + glacier]

shin shin chin chin

shint to throw money at someone [+ **shints**]

shints hints of money |to keep on throwing money at someone

ship a single sheep

shippie to travel by water

shippish a boat urinating-tonguing sea water

shippy smashed glass

ship ship shoo way hip hip hoo ray to a ship that sails away | to wave to a ship and the people on it

shire to hang up a shirt

shiren the shining of a shoe [+ siren]

shirt to hurt

shittage too short

shizzle to put your shoes on the wrong feet

shock troops bullies who bully because they have been bullied

shock-a-block-ice filled with coldness

shock-a-sock-ice when you are **shock-a-block-ice** and unable to feel your feet

shocket a socket that's more likely to shock you than help you

shock-foota 'you've been framed' [+ stock-footage]

shodder a shoddy ladder | a dodgy ladder

shoe rang the luck will come back [boomerang + horseshoe]

shoezukis shoes on wheels [+ *Suzuki*]

shogi several hours

sholja a person who gives backpacks [see backpack] [shoulder + soldier]

shome a degrading home

shoo lace to lose ties | to get rid of a connection | to disconnect yourself | to disassociate yourself [+ shoe lace]

shoolea to take a leash off a dog and for it to shoot off

shooperone to chaperone by shooing

shoopie to shoo someone from the cooking

shoops to have been locked inside a shop [+ oops]

shoot to shout happily [+ hoot]

shooterms the paintball rules

shoperone a sales assistant [chaperone + shop]

shop-gull spendulum

shopping a 'self-funded' treasure hunt

shors short shorts

shot still hot

shotel a showy hotel

shot putch shut up

shoutered to be tired of raising the voice

shout'n'shy to change character, e.g. the sky was shout'n'shy today, first light and then dark

showea in flowers [insp. *the short-winged earwig is most often seen in flowers*]

showears waterproof clothes

showi this is how

show-kin a family member who likes to show off | a hired escort

shrave tired from raving [+ shrivel]

shribber a team who pretend to know [insp. shrubber] [+ fib]

shriver a weak river | weak energy [oppo. **striver**]

shrub to massage in quietness | a group

shrubber a team who vaguely know [**shrub** + shrug]

shrugsborough a time of 'shrugging'

shrugstance the stance of a shrug

shtg shittage

sushial a quiet society [social + shush]

shud no money

shudder milk shake [+ udder]

shudderm flabby skin

shuddrug medication taken to control nerves

shufflee to quietly get away [shuffle + flee]

shuff-puff to fidget due to boredom

shush comfortable shoes

shusher to move your shadows [shh + usher]

shut box to cover as many as possible [insp. *the game 'Shut the Box', where each player aims to cover as many of the boxes as possible*]

shuttlecock to launch a weapon onto a man's private area

shuttlecook re-heated food [shuttlecock + cook]

shydrogen of low water levels

si sig-nature

siamese cat with short hair

si cen sixteenth century

SICK since I couldn't kiss

sick bucket an awesome place | a safe house

sick-feet to be sick on someone's feet

sick-foot to be sick on someone's foot

sick-footage to record someone being sick

sickpes a little sick

siddle suds engear a graveyoda little puddles of oil slither out of the sky and fall onto old stones to make the stones 'new-age'

side cart a portion of chips

sidentical identical sides

sidentification to not give full identification [+ side]

side-sup to have food at the side of the mouth

sievage the act of sieving

sieve soup (in the evening)

sieventh house a soup kitchen [sieve + seventh house]

sievere too much water gone out | to lose too much water [severe + sieve]

sieze the wrong size

sig to look down[+ sigh]

sigh witness an eye witness who holds back or tries not to get too involved

sighre a burning silence [sire + sigh + fire]

signdrome signs of a syndrome

signite ignite by signature

signull no signal, e.g. there was signull so I waited until there was signal

silen siren a silent siren

silfir to often divide [insp. the silver fir tree]

silgull white and silver [insp. a silver gull is white and silver]

sill ill with grey coloured skin

sillegal silly and illegal | for it to be silly that something is illegal

sillo to be missing out because you have been silly, therefore you sit on the side only able to watch

sillord the person who watches TV every day

silvage to make shiny again [silver + salvage]

silver jaws sharp teeth, as sharp as knifes

silver jews silver jewels

silver shoes cyber

silvert to clean in a circular motion

sim beauty

simcard a beautiful message | a beautiful picture | a warm greeting

simful beautiful

simile slimey

simminet to take away beauty from the water without reason (e.g. fishing is simminet) [+ imminent]

simmet simmer signs of dimentia

simolar to like to get your teeth into similar things [similar + molar]

simon's legs long legs | longevity

simplifirst to have the simplified version first

simplist a simple list | basic writing

simplistic cheap plastic

sin bin to curse

sin binge to sin bin a lot

sinc a leaking drip-drabbing tap [+ synch]

sinch a tap in constant use [sync + sink]

sinclination a sinning inclination

sinclude devilish inclusion | the small print on 'terms and conditions'

sinear when the linear sins

sinform to inform sin

singapore to live for singing

singe a song which delivers warmth

single-finded dedicated to focusing on one part only

singulaugh a single laugh

singultusk to have tooth ache in only one tooth [single + tusk]

sininja right on, i'm on it [Na: sìn: on, onto] [+ ninja]

sinistair a sinister level | dangerous stairs

sinput a dark input

sipi a moist condition [insp the sitka spruce tree]

SIPMO she is pissing me off

sippetite a small piece [sippet + petite]

sip-sip soup

sirendipity to have fortunately witnessed a crime [serendipity + siren]

sirsh without men [sir + shh]

sir'tain certain sir

SIS sink(ing) in sand

sishy a shy sissy

sist abyss an annoying sibling

SIT see it through

sitalic for there always to be an emphasis [italic + sit]

S itch an itch S of the back

sittack to squash someone by sitting on them [+ attack]

sitting produck
pharmaceutical
medicines [sitting duck
+ product]

situate cast

SITUATION
suddenly it told us all
to ignite or not

situation castle

situste shu caught
off guard [situate +
shun]

six a new encounter |
a new entry [insp. *the
game 'Ludo'*]

**six minutes past
gateau to de tour**
fifty four minutes to ta
pluto de toe or

**six minutes to
hotter toe in om a
mum** fifty four
minutes past motor
hum

**sixteen minutes
past mackintosh**
forty four minutes to
bish-bosh

**sixteen minutes to
ush moo, shagged
out** forty four minutes
past mushroom rag out

six-pack a pack of
six crisps

sixteeth six teeth

size mattress the
size of the bed matters
(there are two of us
now, you can't order a
single)

sizzabolt to burn
[bolt + sizzle]

sizzled ro-yal [insp.
roy]

sizzlion a burning
body

skate slope to slope
straight away

skaterpillar a caterpillar on a leaf

sketchen a kitchen design sketched out

sketimin an unneeded vitamin [+ skeleton]

skewscumber to sabotage a **scum**

ski schi to contemplate divorce [insp. **schi**]

skill skull

skindred skin of kin(dred)

sking a master of skiing [+ king]

skint squints cheap prescribed glasses

skintography low cost photography

skinvest flesh (in the invest is the skinvest)

skirt to hurt

skirt and shirt to be in lots of pain [**skirt** + **shirt**]

skirtency at the edge of certainty

skit something flying in the sky [+ kite]

skitten a young person who is afraid or jumpy [kitten + jitter]

skittle a losing team

skodapill to sleep in the car [*Skoda* + pillow]

skoff a lot of skiing

skram no marks | bad marks | 'make a run' [+ marks]

skull skill

skullege dead knowledge

skullt obsessed with learning [+ cult]

sky blue and white | a canvas

skyboard a plane in the sky

skyence science in the clouds, e.g. animal experimentation is not science, it's skyence – only a vivisectors dream

skyte to go flying in the air when skiing | to ski off a hill

SLAB stop looking at boys

slab stone cold

slabatory a work place where animal testing takes place [+ **slab**]

slabia a hard labia, one that has been used a lot [+ slab]

slab-slaw cement

slacks matching socks

slacktate the slacking of lactation | to not give your all [+ lactate]

sladders slanted ladders | damaged ladders

SLAG stop looking at girls

slam bid to have enough points [insp. *the game 'Contract Bridge'*]

SLAM slop looking at men

slamb a lamb that is born in spring and dies due to the cold weather

slamention to slam a mentioning

slammanusage to have damaged the **manusage**

slamp a light which shines too bright [+ slam]

slang to sing a song in a different tone

slanterns slanted lanterns | lights on a slant

slanticipation to offer hope [slant + anticipation]

slap jack [insp. *the game 'Slapjack'*]

slape to come round from the **slope**

slapjack speed of hand | quickness of the eye [insp. *the game 'Slapjack'*]

slapparatus weapons [slap + apparatus]

slappendix a very ill appendix [oppo. **happendix**]

slappit-hen to hit someone over the head

slate a cold room

slather to be on the under someone's control | to be a puppet [slave + slither]

slaughter massacre

slaughto the pollution caused by automobiles [slaughter + auto]

slavage disheartening [savage + slave]

slava lava a love od being dominated | to love being a slave

SLAW stop looking at women

slaw born the beginning of **slaw burn**

slaw burn a building up of anger

slayperson a slave

sleak a slight streak

sleaves leaves swept away by the wind [slave + leave]

sledder-hedge to walk on top of hedges [see **slider-hedge**]

sledge to slip off the edge

sleepish to talk in your sleep

sleeve to leave

sleigh scale | a slow death

sleigh'n'slave a horse and cart

slengro beyond the body [insp. *the pronotum of the slender groundhopper usually reaches well beyond the end of the body*]

sleptember to fall asleep up a tree [slept + September]

slicks odd socks

slider-hedge to walk through hedges [insp. **sledderhedge**]

slide light a sun ray

slife a slice of life

slime butter

slime dime filthy money

slinguist to speak more than one language in a conversation

slink a corrupted link [+ links]

slinki a slow transfer

slip the quick sleep where your eyes closed when you **slope**

slipa to kiss with tongues [+ lips]

slipper to slot

slip-pad a place with very little security [oppo. **zip pad**]

slipped-disk a computer problem

slipperch a shoe rack

slippet to lose a piece [slip + sippet]

slit a quick salute

slither to rattle

slithsnap to multi-task

slitter to score open an envelope

slittle that's a little

slob long hair [insp. *the sloe bug has a coating of long hairs unlike the similar bugs*]

slobanon to feel slobbish | to lack niutrients [+ banana]

slobnoxious an obnoxious slob

sloff to climb a cliff against the clock

slood to slide down the stairs on your bottom

sloot a pro-longed goodbye [slow + salute]

slop a shop that is not doing well

slope when the head drops off to sleep when sitting upright or even standing upright

slopes pets [+ step]

slo-pe to hope to sleep

sloph a shop that doesn't promote itself to get customers | a business that loses out due to a lack of 'go' [+ sloth]

sloppo hoppo a big sloppy opportunity

sloppy suit an old 'washed up' suit

slopticle when glasses slide down the nose [slop + optical]

slot that's a lot

sloth a cloth that refuses to pick up dirt

sloti to slip

slot let to slip a letter underneath a door

slots of love depressing love | a violent relationship [slot + lots of love]

slotted spoon to let things slip

slottery the lottery of (fruit) slot machines

sloud so loud

sloud in eare so loud in here (the ear)

slouse to lack self confidence [slouch + louse]

slovakia a vacuum that miserably works, only sucking up the bits it wants to

slow-blow to be shot and then slowly die

slow-hard a slow talking person [+ blowhard]

slowing the process of eating more than supposed to

slowish a little slow(er)

slowkey to wait a long time for marriage when engaged

slowosh very slow

slowvador to slowly become surreal | to slowly graduate into distortion

slucket luck sick in the bucket, tough luck but suck it, you'll get well again

sluggy sticky and luggy

slum berry squashed

slung old (English) slang

slungest to talk in **slung** [+ gest]

slup to mop and leave lots of water on the floor

slur roll

slurdimen falling rocks [**slur** + sediment]

slurs and the sleeps drunken one-night stands [insp. *'the birds and the bees'*]

slycle a cycle of being sly

slyvador to slyly become surreal

sm smell

smack to tell someone off for smoking

smal a little smell

small pea | brief [insp. **beef**]

smallord the smallest person

smark a well-dressed stain [mark + smart]

smarvellous marvellously smart

smash to smoother ashes

smel merely small

smell-born a new smell appears [+ Melbourne]

smell-bourne a domain of smell [+ Melbourne]

smell bowel bad bowels | toilet problems

smellord the king or queen of smell (good or bad)

smil slime [*slime contains the same letters as smile, the same as smile contains the same letters as slime*] [+ smell]

smile gamma

smileage a time to smile

smiler a good similarity | a good match [smile + similar]

smilord person who is well known for smiling | one who is always smiling

smirfk a sickly looking smirk

smirnoff clear as

smockery fake smoke

smoke bung

smoke special methods of killing everything

smo a little smooch

smoo smooth

smoo smoo very smooth | gentle

smoral smothered moral(s)

smother to spread a disease (on toast)

smull a stuffy smell

smurf a blue tongue

smurf nerf police with guns [+ *Nerf* guns]

smurf snuff blue ink

smurfski dehydrated

smyth a common myth [insp. *'Smith' is a common surname*]

sn sense

snack to steal something by quickly snapping it, e.g. I would snack the sunset with the camera

snactor an occasional actor [+ snack]

snactress an occasional actress [+ snack]

snad less than twenty minutes [insp. *the duration of the game 'Snakes and Ladders'*]

snail @ | pattern

snail ale moving patterns

snails slowly growing nails

snailysis slow analysis [+ snail]

snake negative

snakeflie long neck

snakes a group of young women

snakes & ladders ten x ten measurement [insp. *the game 'Snakes and Ladders' where there are ten snakes and ten ladders present*]

snake-spit venom

snake-up to be woken up earlier than you wanted to be

snapposit when a photographer organises positions for people to stand for a photo [snap + posit(ion)]

snare loud snoring

snash to fall asleep in the bath and wake up nearly drowning or choking on water

snaz razz to snare a hole in the clothes when stretching, e.g. when you squat in tight trousers you may snaz razz

snaze a wet sneeze | for the nose to water

snear-cuh it's near a church, near a circle

snee-nario a scenario where you feel like you are going to sneeze but you don't in the end [sneeze + scenario]

snick to laugh [insp. **noo-snick**]

snickers shitty knickers

snigety to make fun of a fussy behaviour [snigger + persnickety]

sniggly a little niggly

snooker pockets targets

snookerb to improve you snooker-playing skills

snookerballs shiny big eyes

snoonario a scenario where you feel tired so you go to rest and you can't actually sleep because you find you're not tired [snooze + scenario] [insp. **sneenario**]

snose a cold nose [+ snow]

snoticeable clear as white [snow + noticeable]

snow so now

snow beard icecream around the mouth area

snow bow a festive present

snow tash white powder under the nose

s'now it's now

snowhere it all looks
the same | blank in all
directions

snownen so (every)
now and then

snowone not even
one

s'now o nev it's now
or never

snowsports sports
played in the snow

snuff curly pube hairs

snuz a coma [snooze
+ snuff]

**snuzzle tone nuzzle
so floafth open fuf**
to softly float upon the
fluff | to ride a cloud

so shawl to put on a
layer | to put on a
social front

so so bear to be
sober, but fuzzy

soap soprano

soaperate to lathe to
hands

soapi animal sweat

soap on a rope
saved from a tricky
situation

soap opera to lathe
the body

soaps hard to get to
grips with | hard to get
hold of

SOB suppression of
botany

sobanon to be
without bananas [+ sob]

sobitat the habitat of
despair

sobra a **bra** where
most people are sober

sobrass to freshen up after a night of drinking

SOCKET speed of car kills every torso

SOC state of confusion

socatoah when a toe sticks out of the sock (due to a hole)

SOCK since others couldn't kiss [see **SICK**]

sock suck

socki to shock

sock my balls cover my balls, they are freezing and it sucks

sockroach a sock containing huge amounts of bacteria, so much that it is possible the sock may just crawl off [+ cockroach]

sock soot the bits that come off a sock

onto the feet when the feet get a bit sweaty [*usually happens with black socks*]

sockport sock fetish [insp. *the Stockport sock man*]

sockput to be shot in the foot

SOD sense of direction

SODA stay over, dance about, e.g. won't you come SODA (with me)?

soda gossip

soda rake to gather phlegm from drinking fizzy drinks

sodabreed to stir gossip

sodarape to drink all of the fizzy drinks

sodasoma an unhealthy body

soderm soft skin

sodrome running after both

sof soft

sofa pockets of what the sofa collects from other pockets

sofa-duck to pretend to not be in when somebody comes round

sofa-suck to know someone is sofaducking when you visit them [see **sofa-duck**]

soferrous soft metal

sofflé sweet and soft

soft seal

softball an easy game | a basic activity

soft ball only a little hit

soft cell easy prison living

soggy-blog a blog which lacks interest

soil so I will | so I'll

soil oil natural oils

SOL speed of light

SOLAR seed of light at rear

solar punel a warm and witty energy [+ solar panel]

solari a colourful and vibrant sari [solar + sari]

solar-lar enlightment

soldiers spacemen

soldoor to join the army [soldier + door]

so-le as long as it's not a problem

solear to listen to vibrations [solar + ear + learn]

solepsy to seizure the feet | to shake the feet [Gk. lepsy: seizure]

solicite to advise on something cited

solid brock

solly visually [+ sol]

solostrum to go solo (in music)

solute to say bye only person [solo + salute]

solve solvereign

solvereign solve

som some

soma a changeable sum

somafai faithsoma

somathang to gnaw at the body

somefang to have something in the teeth | something sharp

someming something swimming | something in the water

someong something wrong

some thigh something to hold onto

somewing something flying | something in the air

somight something right

somsoma a somebody

sonic insomnia to play games instead of sleeping

sonic manic to play too many games

sonnet-drone to be knocked out by a fourteen year old

sonnut a book of sonnets

soot hut a dusty place | a choker

soot-called spoken with a sore throat

sootput a dark output

soperate to operate in soppy mode

sophia sphere

soprance to apply soprano [+ prance]

soprano soap

sorebit a sore subject

sornament a bright red burn that is in a noticible place [+ ornament]

sorridge a bowl of sorrow | a slop of sorrow

sorrowgin a sad beginning [sorrow + origin]

SOS shoes on socks

SOS ROLL speed of sound, rolls on launder live

so-so-bra a half-arsed bra

SOSOF shoes on socks on feet

SOSOFOL shoes on socks on feet on legs

SOT strip or trot

soted soup of the day

sou haw still water [insp. *the southern hawker dragonfly breeds in still water*]

souche "such a douche"

souffray when a soufflé is badly made

soul lid to contain soul

soul lip to speak the truth

sou-led from deep within [+ soul]

soulepse a seizured soul [+ eclipse]

soulker a sulking body

soundwich a crunch sandwich

soup a round face

soup kitchen for christmas very helpful

soup spoon a gullible person

souperman the superman of soup

southern comfort the softness of pastel colours

south-specific to get to the bottom of

something [South Pacific + specific]

souvenir shop a memory of buying something

SOV state(s) of victoria [see **victoria**]

sow & barrow gardening

sowift soft and swift

sox to wear socks during sex | comfortable sex

soz roy

spa an empty space

space ayax

spacemen soldiers

space-stem a meteor shower

spaghetti to get close to one another [see **passen**]

spam-spams funny
junk mail [+ pom-poms]

spa-niche the niche
of hygiene

span sa-hara the
span of humour [*Span
Sahara is a place near
Morocco*]

spank panther to
flirt [see **pink panther**]

spanner a two way
tool
| a two way
relationship

spanner man a
handy man

spar mild [insp.
sparrasis]

sparassist to assist
physically

spare at plus

sparental people that
provide temporary
living for others |
temporary parents

sparevasive sparing
the pervasive

sparklore a
passionate story | a
house fire

sparrow a special
arrow | a private road

sparticipant(s)
always strong
participants

sparticle a strong
eyesight

S (past) one letter
past R, two letters past
Q, three letters past P,
four letters past O, five
letters past N, six
letters past M, seven
letters past L, eight
letters past K, nine
letters past J, ten
letters past I, eleven
letters past H, twelve
letters past G, thirteen
letters past F, fourteen
letters past E, fifteen
letters past D, sixteen
letters past C,

seventeen letters past B, eighteen letters past A, nineteen letters past Z, twenty letters past Y, twenty one letters past X, twenty two letters past W, twenty three letters past V, twenty four letters past U, twenty five letters past T

spatin to wash dishes in dirty water [L. patina: a dish] [+ spat]

spatlight an irritating strip light which jitters on and off

spat-put to put something in bad terms

spatula to wipe up spit

spatulant petulant | to make farting noises with the mouth

spay to scoop low | to dig deep in order to pay out [spade + pay]

speariod the time when spears and wooden shields were used in battle | the time of handmade weapons

spearoom the time in a kitchen when having a battle and using utensils, e.g. for a spearoom we normally use wooden spoons, knives and plates [insp. **spearoid**]

spearnick one whose pernickety hurts and starts becoming a pain [+ spear]

spec-tac when the eyes can't stop staring

spec tin a special or specified container

specifiction specific fiction

speciminute to take a moment out to think about equality and how another may suffer

spectacled a so-called vision

specture a specific image

speech impedal to strive to overcome a speech impediment [+ pedal]

speech-therapy the doorway to a speech experiment | to play out new speech

spefecies a specific species

spellution the pollution of misspelling

spelt many showers of pelting rains

spendex one who spends money on irrelevant items [+ spandex]

spendulum to always be shopping [+ dowse]

spentry money spent on food | money for grocery [spent + pantry]

spermatron a person who produces a lot of sperm (especially one who makes money from it)

spev sport event

sphere (a)round here

spice when a spy is found out

spice girls variables in spice [see **posh spice, scary spice, ginger spice, baby spice, sporty spice**]

spick to suck up long pasta

spick pockets pick targets

spictrum a hypnotizing picture | a fractal | the G-force visuals of Windows Media Player

spid to speed many ways [insp. spider legs]

spidear widow

spider to climb

spiderm flaky skin [spider + derm]

spiduh to lack knowledge in many ways

spie a spicy pie, e.g. a samosa is a type of spie

spike to twist what someone has said

spikey innovative comedy [insp. *Spike Milligan*]

spile to mess up an organized pile [+ spoil]

spilkrunch to pour liquid and for it to set to a solid

spill rag to spill something on the clothes

spinaboo a clothes dryer [insp. **roundaboo**]

spinata for the piñata object to spin around when it is hit

spinocchio a whole range of lies [spin + Pinocchio]

spinoza contrasts [insp. Spinoza's philosophy]

spintellect a clever way

spip in groups most of the time [*the spinifex pigeons spend much of their time in groups*]

spirally to watch a rally lap after lap after lap after lap after lap after lap until you forget which lap it is

spiratoish to feel sick when travelling [+ spiral]

spirect to spiral into many directions [+ direction]

spiris good eye sight [spirit + iris]

spirit-level order

spirot a bad spirit

spirritable evil [spirit + irritable]

spirt jump the game of seeing how far you can spit

spisustain hard to sustain [insp. *sissus: in prescriptions*]

spit a race between two people

spitch to degenerate into chaos

spitefire in fiery | in spite

spitfire to spit at each other

spit-ladle to pick up something on the fryer that is spitting

spitta bread wet bread

spitter spatter to bad mouth the bad weather

spitting fire in anger mode

spitulant when somebody spits whilst they are talking [+ petulant]

splace to work in different parts of the country every week

splack to whack on a heavy amount of sun lotion quickly [+ splash]

splain to accidentally spill something (e.g. coffee) over something important (e.g. a birth certificate) [stain + spill]

splant gasping for air [splash + pant]

splatinum to buy expensive goods | to splash out on the unnecessary without looking at price

splazzatory to go many ways

splendour the fun of working as a clerk

splenter plenty of stingers

splesh a special drink [+ splash]

split peas

split banana splat bonanza

split splash pea wet

split splat mushy pea

spliterate to read something in a different way [split + literate]

splolly a melted ice lolly [+ splash]

splurk to wait for too long [splurge + lurk]

spoc to speak in a distorted voice

spocker a distorted speaker [+ **spoc**]

spocosu spontaneously combustible substance

spoil rag to purposely spill something on someone's clothes

spoilitic to gategrash a political event

spook spack to spook someone | to fool someone into believing a place is haunted

spoon spool to bend a spoon (Uri Gellar style)

spoon-feed to add spoons to your cutlery drawer

sportrait a portrait of a sports person

sportray to portray sport

sports orange [insp. 'Tivial Pursuit' colour]

sporty party a party involving physical activities, e.g. climbing frame

sporty spice spices that enhance fitness levels

spotato a lazy teen [potato + spots]

spoten a group of tents pitched close to each other on a big piece of land [+ spot]

spotissim to pick out the best [L. potissimus: best of all] [+ spot]

spot-put to put something in good terms

spourt to pour something too fast and it spurts, going everywhere

spout to be tired of pouting

spradiste a hot shower

sprai spray paint | to read a whole book in one sitting

spraint a painting gone wrong [+ sprain]

sprait the breathing which occurs when sprinting [sprint + pant]

sprant to sprint and pant | losing breath

sprawl a long story

sprawlful always having a bad posture [sprawl + awful]

spray on sunshine a 'holy' shower | a solden shower

spread to vibrate

spread toast to spread good news

sprey sea prey

spri spring

spring fresh

sprin sprout to run on energy

spring to hop

spring spring to give good news by phone | the bearing of good news [oppo of **pring pring**]

sprinter a very fast printer

sp'rt the sport of spirit

spruce forsyth an entertaining evergreen tree [+ *Bruce Forsyth*]

spuddles deep puddles [+ spud]

spull to pull off a story [+ spell]

spumess the mess made by a foam fire extinguisher [+ spumescent]

spun spoon

spunnet a punnet of squashed fruit

spure pure energy [spurt + pure]

spurified so pure it makes you spew [+ purified]

spur-of-the-momint an unexpected freshness

spur-spun ready to speed off

spydear a nosey neighbour

spyse to try to identify the smell or taste of a spice

spy-stray to not have been looking hard enough

squabble scrabble to have words over words

squad room sardines, **pillchard** or pilchards in a tin

squalid to have sore eyes from hayfever

squalips dirty lips

squalord the owner of a squalid building

square bears care bears who only care about conventions

square root anything which is learnt from the television, e.g. a quote from a TV programme is a square root

squartered for sandwiches or cake to be cut into quarters

squash dilute

squashed diluted

squa shed an extremely cluttered shed

squashed tulips reeking | a bad spring [see **spring**]

squat to morph

squeak heart a kid at heart

squid room to be 'sleeping with the fishes' [squid + **squad room**]

squidgy crashberry

squirtle to squirt water at someone

squrec to stretch a square out from two sides so it becomes a rectangle

sqwarm when the heat melts, e.g. the sqwarm chocolate started to look unappetising, especially when it started to melt onto the floor like a puddle of dung [insp. sqworm]

sqwear to only wear the type of close everyone else is wearing [square + wear]

sqworm a squashed or squished worm

sqwuish an unlikely wish

sqwwinter to keep out the cold [squint + winter]

sr surreal

srow sorrow

ssob not a very good boss

sss three in a row [see **O's and X's**]

ssss four in a row [see **FIAR**]

stabacco a smokers cough

stabajo a job to kill

stabba yabba a voice which causes your head to ache

stabberwocky to stick a needle in someone

stabilize chic

stabilizer a walking stick

stacey stay, see

stackstick to stack food onto a stick, e.g. we would stackstick to make a fruit kebab

staffern a stiff pattern (with no curve)

stagado the night of a stag celebration [insp. henado]

stagnatal an idol birth | an unwanted birth [stagnate + natal]

stair lift to run up and down stairs | to constantly go up and down the stairs

stair lift steroid when a person with huge muscles finds it hard to walk up the stairs

stairoid the levels of steroids

stairs of despair never ending work

stake-away to order an anonymous dish from a take-away [+ stake]

stale an old style

stale away to stay away from anything rotten

stales grown out tales

stalkloss to lose track [+ stalkless]

stall leto to slip up |to make a mistake [+ stiletto]

staminute a moment of stamina [+ minute]

stammer hammer

stamping ground to try and control

(straighten out) **stumpy grounds**

stampoon stamp plus lampoon

stan to stand

stands sans

stanigathan Afghanistan

stank a stinking thanks

stankard a stinking public toilet [stank + tankard + standard]

stanza cancer for a poem to weaken towards the end

star-bucks the mass corporation of Starbucks

starc surprisingly sarcastic [+ stark]

starcasm the main irony [star + sarcasm]

starch same [insp. the sago palm tree]

starchi to stay in top position [+ starch]

starchoo choo a rise in the consumption of starchy foods

star-hive stars close together in a night sky

starine to stand and pee yourself [insp. **citrine**]

star key more options

starm to pretend you have a cold, a sore throat or bad eyesight so you can avoid having to talk or read [stutter + armour]

starray golden [star + array + ray]

star-room the part of a store-room where the valuable items are kept

stars in your eyes to have smoke in your eyes | caught up in cigarette smoke

star-stark a star of complete madness

star stir to pass on good news

star-tar a good headstart

startifice a made up introduction [start + artificial]

startle to open out the hand and fingers then to close, putting hand in punch posture

starvsoma a starving body

star wave "wish you were here"

stashue a delicate stash [statue + tissue]

statam to be stood still when everything around you is moving [*warning: statam may cause motion sickness*]

statant on all fours

statch an immediate stitch [+ stat]

statick-tock for time to stand-still | to put something on standby

statock a clock showing little or no change in time

statrack a motionless song | a dead path [static + track]

statsit to immidieately sit down, e.g. in the game 'Musical Chairs' you have to statsit in order to win [+ stat]

statwistic a twisted strategy

staxel stacks of gifts

staxi a long row of unoccupied taxis

staydium for there to always be something going on [stay + stadium]

STD save the day | since the day

steadhead one with a steady head

stealth is steelth jackie-channeling is a BT-free-spirit

steam when driving and unable to see properly because the sun is too bright

steamer a steam train

stear to make yourself cry [tear + steer]

stedders step ladders

steep a sleeved top

steeple people people up a mountain

steerio a change in tone [+ sterio]

steerish to slightly move [steer + ish]

steerjerker a pathetic joker | a sneaky driver, [+ tear jerker]

steerwhile to have currently been travelling

stelephone a strong telephone [+ steel]

stempa the growth of temper | towards anger

stemper stantrum when flowers insist on not growing

stemperature the temperature of soil

stemple the temple that is 'nature'

stemulation when a flower is stimulated | to stroke the skin with a flower or leaf

stephen every so often

step toe and son the traditional tactics of a group of bullies

stereotopical the stereotypical topic

sterry oid when a person takes steroids in order to cope with things [+starry eyed]

stewba a stew that is music to the ears [+ tuba]

stewdent to put off going to the dentist – to stew for a while

stewpig stupid

STI save the initial

stick hassle [see **joystick**]

stick-tock to be low on stock

sti(l)letto a bad ending [still + stiletto]

stick to your gums don't let the dentist take them out

stickle to poke a ticklish person

sticky hands hands with 'come' on

stide a steady tide

stiff little fingers fingers that can't move because they have been in the cold for too long

stiff riff a song without any 'oomph'

stiffler's mom a mom who has sexual activity with her sons friend

stiff shirt a tight shirt

stiff staff colleagues who you find hard to get on with

stiff-stoff stiff movement

stiff-stuff stuff that is unlikely to change

stiletto a house which has been on the market for a while and has had no interest [still + 'to let']

still high heeled shoes [see **anime**]

stilt height [oppo. **stunt**]

stimolar to give a love bite [stimuli + molar]

stimuesli the energy gained from eating muesli [+ stimuli]

stimulinger to linger in the stimuli

stimulled wine to mull in the stimulus

stin to stand in a crowd

stire to become tired of restraint [stir + tire]

stirish a little stir

stirmoil a chaotic stir | an electonic whisk on full-power and out of control [+ turmoil]

stirosh a big stir

stissue a sticky issue

stitch-tits breast surgery gone wrong

S (to) one letter to T, two letters to U, three letters to V, four letters to W, five letters to X, six letters to Y, seven letters to Z, eight letters to A, nine letters to B, ten letters to C, eleven letters to D, twelve letters to E, thirteen

letters to F, fourteen
letters to G, fifteen
letters to H, sixteen
letters to I, seventeen
letters to J, eighteen
letters to K, nineteen
letters to L, twenty
letters to M, twenty one
letters to N, twenty two
letters to O, twenty
three letters to P,
twenty four letters to Q,
twenty five letters to R

stobill a stable
amount

stobtub a postbox

stockhausen
motivational music |
music which motivates
you

stock-king-kong a
large delivery

stockonomy a pile of
damaged stock [+
economy]

stockport a large
serving of port

stodge to stand for a
long time

stods flour and yellow
maize foods [+ stodge]

stomacho a muscly
stomach [+ macho]

stomaga the contents
of the stomach [Spa.
estomago: stomach] [+
magazine

stomata for the gas to
go off and on, e.g trying
to hob-cook on a gas
cooker

stommage to cover
the stomach

s-tone a dead tone [+
stone]

stool both chair and
table

stop ex

stopcock a broken
stopwatch

stopdock for a tail to stop wagging | when a clock stops working | when a pendulum stops swinging

stopingpong to keep on stopping | to constantly stop

storage pockets

storare a rare story, one that is rarely ever told

store-matron to look after someone's possessions

storkloss to not grow any more

storm-stalk to heavily analyse [+ stalk]

storpid stupidly sluggish

stourport a large serving of stout [see **stockport**]

stout still out

stoutskin thick-skinned

stove to stand still and not move

stowe to put away the towels [+ stow]

sto-xic to feel dead | to feel empty [stoic + toxic]

strack a dish that falls on the floor (and strays off track)

stracky a shoddy sock [tacky + strike]

straightosphere no such thing

stram to quickly organize into sections [strum + ram]

strang string along the strange

strap a bond

straphinger a door coming off its hinges [+ strap hanger]

strapple having no gravity

strathedge when a plan gets put on hold [strategy + edge]

stratomato an area containing lots of red objects [stratum + tomato]

strat-tee-shirt-gig to consider getting a souvenir

stratummy bug bed bugs

strawbeer to drink beer with a straw | a young person

strawberry beer to seem friendly

strawberry laces velcro shoes

strawgut a gut full of strawberries

stray stride

straytion to migrate the station [+ stray]

streeld a curved road [+ yield]

streem a flooded street [+ stream]

strefi a street fight

stresstimony to stress a testimony

stretchameet to greet somebody with a hug

stricks tricks which get you into sticky situations

stricky to hit a problem [struck + tricky]

stride a stimulating ride

strike to blow all the candles out

strippers stripes

strip-toe to take off shoes and the socks in an enticing way

strip-win a change in volume [insp. *the stripe-winged grasshopper's song volume rises and falls*]

stritch to try and stretch out stitching to save time

strive five to six

striver a river with strong flow [oppo. **shriver**]

stri-win ripe orange(s) [insp. *the stripe-winged grasshopper's abdomen is orange only when mature*]

strobe all lit up | pure

strobee a swimming towel [the strokes + robe]

strobe flash to experience purity

stroke to light all of the candles [see **strike**]

strokes a swimming baths

strolletto to stroll around in stilettos

stromp impassionate activities | aggressive passion

strongue a strong accent

stroop to be hit with a strap or a belt on the top of the back [+ stoop]

strop to start taking the top off

strop clause a strop from an agreement is terminated

stropes the lane dividers at the strokes

stropi in groups of five

stropponent a stroppy opponent

strotch to smear | to spread a blotch [+ stretch]

struct a strict structure | many rules

strug to stop shrugging | to start to understand [+ struggle]

strumach when the stomach makes noises because it is hungry [+ strum]

strumble to waste time | to mess about

strum-bum to scratch the bum with the fingers

strumina the stamina of strumming

strumolar to wash the teeth with a rhythm [strum + molar] [insp. **strum-bum**]

strum-tum to rub the stomach

strye sleeping on hay [+ straw]

stub gad

stub stain a carpet stain

stub'n' born always remaining

stubbelt to fit carpet

stubble carpet

stubble bubble chewing gum (stuck) on the carpet

stundard a standard pain [+ stun] [see **stundead**]

stuffingers chubby
fingers | clammy hands

stuffspring over-
weight children

stummber to stumble
into summer

stummer hummer

stumpy grounds
naturally up and down

stum stun almost
there [Na. stum: almost]

stun to stand in
surprise | stone

stundead a deadly
pain [insp. **stundard**]

stung badly sung

stunt short [oppo.
stilt]

stupid stewpig

sty-dye a colourful
mess

styli solitary [insp. *the
flower of the sweet gum
tree is solitary*]

styload to build up a
style [+ stylo]

stylone a low-key
style

sty mess

sty hones an honest
mess

su su 'shut up, right
now'

subdusa to overcome
more than one
[medusa + subdue]

subi a summer bird,
e.g. a seagull [oppo.
wibi]

subi wiki summer
bird facts

sublemonal a hidden
bitterness [lemon +
subliminal]

subliminade hidden ingredients [+ subliminal]

sublimbo a series of subliminal messages [sublime + limbo]

sublimited a limited sublime

substitoot to substitute a toot | to alternate a greeting

subsystem a system to manage life

subtr action the action of having or giving less

subtract the necessaries | the free livings | less expensive

succault successfault a wise mistake [success + fault]

succomb-over to run through an alley [succumb + comb-over]

succrumb to give away a little | to give a hint [succumb + crumb] suchin – such situation

suchkin such a 'suck' situation

suck hoover | sock | tongue

suck book to steal someone elses words | to pretend a quote is your own

suckering for a single parent to raise a handful of children

sucket a socket that does not work

suck faces to powerfully kiss with tongues

suckill to over hoover | to over suck

suckin a 'suck' situation

suckle hoover a little

suck-like not similar [oppo. **such-like**]

suckrolose a fly feeding on sugar

suck sock to gag

sucrew to suck in tight [+ screw]

suction when something is boring

sud fudge to suddenly become stuck

sudan a sudden, e.g. all of sudan

sudden a dead tree

suddenly many dead trees [+ **sudden**]

sudder suddenly sinful

suffishcate to take something out of its place

suffixcate suffocate with suffix use

suffocat a featherstuffed pillow

sugar a weight-gainer

suggesture to hint at by body movement

sul-de-sac to be stuck in a gro(o)ve of sulk [+ cul-de-sac]

sulinen to spend a lot of time in the bedroom linen plus [Na. sulìn: be busy] [+ linen]

sum summer

sumblime to have a faint lime taste, colour or smell [+ sublime]

sumbrell to put off calculating [sum + umbrella]

sumbrella an umbrella used in the summer | an umbrella used to keep in the shade

sumbrero a flexible sum [+ sombrero]

summer to relax

summitre a highpaid wage [summit + mitre]

summonochrome to take away colour

sun yellow and orange

sunburst plenty of sun | lots of warmth

sunbust no sun | without warmth

sund under the sun

sunder thunderous sun

sunflower patch an ear containing earwax

sunflower said a saying by Vangogh [+ *Simon Said*]

sungurn when you eat something too hot and you move it around in the mouth to try and cool it down [sunburn + gurn]

sunion sweated onion

sunse sunset [see **suri**]

sun slit to find happiness in self-harming

sunable brightly unable to [insp. **sunlike**]

sunback a sunburnt back

sunblunt without sun

sunburst with sun

sunbust without sun

sunstitch to black out

sunday buest
Sunday I was [Wel.
bues I: 'I was') [+
sunday best (clothes)]

sunflower to dance in
the sunny weather

sung to add [oppo.
gnus]

sung hun one who is
a good adder-upper [Na.
sung: add] [+ add]

sung hung to add no
more | to stop adding
(up) [Na. sung: add] [+
add]

sunga toga a long
dress (worn by both
men and women) [Na.
sung: add] [+ add] [+
toga]

sunglaze the glaze of
the sun | for heat to
melt an object

sungun to add up on
a calculator [Na. sung:
add] [+ add] [see **sung
hun**]

suniform a costume
[sun + uniform]

sunlike unlike in a
good way

sunseat a deck-chair

sunser when shops
close on a Sunday |
Sunday service

sunshi a yellow
balloon

sunsports sports
played in the sun

suo local a local of
the place [L. suoloco: in
one's own or rightful
place]

suo locust a local
stuck in the place they
come from [L. suoloco:
in one's own or rightful
place]

sup-chin to have food
on the chin

supear a curvy body

supera ice bundant
'the icing on the cake'
[superabundant + iced
bun]

superdrug not tested
on animals

super-market cheap
to only buy the
cheapest products

super-market chic
to only buy labeled
products

suposession to
pretend to have
something, e.g. she
would suposession
fame and you would
suposession a session
on algebra [possession
+ suppose]

suppare spare supper

suppart to partly
support

supplesit supposedly
pleasant

suppocket to check
the pockets [+ suppose]

suppodium to
wonder whether to
move the foot or not
[suppose + podium]

supprim supprisingly
formal [+ prim]

supshy a person who
doesn't like to eat in
front of people [supper
+ shy]

surclude to
permanently preclude

sure-gery therapy [+
surgery]

surenought definitely
never

surfage to look over
the surface [+ surf]

surferris to run
around in circles until
you feel dizzy [surf +
ferris]

surgerry a life support machine

surgery sure Gerry

suri sunrise [see **sunse**]

surpassion beyond passion [+ surpass]

surpraise unexpected praise [+ surprise]

surprice to find money [surprise + price]

surprism exciting colours [surprise + prism]

surrend to come to a corner

surround to come into the middle

sur-round a definite rounder

surveilense the allseeing eye [surveillance + lense]

survilence a vile sighting caught (on surveillance)

survivital vital for survival

sushicidal death from seafood

SW some way | South West

SW itch an itch SW of the back

swamp when a drink curdles

swamp socks unwashed socks

swamp thangs smelly teeth | unbrushed teeth

swamp thongs smelly or/and unwashed knickers

swamp whimp one who is afraid of dirt

swamp a mind of its own

swan twenty five thousand [insp. *a swan may have as many as twenty five thousand feathers*]

swana white with a little bit of orange | mostly cloudy with a chance of sunshine

swano stodge [*swans are fed bread*]

swander to float around with the head up in space

swansea swans in the sea

swanswoo(p) a speedy transaction

swatch a candy watch

swavvy a savvy surfer [+ wave]

sway to speak about your emotions

swe'dish a sweet dish | a pudding

swear sun wear | swim wear

sweat a sticky sweet

sweat lettuce lettuce which is left out in the heat for longer than it should be

sweats and sins a feeling of guilt

swee a slow wee | a long wee

sweegut a gut full of sweets

sweep to go into a dream state when sleeping

sweet cake

sweet sweep to put pieces of cake into serviettes

sweet shop sweat shop

sweet tray cake tray

sweetener the death of rats [insp. *Splenda*]

sweetrot to get rotten teeth from eating too many sweets and sugars

sweets bones

swelding build the setback of building work due to extra costs

swell cream from a cow

swell wagon an icecream van [insp. **swell**]

swen old news [+ news]

swep a week which goes by like a day [+ sweep]

swet a sugary drink [sweet + wet]

swete a wet summer | hot rain [Fre. ete: summer]

swillow to swallow what was swilled

swim ming to be feeling rough | to be feeling sea-sick

swim mong to be feeling monged | not in top condition

swimmingly fish-gist

swineger to binge [swinger + swine]

swing for the fingers to swell

swip to be banned from something

swipe to sweep fast

swir twist

swir head a twisted head

swir heard to twist something because you misheard

swirbodied having a flexible body

swird to twist words

swird herd a group of people who twist words

swivelvet to enjoy being swiveled around

sword to wave a wand or stick

s-word an evil word

swosh a wish that never came true

swoshing moving freely from side to side

swy to say something in a questionable way

sylpi one of three | poor [insp. the scots pine tree]

symbalti the status of the spice, when very hot symbolises a strong person and mild is a weak person who won't try and can't handle more spice

symbol object

symbowl the chosen object [+ **symbol**]

symbowling talking in symbols [insp. **symbowl**]

symmode a mode of symmetrical

sympodium the podium at a symposium

symposer a poser at a symposium

synchronical a record of events that happened at the same time

syncringe for a sound to resonate inside you [sync + syringe]

syndicope to change groups [syndicate + syncope]

synthesise new order

sy-rho diamond-shaped [insp. *the syromastes rhombeus bug is recognised by its diamond-shaped abdomen*]

syria serious

sys system

sys anal the whole bum

sys analys systems analysis

sys eng systems engineering

sysmic systematic

system sys

system of a down for a system to go down

system of an up for a system to go up [insp. system of a down]

systemath a logical amount [systematic + math]

systerm a systematic term

Tt

T *pic* pylon | a headless cross | gallows | double street light

TA talking about

ta tao

ta lud to be thankful for having parents | nto be thankful for being looked after [+ adult]

tabashco a group of people who love hot spices [tabasco + co.]
tab-back to keep back | to keep away

tab-boo a feared bill | a worrying amount

table to sit around

tablet a small table

table-top hair that has been flattened on the top by a hat

tabloid to share conversations around the table

tabsolute one who lives off medication and prescriptions | the pharmacy world

tadder to use the smallest amount of tissue when on the toilet [oppo. **wadder**]

tagore to refuse a kinghood [insp. *Rabindranath Tagore refused a knighthood*]

taicheese non-animal cheese [+ tai chi]

tail a pull cord

tailer to carry on

tail tile to carry on through the night

tail-chase to follow someone

tailfilms *Carry On* films

take a chance of mean to say it like you mean it, and you mean it to be 'mean' [insp. *Abba*]

take-a-feet to ask someone to stand back

take-a-rake to not take a break, but to take a rake and get working

talc to walk barefoot outside

talentil a growing talent [+ lentil]

tale-talent to make up a talent | to lie about a skill

talipot a posh teapot [+ "tali-ho"]

talk to yip

tall tool

tall-tell told many times

TAM talking about my (generation)

tame a tape measure

TAN they are nice

tang when shirt is not tucked in [+ hang]

tan nic acid ta Nick ai said

tanden a place for two people, e.g. a hotel room which has only one double bed [insp. **tandigs**]

tandev a car that only seats two people [insp. **tandigs**] [+ rev]

tandigs clown pants which fit two people [+ tandem]

tandin dinner for two [insp. **tandigs**]

tandolin when two people dine and there is a serenade [**tandin** + mandolin]

tanfold tan lines

tangateau a sweet taste [tongue + gateau]

tangenitial to go off tangent to the genitals

tangleble uncapable of being touched without feeling a discomfort [tangle + tangible]

tangle neckle for hair to get tangled up in a necklace

tanglow the colour of the night dominated by orange street lights

tanguage the language of touch

tangwage to savour money

tank to thank

tankage the process of writing a tanka

tannag the nag brought on from too much tanning, causing irritating sun burn

tanout lights out [*Tanout is a place in Nigeria*]

tantrara the sound made when being massaged [tantara + tantra]

tanx a taxi rank

tao all things happen and exist

taoday tao today

tap latex

tapast a healthy past [+ tapas]

tapas typos to eat your lunch at the computer

tap-dance to turn on the taps and change the strength of output

tapduns to try and wake up the brain

tape a class A type

t ape to play on being cheeky [ape + tape]

tape duck domesticated ducks who are fed bread [tape deck + duck]

taperm to always have one end shorter or thinner than the other | for the two sides to always be different

tapioca to tap then poke

tapisdance to make a tapis | the process of making a tapic

tapisho to hang up a tapis

tapistol to stick down | to staple down a tapis

tappitit to hit someone in the breast area

tapple-ware tapping on surfaces

tap poe poetry made to the beat of a tapping (usually by the fingers or feet)

tapsoda one who does not waste | to not waste

tapsody to impro and work with what is already there [rhapsody + **tapsoda**]

targets snooker pockets

tar good manners

taric acid the passing on of good manners [+ **tar**]

taro turn around

tart when curtains are too short for the window

tartar thank you very much [+ **tar**]

tartar, cream of the good manners of *please and thank you*

tart break to finish eating jam-tarts

tarticle the 'page three' article in The Sun newspaper

taser a bad taste

tasko a team task

tati to tattoo yourself

tattoo a permanent transfer

tawcoc to be found in trees [insp. *the tawny cockroach is often found in trees*]

taxan a lot of tax [Na. txan: much]

taxicity a city revolving around taxi's taxis | the route a taxi takes

TB thunderbird | too basic | to be

TBC to be cruel

TBF to be free

TBT two by two

tc touch

TCP 'take care' parents

TCTH too cold to handle [oppo to **THTH**]

te liberate ourselves from convention

te cen tenth century

tea-bags dark tired eyes

tea-cap to cover a hot drink with the hand

tea-cope job a long job but can be achieved with copious amounts of tea

teadious a person who will not drink anything else other than tea

team group to rain off and on and off and on and off and on and off and so forth

tear tier

tear gadget the weapon of tears to get your own way

tearminate to stop crying [+ terminate]

tearmo to cry for a moment

teartilla to cry from mexican spices

tearwhile to cry for a while

teaspun a bit shook up [teaspoon + spun]

teat a sugary tea [*in rhyme with sweet*]

techniche a performance role [+ technique]

techno hero [insp. Technology]

technohead fast energy | a quick impulse

technology heroin

technote a chaotic note | a note which is almost unreadable

ted to talk someone into something | to make it sound innocent

ted to debt to all of a sudden have money problems | to have independence when you are used to being dependent

teddie to make rough [+ die]

tedditory it is mandatory to have a teddy

teddy current a massive teddy wrapped up or in a box [+ eddy current]

teddy talk light or soft talk

tee junction a time when you take off your clothes, especially in a relationship for the first time [+ tee shirt]

teel to lounge around the house [Wel. tee: house] [+ 'l' for lounge]

tele com to skype chat

telejack when you have nobody to call | nobody to talk to

telemoo black and white TV

telepardy something which comes on tv that should not be seen by the other persons watching it, e.g. to avoid telepardy do not let your children watch television after nine o'clock

telepat to experiment in telepathy

telephant a largesized mobile phone [+ elephant]

teleport to ring up and order drink from an alcohol take-away

teleprick to predict or have a feeling someone will be a prick before you find out they actually are a prick

telethesis a sensitive thesis [+ telethesia]

teletubby a massive television screen

televise a stand or holder of a tv

tell to dob

tell-o-path to be able to talk someone into doing something

telly phish to pretend to be watching TV

tempast a violent past [+ tempest]

templant religious guidance [temple + template + plant]

tempriorise to plan to take it slow | to decide to keep back [prior + temporise]

tenacry to put the emotions on hold | to refrain from crying

ten minutes past mon peel paint fifty minutes to bon heel i ain't

ten minutes to aren't you a dresser in hare? fifty minutes past aunt is a hairdresser

ten penny court an unlevel tennis court | a tennis court in a poor state

tenatrance to keep hold | to be held in a trance

tenantwich to be a person living in Nantwich [+ tenant]

tenebriff a dark song [tenebrific + riff]

tennest to live in a word of tennis

tenniche a niche which goes back and forth

tennichez to string together

tennis balls healthy genitals

tennis ricket a wrong appliance | an unsuitable appliance | an unsuitable object

ten-pin bowl to knock something down

tense sack a tense stomach

tense sense to hold back [oppo. **tons sense**]

tensoma a tense body

tensor a spanner | a screwdriver

tent fest

tentickle a ticklish person who does not like being touched due to this [+ tenticle]

tent pin bowl to apply boundaries in a conversation [insp. *in tenpin bowling where the sides can be lifted up to prevent the ball from falling into the drain*]

tent pin bowling when you put the sides up when playing ten pin bowling | for something to have boundaries

tep when a pet goes missing

tepan anchor [insp. the screw-pine tree]

terror-ball to play into a game of bouncing off badness, e.g. getting involved with gun gangs and carrying out messenger deeds

terrorism heroinism

territorn to have lost power or grounds [territory + torn]
terrix territory

TESCO til every sun cries over

tesco take it because

tessen to travel somewhere new

te-tastol to give up sweet and chocolate in order to try and lose weight

te-tootal to not drink because you are looking after your voice [+ **toot**]

tetrarch the main room [*tetrarch also means 'a ruler of a fourth'*]

tetrarcher somebody who owns a quarter of something

tetris to get into a line

tetris scan a scan to see everything is in order or good shape
tex a short text, e.g. "yes"

tex ho seven to ten [insp. *seven to ten players in the game 'Texas Hold Em'*]

texaco to get in a taxi with a group

texas to get in a taxi on your own

texchange to exchange texts | to forward on a text or a contact number

textoid one who is always texting

text-shy to not like people looking at your handwriting | to dislike people looking at the computer screen whilst you are writing

texture a conversation by text messaging

teye to stop looking [Na. txey: halt]
th Thoreau

thank to tank

t-hank to cop

thanxious anxiously thankful

the ball's in your court it's up to you to have a good time [see **ball**]

the ball's in the court the words are there | the words are on the tip of the tongue, waiting to come out

the cloud room the space when or where dreams happen

the coasters people of the coast

the cribs the place in a hospital where babies are taken

the damn age the age off the damned damage, the damn age could be teenage-years or a mid-life crisis

the decimal the placement of hierarcy

the distillers the simplistic people

the futureheads people of the future

the hurls are alive! the act of puking to make yourself feel better | the act of doing bad to do good

thembray unborn people

the para rubber a
full latex suit [insp. the
para rubber tree]

the presets the
people who plan ahead

the red paintings
the expressions and
messages in a painting

the sky at night TV
between 1am to 5am
then hen to then lie
down

the streets the urban
world

the strokes forward
slashes in an internet
address | a swimming
baths

the world next door
the land of dreams and
fantasy

theatree the growth
of theatre

the microwave an
expensive stopwatch

themshelves people
who put themselves
down | people who put
themselves on shelves

therapest for therapy
to be hassle

therapeti little
therapy

therapie lots of
therapy

thermill to spread
around hot water in the
bath

thermocoup a
passionate couple

thermoon a bright red
face | a red balloon

thermouse a small
warm patch

thi cen thirteenth
century

thickups strong
hiccups

thig a tight and uncomfortable hug [see **thug**]

thighway long way to the thighs | a measurement of the thighs

thin-de-ano-shun to not let someone get any thinner [indian ocean + shun + thin + anatomy]

thindulge indulge on healthy food

think to cap

think-thigh to kick ass | to solve a problem

thips toned hips [see chips]

third eye the creative visions

thirdid to do on the third time

thirst & foremost to drink water before doing something, e.g. just woke up, or another, before bed

thirteen minutes past pastrial forty seven minutes to pantry go i'll

thirteen minutes to son's a mayor but a ruck forty seven minutes past mon stair truck
thirteeth three teeth

thirty eight minutes past chug twenty two minutes to chew ug(ly)

thirty eight minutes to new york before london twenty two minutes past ny-lon

thirty five minutes past mini skillet twenty five minutes to mine is a skill, is it?

thirty five minutes to es lumer an 'oh' twenty five minutes past slumbro

**thirty four minutes
past bottle** twenty
six minutes to boat tall

**thirty four minutes
to pie cut but kept
all** twenty six minutes
past picket kettle

**thirty minutes past
train thomas** thirty
minutes to rain in home
(mess)

**thirty minutes to
rain in home (mess)**
thirty minutes past
train thomas

**thirty nine minutes
past bucket lit**
twenty one minutes to
book tilt ket

**thirty nine minutes
to wa(te)r dr drib**
twenty one minutes
past wardrib

**thirty one minutes
past for lorn** twenty
nine minutes to four
lawn

**thirty one minutes
to meh oh apply lo
shun** twenty nine
minutes past eh motion

**thirty seven
minutes past bizz
quite** twenty three
minutes to a hibiscus
kite

**thirty seven
minutes to barry's
back** twenty three
minutes past berry
black

**thirty six minutes
past manda tore din
aire** twenty four
minutes to motor door
in the air

**thirty six minutes
to inch torch tran
ton** twenty four
minutes past tractort
con

**thirty three
minutes past plast
stair** twenty seven
minutes to past the lass
a stare

thirty three minutes to char hurt is huh twenty seven minutes past chart art is ch

thirty two minutes past haemorrhage twenty eight minutes to hey me more rage

thirty two minutes to hands sell his twenty eight minutes past hassle hiss

thistory the present and history

thomas the petrol cap [insp. *Thomas the Tank Engine*]

thomas the wank engine sexual foreplay on a train | a late train

thoreau wild | rudiment

thornament a valuable ornament that you are not allowed to touch

thrap to really get at a rash through the form of scratch

thread read thoroughly

three hundred and sixty all the way round

three minutes past crows spare crows fifty seven minutes to cows are sparrow

three minutes to fiver a ukulele ridden by a nun fifty seven minutes past funkel bike with an uncle on

threesome a group of three

threesum a three figure sum

three wees men three men wisely having a wee

threject for power to go out of something [throb + eject]

threshold how long you stay 'held' on the phone for when you get put on hold

thrice thai rice

thrick to keep holding on [+ think] [insp. thrink]

thrink to thoroughly think

thrihatch to give birth to triplets

thrips to have no shape [insp. *thrips are tiny winged or wingless black insects*]

thrispecs three-dimensional glasses

thro throat

throap to **thrap** with beat boxing thrown in | to rap to beat boxing [+ throat]

throast to throw something into the fire

throat thro

throbbat to hang upside down and the head to throb because the blood has gone to the head

throbject a vibrating object

throbs-born to feel the body pulsing in many places

throlace a poloneck | to cover the neck [**thro** + lace]

throttle hatch

throught thought through

throwboat when the boat is thrown around by choppy weather and rough seas

throwing cotton to share dreams

throwst see throast

throw-throat to be able to throw your voice

throw-throw-throw the boat to sink a boat

thrunder to run like thunder

thrust byte cyber passion | cyber flirting | to have feelings for someone you have only met on the internet and not face-to-face

THTH too hot to handle [oppo. **TCTH**]

thu most ambiguous

thug a tight hug [see **thig**]

thumb mature [insp. immature]

thumberella a cocktail stick used to shelter the thumb

thumb-print identification

thumb-suck immature

thunder-belt to loosen a belt after eating too much | the sound of a belt unfastening

thursday buest Thursday I was [insp. **sunday buest**]

thrustler a player [thrust + hustler]

thy unusual (of its kind) [insp. the doum palm tree]

ti time | in [see **tide**]

TIA talk in ale [see **tia maria**]

tia to take it | a plant pot

tia maria an evening of drunken conversations

tiara a crown of thorns

tiarantella a fairytale story [tiara + tell]

TIBET two is by ever two [see **TBT**]

TIC tongue-in-cheek

tictac to sacrifice in order to create opportunity [insp. *the tactics in the game 'Draughts'*]

tide in and out

TIE take it easy

tie a bowling pin

tie knot a corporate knot

tie una favourite aunt

tie uno favourite uncle [insp. **tie una**]

tier tear

ties'r'us a massive selection of ties for a business man | a very boring place for a child (who wants toys) [oppo. **toys'r'us**]

tightan to open a very tight jar [insp. Titan]

tightin a lid or top of a bottle or jar on too tight

tight jeans too uncomfortable

tiith wobbly teeth | a loose teeth [+ tit]

tik to be missing ingredients [+ kit]

tila time-lapse

tillymouth to wash the mouth out

timbir time of birth

TIME testify in my ego

time dime time means money

timeid timid time

time team numbers one to twelve

time-warp to manually delete email messages on hotmail

timidst fo feel sick from nerves [timid + midst]

timothy 'what time is it?'

timposs an impossible time

timpulse impulse of time

tims Z times two [see **Z**]

tin tin man knight in shining cleaner

tink to stick out the tongue

tinny a tin taste

tintimidate to intensely intimidate someone

tintro to give a bit of a twist to an introduction

tioth a wobbly tooth | a loose tooth [insp. **tiith**]

TIP tourist information point

tiposs an impossible target [insp. **timposs**]

tipsoda of good advice

tissley to be shy of blowing your nose in public space

tissue-whack to use a tissue until it is completely bunged out

TIT talk in tongue | tell in tale [see **TIA**]

titch sand between the toes [itch + tickle]

tit tit tit pretty please talk in tongue

tix enter [+ exit]

TL too long

tl tools

t'laf a flat laugh

TLC tea loves cake | too long coming

tloud too loud

tm to make

TO too obvious | tin opener

to lettuce to eat healthily

to morro climb around [+ morro]

to ode toad to kiss a toad

toad to add

toask to ask a question you have been wanting to ask for a long time [+ toast]

toasted worrye when something that worries you burns your insides and hardens

toaster one who celebrates

tobago a bag too big

tocsin a nuclear warning

todada today is dads | father's day [see **tomoda**]

todouche to do in a douche-like way

toebago to kick a bag

toedge feet that walk to the side [see **t-toetal**]

toegad to stub your toe

toene a distant sound [tone + toes]

toepick to pick something up with the toes

toe rag a towel to dry the feet

TOF tongue of fire
toffee tea and coffee

tog not got | tried to get [+ got]

toga to give something [+ yoga]

togaeau to stop eating cake or sweet foods to be able to fit into an piece of clothing [toga + gateau]

togo to walk off

toh-dye-tye lots done | done a lot

to-iat the outside... is a toilet

toidoh to realise the toilet cubicle contains no toilet tissue when you are in need

toiletiquette good bathroom/toilet manners [+ etiquette]

token yoyo a good balance

tolerate due

tom & jerry hide and seek

tomato to talk about something else other than that which is being spoke about [*the tomato is a fruit, not a vegetable*] [see **coco nut alliance**]

tombin for two people to be embarrassed at the same time [insp. **combin**]

tombourine to not want music any more | to not have music for a while | when a place plays the same (dead) music

tombtable a timetable of burials in a funeral service

tomoda a day tomorrow | mother's day [insp. **todada**]

tommy a tomato

ton not a lot [+ ton]

tone and tonly many tones

tong to pick coins up from a flat surface with two fingers

tonga tongue

tonglue two tongues tied together kissing

tongue a flappy pocket opening (like a shoe tongue)

tong-tune to experiment with making noises from the mouth

tongua to wear a dress that makes people drool | which brings lots of attention (tongues out) [+ toga]

tons sense to not hold anything back [oppo. tense sense]

tony only a ton

tooche to touch the teeth | to look at your teeth in a mirror [+ touché]

toofre too frequently

tool tall

t'ool to fall

t'oil to fail

tool iao heart to fall in and out of love [see **IAO**]

tool stool to fall off a stool

tools ba a fast goodbye [oppo. ab sloot]

toot to sing about | to let out a chirp

toot pinto to drink heavily and have no hangover

tooth god

tootha audio

toothcake 'god is sweet' [see **toothtooth**]

toothpaste an oral activity

toothaste to get something stuck inbetween the teeth

toothtooth 'god is god' [see **h'toot h'toot**]

tootier to sing on many levels | to have many tones

tootless to talk less | without positive talk

top hat a favourite hat

topal a favourite sweet [top + opal]

topaz to pass

topical forest of how a topic grows

topple ware to bottled up your feelings (in a tuppleware box) in order to keep going and then you are able to come back to them after [+ top]

torch scorch

torpid kid a child with no energy | a sluggish child [oppo. torso kid]

torquay a broken key [+ torn]

tortle slow torture [+ turtle]

torso kid a child with good energy |a child with good movement [oppo. torpid kid]

tortle slow torture [+ turtle]

tortoi between a yellowish brown to almost black colour [insp. *the tortoise bug ranges from yellowish brown to almost black*]

toshiba to have beer in the moustache

toshiva god is TV [*Toshiba* + Lord Shiva]

toss and tail to be uncomfortable in bed and to change sides of sleeping [+ top-and-tail]

tossung a kissing corner [Na. Tseng: place] [+ tongue]

toster a toaster which only toasts one side of the bread

tosu toxic substance

TOT train of thought | tomatoes on toast

totaxillarian to always use taxis

totot a short total

tots tv a childrens show | child's play

toucha the dance of touch

toughpaste something hard to get into | something difficult to understand

tourestrial overcrowded with tourists [+ terrestrial]

tourist shop time to wander

tourito to study a subject [tour + territory]

tourito dorito to study the cupboard to work out if it contains snacks (preferably nachos) [insp. **tourito**]

tourn travel sickness [tour + churn]

touwrist to move the hands [tourist + wrist]

towel bow for nothing to be coming [insp. **towel bowel**]

towel bowel a dry bowel | no output

towel soot bits of fluff from the towel onto the body when you are drying yourself

tow long truckers to tow and truck long hours for little money [+ 'so long suckers']

toxi city a toxic city

toys'r'us a massive selection of toys for children | a very boring place for a business man (who is looking for ties)

T (past) one letter past S, two letters past R, three letters past Q, four letters past P, five letters past O, six letters past N, seven letters past M, eight letters past L, nine letters past K, ten letters past J, eleven letters past I, twelve letters past H, thirteen letters past G, fourteen letters past F, fifteen letters past E, sixteen letters past D, seventeen letters past C, eighteen letters past B, nineteen letters past A, twenty letters past Z, twenty one letters past Y, twenty two letters past X, twenty three letters past W, twenty four letters past V, twenty five letters past U

tracey head one with a hangover [Gk. trachy: rough]

trackea to be out of breath when running round a track [+ trachea]

tractrivials comical drawings | comical writings [tractive + trivial]

trada a tragic happening | a tragic introduction [+ tada]

trade-discuss old news [trade-discount + discuss]

traffack the annoyance of being caught in traffic

traffic moon a lot to look at in the night's sky

traffork traffic all ways

trafforkrike being caught in traffic when you have to be somewhere in a hurry

trafi a fight on public transport or a fight to do with transport, e.g. a trafi on a train or trafi because of road rage

trague a vague traveller

trah la blah an expected conversation | to find the general conversations of 'how are you?', 'what you up to these days?', 'you working?' very boring [trah la la + blah]

trail & era a historical walk [trial + error]

trail oil water for to keep hydrated when walking

traimpse to walk heavily or tiredly around the streets/city centre [+ traipse]

train torrential rain

trake to try different cakes | to sample cakes

trale an ale trail | a pub crawl

tramatic deadly dramatic

tramble to nearly get runover by a tram [+ tremble]

trambli to trip over a tram track in the road

tramce the void of 'hours-long' train journeys [tram + trance]

tramp a ramp in a tram line

tram-tracks sprayed tan lines

tranc the patterns on tree bark [trunk + trance]

tranci a rancid trance

trancid rancid trance [*a new genre of music: chaotic, rotten sounding trance*]

trangle tangled in three places

transclothes clothes which can also be worn inside out

tran send to pass on key advice [+ transcend]

transerp having two curves [transept + serpent]

trans-fat an overcrowded train

transfire to change the colour of a fire | for the colour of a fire to change [+ transform]

transfor for a change | into change

transight to temporarily see [+ transitory]

transmits gloves which can be worn both inside out and outside in

transpis to get on the wrong train, bus or tram

transportrait a portrait of the face of transport

transprite to transfer into a sprite, goblin, fairy or elf

transpur to steal a car

transpy to 'peoplewatch' on public transport

trash rash a rash or mark on the skin from bad hygiene

traumatch a highlighted trauma [traumachy + match]

travelour a soft-easy going traveller [+ velour]

travelslime late bus transport

travel-suck boring travel | a long-lasting travel sweet

travelvet luxurious travel [+ velvet] [oppo. **travile**]

traverse poetic travel writing

travessel backpack(er)

tra-vest a drawn on vest

travile poor travel [oppo. **travelvet**]

travis to travel around an island

travobot a satellite navigator

travogue to travel in style

travolt travelling experience [+ volt]

travolve to change travel plans [+ evolve]

travulgar the transportation of animals for livestock [vulgar + travel]

tray bien a good tray | a healthy serving | a good-sized portion

tray mal bien a bad tray

tray-tire to be tired of serving

traytongue to offer yourself as a taster

tre gre a romantic way of saying 'regret'

tre hu treasure hunt

treasure juice

tre-at at the tree

treckage a walking path

tree god | to have constant or a lot of food and water

treeper a protector of trees [tree + trooper]

treest a row of trees [+ street]

tree talk wild talk | when the wind blows and the trees make a sound | the sound of trees swaying in the wind

treed to tred in a woods

treesome many trees | a group of trees

treeson to perform treason on trees

treffor a terribly over-priced amount

tremblend a dangerous mix [tremble + blend]

tremmer traj tremblimg with tragedy

trend ival

trender to take in a tre nd | to adopt a style [+ render]

trent the path to an entrance

tresh-trash treasured trash [ones *trash is another's treasure*]

trespassion the passion of trespassing the most private areas

trespiss private wild lands

tre-ut near the tree

treval to sit on a train seat that is travelling backwards [+ travel]

tri che an arrow | three points [see **chin check**]

tri gam yeasty smell [insp. tricholoma gambosim]

triaflan a trio of desserts [+ triathlon]

triangle fire

tribless to pray three times a day

trick ramble

trickster rambler

tricksuit expected attire [trick + tracksuit + suit]

trident to try out a new dentist

trifault too many layers [+ trifle]

trifle a person who eats many desserts

trightin to try and open a bottle or jar where the lid is on too tight

trigmarole to be in a long complicated procedure of being threatened

trigtor an allergy warning [+ trigger]

trim-bush a hair cut

trimena to cut your stamina down | to cut out an exercise

trippage a time of travelling

tripsoda adventurous tripsody an improvised trip where there are no set plans or directions | to saunter [rhapsody + trip + **tripsoda**]

tripull to pull three times

trisa short life [insp. the pawpaw tree]

trisco a contract is made [insp. the game 'Contract Bridge']

triv purse the five W's (who, what, when, where and why) [*the*

game 'Trivial Pursuit' is based on these questions]

trize to value someone for trying | to appreciate the effort [+ prize]

tro january the start of hard work | the beginning of a hard working period

trodder a baby tree

troff not the truth

trolur smoothlyrounded [insp. *the troilus luridus bug has smoothly-rounded shoulders*]

tropaz a shining group | a well achieving team [topaz + troop]

trophobia to have a phobia of any nutritious foods

troth tooth to eat out of religions hand | to feast from religion | full of religious signs

trotten rotten and treaded on

trouble red

troublesum more red

trough tough trouble

trough plough to work with depression| to work while depressed

trous ¾ trousers

trout to hang up trousers

trubacco to smoke a pipe [true + tobacco]

truck terribly yuck

true glue an honest connection

tru mate a trumpet it is true, your mate is indecisive

truffle a warty appearance

trunk a fat leg | a swelled body part

trunk cut heart broken

trunki to hold something up to the light, e.g. a 20 pound note to see if it is real [insp. *the job of the trunk: to hold the leaves up to the sun*]

trunkulate to put underwear on

t'rust to rust

trustament the testament of truth in a relationship | science

tryfle one who always tries something new

TS too short

TT too true

T (to) one letter to U, two letters to V, three letters to W, four letters to X, five letters to Y, six letters to Z, seven letters to A, eight letters to B, nine letters to C, ten letters to D, eleven letters to E, twelve letters to F, thirteen letters to G, fourteen letters to H, fifteen letters to I, sixteen letters to J, seventeen letters to K, eighteen letters to L, nineteen letters to M, twenty letters to N, twenty one letters to O, twenty two letters to P, twenty three letters to Q, twenty four letters to R, twenty five letters to S

t-toetal feet that walk straight on [see **toedge**]

t-totaxillarian to never use taxis

ttt three in a row [see **O's and X's**]

tttt four in a row [see **FIAR**]

t t t t t a train noise

tubacolosis the damaging of the voice [tuba + tuberculosis]

tubercoliseum the building up of tuberculosis

tuesday buest Tuesday I was [insp. **sunday buest**]

tuftpaste something to pull at

tug of wart a war with warts | to try and defeat warts

tu is it suits [+ suit]

tuli one for one [insp. *the tulip-tree: one seed with one wing*]

tulip a flowerey kiss

tunga a tongue piercing

tunis 'this is a tune'

tunisia 'what tune is that?'

tunt until

turbinary the maximum speed [turbo + binary]

turboi for a child to grow up fast [insp. **turbow**]

turbow to quickly make a bow | to quickly decorate [+ turbo]

turd-faced a polite way of saying 'shit-faced'

turds and the tees youth who wear t-shirts and get '**turd-faced**' [insp. *'the birds and the bees'*]

turfboard slippy grass [surfboard + turf]

turf-surf to gambol down a hill

turf-tariff a green tarrif

turnap to change sleeping position

turnip turn around

turnipples large nipples

turn-table for a table top to be able to be turned

turo turn round

turp to remove

turquoise to ask a good question

turt tongue-like [insp. *the turtle bug has a tongue-like scutellum covers most of the abdomen*]

turtail slowly moving side to side [turn + tail + turtle]

turtle an adult carrying a baby in a carrier on their back

turtle-ahead a place ahead where a turtlehead is required for safety

turtle-head to wear a protective hat

tusky lots of teeth on show

tusky dog an animal with sharp pointy teeth

tussis a fluke [L. tussis: cough]

TW too wrong

tw cen twentieth century

twat bucket a victim we do not feel sorry for | who brings the problem upon themself

twe cen twelfth century

twelve minutes past tumble we dress forty eight minutes to hum a humbless

twelve minutes to wonder about ze toffees forty eight minutes past huno doze off trees

twenty eight minutes past hassle hiss thirty two minutes to hands sell his

twenty eight minutes to hey me more rage thirty two minutes past haemorrhage

twenty five minutes past slumbro thirty five minutes to es lumer an 'oh'

twenty five minutes to mine is a skill, is it? thirty five minutes past mini skillet

twenty four whora
a Spar Convenience
Store

**twenty four
minutes past
tractort con** thirty
six minutes to inch
torch tran ton

**twenty four
minutes to motor
door in the air** thirty
six minutes past manda
tore din aire

**twenty minutes
past umbro shorts
cake** forty minutes to
tumble cords take

**twenty minutes to
dressed up and low
key** forty minutes past
don key

**twenty nine
minutes past eh
motion** thirty one
minutes to meh oh
apply lo shun

**twenty nine
minutes to four
lawn** thirty one
minutes past for lorn

**twenty one minutes
past wardrib** thirty
nine minutes to wa(te)r
dr drib

**twenty one minutes
to book tilt ket**
thirty nine minutes
past bucket lit

**twenty percent
trousers** shorts

**twenty seven
minutes past chart
art is ch** thirty three
minutes to char hurt is
huh

**twenty seven
minutes to past the
lass a stare** thirty
three minutes past
plast stair

**twenty six minutes
past picket kettle**
thirty four minutes to
pie cut but kept all

**twenty six minutes
to boat tall** thirty
four minutes past bottle

twenty three strong
| big [insp. *the game
'Contract Bridge'*]

**twenty three
minutes past berry
black** thirty seven
minutes to barry's back

**twenty three
minutes to a
hibiscus kite** thirty
seven minutes past bizz
quite

**twenty two minutes
past ny-lon** thirty
eight minutes to new
york before london

**twenty two minutes
to chew ug(ly)** thirty
eight minutes past
chug

twice-dice second
roll of a dice

twine when two cars
on opposite sides of the
road pass each other as
if a dance move

twist swir

twist-bint a screw
top

twist'n'shut to
screw the lid back

twist-watch to twist
a watch around the
wrist

twit bucket a person
who reports someone
for their own wrong
doing [insp. **twat
bucket**]

twix when the flame
from a candle dies
down

two cen twenty first
century

two foot ladies in
bingo, two ladies, with
two feet, is two and two
= 44

two minutes past eagles ear fifty eight minutes to seagulping beer

two minutes to peas cull eye treble fifty eight minutes past eagle eye plebble

two pints and a pill to have a hangover after light-drinking

two-sided Jesus Jesus on a game of noughts & crosses [insp. **jesum**]

two-way up and down

tye lots

tye dye over and over

tyeah a lot of positivity | lots of yes's [insp. **tye**]

tye-die a person who passed away but had a colourful life

typesit a typeset that does not change [+ sit]

typy to talk online

tyrement tyre marks

Uu

U up

u unity

U *pic* stubby test tube

u2 you too

ub con to spend time in a daze, staring into space and not really thinking about nothing in particular (between the consciousnesses)

uboat a big boat [insp. uber] [oppo. baboat]

ubertuba highly musical | one who can play many instruments [uber + tuba]

ubiquietous to be quiet everywhere [ubiquitous + quiet]

ubi tubi to be lost on the underground | to get on the wrong train on accident [L. ubi: where/wherever/whenever]

u-cut to exclude yourself

u-cutlery to offer yourself | to offer your services

udabarb barbuda

udder dairy

udder mudder cow's milk

udder murder to chain someone up without their consent

uddle to huddle to create shelter [Fre. ud: wet]

UFO until forensic observation

ufo toy planet

ug a small hug

uganda 'you gander'

ugg the slaughter of at least eight lambs

uglift to be lifted by ugliness | to see the beauty in the ugly [lift + uglify]

UHU you are who? | who are you?

uhu sticky hands

UIN urinate in nature

UK usual kinesis

uk you ok?

u-key-cut to **u-cut** from an idea

ukiyoyo a **bouncy castle** [Jap. Ukiyo: world, life] [+ yo-yo]

ulcer dimension stress | to be rundown | to be in a bad condition

ulemath learned math

ultrance a trance beyond

ultrant an very big rant [+ ultra]

ultrap a big trap

ultrasonic oldskool gamer

ultrinse a long rinse [+ ultra]

umbacan to give reasons for having weariness

umber an umbrella pole [see **ella**]

umbine to reunite [+ combine]

umbrally the fight for umberella space on a narrow street

umbreal to cover up reality | to layer the truth

umbrenous the death of umbrellas

umbrill good shelter [umbrella + brilliance]

umbro a small umbrella

umbronco to try and cover up | to try and umbreal | to ignore bronchitis

umco the latest

umlung strain for it to feel like hard work to breathe properly

un board den to dismantle a **den**

una grena botty one green bottle

una grena botty sitar on de vu-awol one green bottle sitting on the wall

unamp unsound to be employed | unable to work

unawear to not wear clothes

unbalense to not be able to take a focused image due to shaky hands

unbed to wake | to get out of bed

unbever age under eighteen

unblind to be able to see again

unbod to take yourself out of your body

unbronze to feel fresh and awake | to be inspired [insp. *the green shield bug is deep* *bronze colour in late autumn (before going into hibernation) and then bright green after hibernation]*

unbun to be direct

uncanny no ring-pull

unchant to step down | to stop speaking highly of something or someone

unchanto the most unused

uncial turning points [L. uncial: curvy writing] [+ functional]

uncle ben a watch | a wall clock [insp. oxyben]

uncomfordents overlapping teeth | for things to not sit well together

uncomforty to be uncomfortable with old age [+ forty]

unconman an unconventional manner

undead dayd

under ten pre-emptive

undergarm to wear too little

underseed to not have planted enough seeds

undervert a non-extravert

underwater bunker

undo a circling arrow

undoe to take back money

unexpeek something you're not suppose to see

ungob to spit content out of the mouth

ungrin to stop smiling

unhat to lose a thought

unhighlit unhighlighted

unhot to constantly not think

unhumoured onflu

unicarnage to rip up a myth [unicorn + carnage]

unicode to try and figure out somebody's gender (even though we know deep down there is no such thing as gender [see **gender**])

unitcommy community

united state a state of unity

unitrogen a unit of nitrogen

univerge at the verge of becoming universal

unlake now without lake

unlike ekil

unlit and unlifted cigarettes left on the table

unnestercest artificial insemination [unnecessary + incest]

uno dos stress stress due to finances

uno doze stress to be tired of stress [insp. **uno dos stress**]

unone one but none | to feel invisible

unreal genetically modified

unseal to go from soft to hard

unsexpected unexpected gender of baby

unsignal to not bleep

unsine an unseen sin

unsittimol when something goes down the wrong way [insp. *a paracetemol stuck in the throat is unsettling*]

upen to write in pictures | to paint [insp. u-turn]

unsin to become good

unslip no slot

unsness unecessary accessory

unspin to focus

unstarch to not be the same anymore

unstrobe to be all dark

untable to not sit around | unable to relax

untermession to utter words which contain some form of message [under + mission]

until tunt

untot to lose the train of thought

UOTFN urinate outside to feel nature

up and down life

U (past) one letter past T, two letters past S, three letters past R, four letters past Q, five letters past P, six letters past O, seven letters past N, eight letters past M, nine letters past L, ten letters past K, eleven letters past J, twelve letters past I, thirteen letters past H, fourteen letters past G, fifteen letters past F, sixteen letters past E, seventeen letters past D, eighteen letters past

C, nineteen letters past
B, twenty letters past A,
twenty one letters past
Z, twenty two letters
past Y, twenty three
letters past X, twenty
four letters past W,
twenty five letters past
V

up a tree amongst
bushes

upsoda thumbs up

upspidered crawling
an unknown boundary,
e.g. we upspidered on
the ceiling then we
upspidered the
fractions of galvanizing
simultaneous morph
equity - this made us
upspider under the
table

upstair to lift
someone up | to lift
someone's spirits

up sun when the sun
rises

ural to speak out-loud
to yourself [+ oral]

U-rally to compete
against yourself

uranoose to try and
hang yourself for the
seventh time [+ uranus]

urbal the herbal
urban | the organics of
urbanism

urban ruck gull a
seagull at the seaside
[insp. *the rucksack is a
travellers companion*]

urban ruck pig a
pigeon in the city centre
[insp. *the rucksack is a
travellers companion*]

urban's organ the
pace of an urban
environment

urca with care [insp.
kitul palm]

urdu how we do our
hair-do

urinary tractor infection an oil leak on a tractor

urinate dashi

urin eat to drink soup [+ urinate]

ursula insulated

uruguay you are a guy (who's) grey

urv velvet [insp. **urvi**]

urv garm a velvet garment

urvi velvety [insp. lasiandra]

US udder sin [insp. **AN:US**]

USA usually safe as

useless secivres [+ services]

useloss useless but not a loss

use use to use too much | to take advantage | to take for granted

use your fuck use your fork to fuck(ing eat)

UTI urinary tractor infection

util at counter to count the **utilities**

utilities body parts

utility A person with **UTI**

U (to) one letter to V, two letters to W, three letters to X, four letters to Y, five letters to Z, six letters to A, seven letters to B, eight letters to C, nine letters to D, ten letters to E, eleven letters to F, twelve letters to G, thirteen letters to H, fourteen letters to I, fifteen letters to J, sixteen

letters to K, seventeen
letters to L, eighteen
letters to M, nineteen
letters to N, twenty
letters to O, twenty one

letters to P, twenty two
letters to Q, twenty
three letters to R,
twenty four letters to S,
twenty five letters to T

U-torn to fail on
making a U-turn

utroopia a good team
| team spirit [utopia +
troop]

uu whoo

uutha who's that?
[insp. **uu**]

uuu three in a row [see
O's and X's]

uuuu four in a row
[see **FIAR**]

uvinate to urinate the
wine you just drank [+
vino]

Uwho hello, you are?

U-with away with
[Rus. U: away]

Vv

V *pic* an upside down cat's ear | a blown away (upside down) tent | pointy

v voices of vedas and veganism

va blow

VACATE vile as cancer at the evolve

vac ate to be sucked into going on vacation

vaccition to put to sleep for a while [vaccination + vacation]

vaccoma a time table having no free time [see **vaccome**]

vaccomb to blow-dry and brush the hair at the same time [vacuum + comb]

vaccome the time will soon be sucked up | time goes fast | a high powered vacuum sucks up time

vactor to add on a character

vade in place go in peace

vagina a sex pistol

vaglue to stick to a price [value + glue]

vagueitabe a vague person

valab a valuable label, one which comes in handy [oppo. **calab**]

vali erm to stare into the distance | to look lost [valium + erm]

valley a big blow

vallie to lie on a valley

valoot to over-do
[value + loot]

valub to barter a price
[value + lube]

valube a good bond
[value + lube]

valve to hold your
finger over the whole in
a bong to not let the
smoke out

valvue the value in
condensing

vamp ramp an urge
to give a love-bite

vamprint a love bite
[+ vampire]

vampyre red-hot

van blown

vandango to erite
'clean me' on the back
of a dirty van

vandatta to crash
into a van [+ vendetta]

vanilla spice to blow
hot and cold | both hot
and cold, e.g. you had a
fever and your
temperature was
vanilla spice

van lunch to buy
lunch from a catering
van

van lush a camper
van

vanull no blank, no
white

va pour to blow out
smoke

vardi pockets in a
cardigan used to store
things [+ vase]

varse a seat [arse +
vase]

vase hands together in
praying position

vasgina to insert flowers into the vagina. to lathe with perfume

vashush to control someone | to demand that someone stops speaking | to refuse someone of their right

vasore a sore vessel [L. vaso: vessel]

vassamar the usual assumption

vaste the vast taste

vat skip to try and avoid paying VAT

vat vac for VAT to pile up and become a big expense

vat vent to not have to pay VAT

vault a strong fault

vava po to blow a fuse

va va voom to blow a kiss

vax VAT and tax

veal calf | nasty

veali child abuse [+ **veal**]

vealocity to not be able to turn around [*like a calf in its cell*]

veery to let out too much [veer + very]

vegateau a vegetable cake, e.g. carrot cake is a vegateau [+ gateau]

vegemite I might do, I might vegout

veget to be healthy

vegetable a colourful meeting with lively discussions [+ table]

vegg a replacement for egg in cake-making

vegina a healthy vagina

vegout relax

vegun to curse vegetables

vegut a healthy gut

veins wires

vel sha to put up with the cold [insp. the velvet shank]

vel shank to go to a bar to get warm after **vel sha**

velhell comfortable but hellish

velocite to cite velocity

veloucity a soft speed [velour + velocity]

velourcro for a feather to softly fly and slowly fall [velour + crow]

velvet shank to put up with cold temperatures [insp. *velvet shank fungi survive in very cold temperatures*]

vendata to gather evidence for a vendetta [+ data]

vendung machinery a corrupt system [dung + vending machinery]

vendom to protect spite [venom + condom]

veneareal wart to hear something on the radio which gives you pleasure

venison venom

venterlate to deep breathe from the naval [L. venter: abdomen] [+ ventilate]

ventrance a window [vent + entrance]

ventroliqour
ventriloquist plus liquor

ventry to enter
through the window
[vent + entry]

vent til late to live
for a long time

ver cov a very good
cover band [oppo. **nev
cov**]

vera's very good
listener | ears which
are very good at
listening

vercin to be more
valuable than gold
[insp. cinnamon]

ver-ee to vary every
day | to vary each day

veril alternate [insp.
star anise]

verise a high rise

vermihole wormhole

vermiwood
wormwood

vero to feel high |
hero

versci attractive [insp.
parasol pine]

versit test of wit [insp.
the game 'Reversi']

versi water-resistant
[insp. parasol pine]

vertear to break out
into tears

verteabra to drink tea
from the vertebra

vertebra the cup of
the bra

verte bra a bra which
changes colour

verticall to call
someone from the other
side

vertide the action of
opening and closing,

e.g. we vertide the curtains

ververve double verve | double energy

vesell to sell your blood

vess varied essence

vetcorn for a file to not be converted to the format you wanted

vewol a change of energy [+ vowel]

VIAGRA victory is a grand roaring achievement

viagrass herbal sexual aids

via maria the use of marriage

vibrace a race of who can spread the quickest, e.g. sponsor ship: who can get most signings

vibran to make bran flakes more colourful by adding fruit

vibrasion for the eyes to shake

vibrate to spread

vibrun when **vibran** mixes with the milk and turns the milk a different colour

vi-car a vintage car

vicarton *Ribena* - 'the vicar of carton drinks'

vicertify in the process of certifying

vice spice to choose the non-wild

victim taste

victoria victory

victorn steal of the limelight [victory + torn]

viddie for a video to keep on stopping and the screen freezes on a certain part

videar a film star [video + dear]

vidiconundrumince to try and figure out the plot of a film [video + conundrum + mince]

vietname a Vietnamese name

vigilonce to watch for a long time [vigilance + long]

vigisimomentum of twenty minutes [vigesimo + momentum]

vigology a study of vigils

vigore a scary strength [vigour + gore]

vigorg the power of beauty [+ gorgeous]

vigorge gorgeous vigour

vigorust to lose strength | to weaken in old age

vijun slender [insp. the red cedar tree]

vikes a historical version of 'yikes' [+ viking]

viking day a day when your'e not sure what actual day it is

vilifry to embarrass someone by vilifying them [vilify + fry]

villactic dairy farming [villatic + lactic]

villa la hardhouse music [villa + la la]

villatte village news [+ latte]

ville ill and vile

villust a shaggy lust

vimto to dash to | to give spirit to

vincent a person who spends their last bit of money on alcohol (preferably wine) [vino + cent]

vindif the differences between wines [+ vino]

vinegarn to garnish with vinegar

vinegore too much vinegar

ving to take off your marriage ring ['V' is for 'vacant']

vinote to write after drinking a large amount of wine [vino + note]

vintage mini young male surfer

vintil vintage until (antique)

violins til sad until angry [+ violent]

vire bot a green bottle [+ virescent]

virust a computer left to suffer with a virus | an untreated computer

visent the gift of vision

vishpee to pretend to be having a wee [+ peevish]

visor car a car with no roof

visort no covering of the head | to show the head [visor + sort]

vista visitor

vista bok visitors book

vitalite vegan | vegetarian

vitalit vital literature

vitall a good grow

vitalmins vital vitamins

vitalot a lot of vitality

vivisectionist a cold-hearted murderer

vitamins mcvities

vizgina comical foreplay, involving interesting objects to be placed in the vagina, e.g. an alarm clock

vizkiss to blow a raspberry on the skin

vizolate to read viz alone

vocull to kill the voice

vodcat to crawl as unable to walk due to drinking too much (vodca)

vodcat got the cream to finally reach

bed after having to **vodcat** to it

vodeo a fashion video [+ vogue]

vo-hiss very quiet talking | a wispy radio

voidentification unknown identification

volcan to choke on alcohol

volcanic eruption to be wanked by the devil

volcanny a controlled flow, e.g. volcanny in pouring the water into the glass

volcanvulnerable a place that is vulnerable to a volcano fiasco

volcuncanny highflying | to unleash spurts of energy

volium to breathe in hot air [valium + volcano]

volvic tap water

vommittens sick-looking hands

voom kiss

voom and craft to kiss and make up

voom and witch craft to kiss and cast a love spell

voom chase kiss chase

voom pace the pace of a kiss

voom vac to suck faces

vortax unknown territory – where's tax going – is it here? [vortex + tax]

voseacull to kill the voice from shouting at sea

votch to watch visuals

votest a vote of complaint [+ protest]

vouch voucher

vowcock a penis that is saving itself for when it gets married [see **vowgina**]

vowel energy

vowgina a vagina that is saving itself for when it gets married [see **vowcock**]

voyn travelling funds [voyage + coin]

voy spag to be stuck inside a post box [voyage + alphabet spaghetti]

V (past) one letter past U, two letters past T, three letters past S, four letters past R, five letters past Q, six letters past P, seven letters past O, eight letters past N, nine letters past M, ten letters past L, eleven letters past K, twelve letters past J, thirteen letters past I, fourteen letters past H, fifteen letters past G, sixteen letters past F, seventeen letters past E, eighteen letters past D, nineteen letters past C, twenty letters past B, twenty one letters past A, twenty two letters past Z, twenty three letters past Y, twenty four letters past X, twenty five letters past W

V'room a room of peace

V (to) one letter to W, two letters to X, three letters to Y, four letters to Z, five letters to A, six letters to B, seven letters to C, eight letters to D, nine letters to E, ten letters to F, eleven letters to G, twelve letters to H, thirteen letters to I, fourteen letters to J, fifteen letters to K, sixteen letters to L, seventeen letters to M, eighteen letters to N, nineteen letters to O, twenty letters to P, twenty one letters to Q, twenty two letters to R, twenty three letters to S, twenty four letters to T, twenty five letters to U

vulgaris pleasantly vulgar

vulgart vulgar art

vulgar wheat bleached wheat products

vulgarnish to put salt in someone's tea | to dab someone's toothbrush into toilet water | to give someone who asked for a glass of water a glass of vodca | to lace someone's food in hot peppers | to pour vinegar in someone's wine | to spit in someon's food | to fill up the shampoo bottle with clear glue

vulgoat vulgar on all fours

vvv three in a row [see **O's and X's**]

vvvv four in a row [see **FIAR**]

Ww

W West | walk | way

w Wordsworth

W *pic* concertina | buck teeth

WAA we are a

WAABOF we are a bunch of flowers

wa-bi the sound of a free-wheeling bicycle [insp. *the wart-biter cricket resembles the sound of this*]

wache bedsores and aches from staying in bed for too long

wad cheque

wada yada money talks

wadder to use a lot of tissue when on the toilet [oppo. **tadder**]

wad pad a stuffed house |a house with plenty of clutter

wadpod wadpad

wad rob to steal money

wade a big wad of money

wade to wade work to live

wadpad cheque book

wadpid a bounced wad

wadpiddle the embarrassment of a bounced wad and how it lets your rep down

wadpod a cheque processing

wads long legs [insp. wading birds have long legs]

waffle a wobble | an insecure wall

wage ho the legal age you have to be before you can work [+ how age]

waggarments garments worn to for disguise

wagpuss a puss that does not come home at night time

waifer to threaten leaving

wailray many train tracks | over-crossing rail tracks

wain the painful way

waink an unseuccessful wink

waise to be wise about the waist

waister a piece of clothing (usually a jumper) tied around the waist

wait bleached (white) wheat | unhealthy

wait huh wait, what was that? e.g. to be walking at night, and you mentally ask the body 'wait huh' and the body stops to listen out | inner dialogue of security

waiting for godot nothing is everything

waiting roam to wait for a car park space [+ waiting room]

waitrest a waitress at rest

waitrose wait, flowers

waitus wide feet [**wait** + **feetus**]

wakeonay to sleep amongst

wakish a little awake | not fully awake | not fully turned on | low volume

wakosh very awake | fully awake | full power | high volume

walkdom organized randomness | a borderline random

walkdome a place of experiment [see **randome**]

wall a block

wallace collection a collection of savoury crackers [insp. *Wallace & Gromit of Wallace's love of crackers*] [see **gromit** *for Gromit*]

wallayby to be at someone's side while they are having an epileptic fit [wallaby + lay-by]

wallet wol

wallord a lord of strength (as strong as a wall)

wallord paper to find the soft spot of a strong person

wallord papered to have activated the soft in the wallord, therefore becomes less of a wallord

wallpost a political message [wallposter + goal post]

wallrus to lean against walls

walnut coffee coloured

waltzer fun but sickly

wa me sensible |what, me?

wan to want a little

wand to put hand up to ask a question, w is for wait

wanda to want a lot

wander to wand for a time

wanderm flabby skin

wandesk to move tables around

wand hut a magical place

wanding wingding to ask a bizarre question

wandisc to move around in circle

wandisco to move around when dancing

wandive to wander around in dung

wandude to go about things in a nonstressed, relaxed and mellow way

wang to hang your head out of the house window

wang panda to wang at night time

wank to not be able to

wank shake to shake hands with someone using the hand you've just wanked with

wank tank a tank in a vehicle which sucks up petrol or diesel far too fast we should call it mechanical gluttony, but instead lets call this a wank tank

wanky-panky only foreplay [insp. hanky-panky]

wapi durable [insp. the blue pine tree]

WAR wheelchairs are resourceful

wardrobe den

wargame to triumph through cunning strategy

warhol a tin can

warhol invasion a whole isle of canned food

war hut a prison camp

wark warp, whack and war injuries

warltz the dance or appearing of warts and how they come and go

warmhole an open fire

warmong to lie for too long in bed when awake

warner bros signalers

warriot war against war

warrust when a warrant is dropped

warry to try and discard worry with much force | to be at war against your own worries

war spurs intense arguments here and there

wart whisky and water

warter dirty water

warx a decrease in population due to a war [+ axe]

wasabeer green beer

w-ash to scatter ashes in the sea

wash bun soggy bread

wa shed a place where you wash your clothes

wash hands when a fly puts two arms together in act of feasting

washing not wishing [oppo. **woosh**]

washing pig a big garment which takes up a lot of pegs

wash-machine repetition

wash-pout to wash out the mouth

wash-tin a tin bath

wasp to quietly speak

waspers hurtful whispers

waste a horrible taste

waste-band a person who does not eat and lets their body waste away

watch a scientific accessory

watch haze witches hour | to keep on track of the lunar cycle [+ witch hazel]

watch-click a stop-watch

watchoo choo to wait for a train

watchual to time a visual

WATER we've all tried every reason | when a tent emerges roar

water brother a brother who was born from a water birth

water candy sugary drinks

water criss-cross criss-cross patterns in the water

waterho waterproof

water hoarder a hoarder of water

waterhoofs waterproof shoes

waterhoot a flying land bird able to go in the water, e.g. seagull or goose

watering ring a tap that has been left on and is waiting to be turned off [+ "ring ring"]

waterion a place of water

waterjockey one who rides waves not horses

waterms loose terms

water nose a wet nose from having a cold

waterport for water to pass through the drain and into the sewers

waterportal a drain to the sewers

waterproof reading deep into proof reading | checking for a leak | a plumber at work

water purse the bladder

water rays sunny rain

waterritoral the territory of water

waterrix a territory of water

watershod lacking water

water sister a sister who was born from a water birth

watersocket to put your ears under water and hear distorted sounds

water the flowers to spit on someone's food

watray a serving of water

wa-tres bien a refreshing intake of water

wa-tres bin polluted water | a refreshment containing toxics and chemicals [insp. **wa-tres bien**]

WATT with a timed task

watt hut a power station

wattlag to lack power

WATTS when a task tumbles sideways

WAV wrong, angry, vile

wavage the act of waving | the motion of waves

wavefunk to dance in water

wave lettuce a small portion of salad [insp. *wavelet: a small wave*]

wave-line the family tree of friendship

wave wave a side-toside hand wave

wāw a 'wow' regarding something written [insp. *'wāw' is the 27th letter of the Arabic alphabet*]

way sel always well

way-hay the next turn [Na. hay: next]

wayhey to wee outdoors

w-ding-ding bell service at wedding

weakponder to ponder around when at fragile level in life

wearinest a home of weariness | the birth of weariness

weaponder to ponder grabbing a weapon

wear-row to not let an argument pass

wear socks protect the feet

wearth to be naked | to wear a natural skin | to have a natural skin

weather cock a thermometer

weave wedge to get pleasure from giving a wedgie

webboil when the water starts to boil [+ wobble]

webrents house spiders [+ rent]

wedday day of wedding

wedding day wedday

wednesday buest Wednesday I was [insp. **sunday buest**]

wed to weed to be attached to weed

weeeeeeeeeeeeeeeee eeeeeeee a long wee

weed the decline in the number of whiteeyed ducks due to drainage schemes

weed to wed short of weed

weekent the weekend was spent...

weekinned a weekend spent with the family

ween to wee in public, e.g. to ween in urinals or outside

weep cup | to whip

weepingpong two people crying together

weigh in a manger for people who have eaten too much over the christmas period to then worry about their weight

weighsleigh a weighing scale

weighting waiting for trouble | waiting for weights

weitri the domination of the modern [insp. *the long jack tree dominates forests and the old*]

weke to emerge weakly | to not want to wake

weld to live for work [see **wild**]

welding build there's good work being done on the building | it is coming along well

well know to know well

well no not well

well o if you say so | if it's like that | that's'all

wellington to do very well | a place of well-being

welly done done good in bad weather

welly toss to see how well you can achieve

welly well a good try

welse for somewhere else to be good

wem when are they?

wenjam a sauce | a juicy sweet

werewolf a hairy leg

werewolves hairy legs

WERNER we are never, we will never [*werner is in the fourth quadrant of the moon*]

werrant a warrant to to stray from the course | to go East

westlife life of the West

wet lettuce we'll have to stop meeting like this

wetsee to spot a leak | to see something shining

WEWEHESS wake, eat, work, eat, home, eat, social, sleep (the process of the day)

whale while

whale ale drinks containing fish (most wines and beers)

whale tracks routes taken by sea

whalense to see under water

whaleray the surface area of the water where a whale is under

whalloy to look at what's left [insp. **loy**]

what's laws is mine whatever the law has I also have, if they have legalities and illegalities, then I will have them to, or if they have the right to rule out something then I do too, I can take the law into my own hands

what's mine is laws when the law or governing body rules that everything you own is theirs (e.g. debt people)

whatshit an underlying problem

whatsnot unknown and forgotten problems

wheat too much [see **wait**]

wheel air recycled air

wheel arrow undo

wheel well have a good cycle

wheesil a tyre lacking air

wheeze to puncture a tyre [see **wheesil**]

when SOCK when states of confusion kill

when SICK when states in confusion kill

when-party a surprise party

wherewhile to not know where you have been formerly | to have forgotten what you were talking about

wherolous where we roll around as louse

whether weather plans decided around the weather forecast

whey to dry yourself with a damp towel

whey neigh no way

whez not much of a wee | a few drops

whifa a very white face [insp. *the dragonfly called the white-faced darter has a very white face*]

whifir erect [insp. the white fir tree]

whilercok a cook with no deadline | to cook with unlimited time [oppo. **countercook**]

whiling to wait around for a while

whilling willing whiling

whinedow a whining mouth which keeps opening and closing [whine + window]

whip to weep

whipped cream
weeping eyes

whipped crem
severely beaten

whips wounded hips
[see **thips**]

whirlitated to be
irritated by a whirling
action, e.g. to be
whirlitated when sitting
on a roundabout

whirritated to be
irritated by a humming
sound, e.g. the boiler
gets you whirritated

whirsle for the area to
spin around you

whisper and whisks
the heat of a
competition

whist about one hour

white why no words,
why blanc?

white paper awaiting

ideas from experience
[insp. tabula rosa]

white shoes sun, sea
and disco

white tooth a person
who is constantly
cleaning

whitechapel least
profitable [insp. the
game of 'Monopoly'
where Whitechapel is
the least profitable
place to buy]

whiting bay a late at
night walk to the phone
box

whittalc when the
phone in a phonebox
does not work

who which one?

whodoo who do
voodoo? who made this
magic?

whoe where's **HOE**?
[see **HOE**]

whomans who are these people? | unknown persons

whome not sure who lives there

whoot to mime [who + **toot**]

whoratio person who has sex with many (who overkills)

whore who are you? | questionable

whorn of who's target

who-tell not too sure of who runs the place | not to sure of who is in charge [+ hotel]

whouse a squatted house [who + house]

whydah wider [insp. 'whydah' is another name for the widow bird]

why ross why sorry?

wibi a winter bird, a red robin is a wibi [oppo. **subi**]

wibi wiki winter bird facts

WIC who's in charge?

wic-kid a young witch

widark a widow's loneliness

widawn when a widow finds a new lover

wide-died very dead | eyes forever closed

wide-down to become tame

wif what if [insp. **wof**]

wi fi why five?

wig ro tel to live anywhere

wig-wag-bam fun in a tent [+ wig-wam]

wig-worm underground shelter [+ wig-wam]

wike to wake wide-eyed

wiki fact

wild to live

wildabble to take risks now and then

wilde exciting

wild fungi misunderstood

wilder old tree

wildle to live idly

willisecond the quickest time of **willy** play

willore lores of 'will' and 'power'

willow medicinal

willy free-will

win gin and white wine

winc as much in your hand as possible | to take a large portion

wincan showy [insp. the canella tree]

windemere a bay window

winder a winding winter

wind-hurl to be sick and for it to go in the hair

windie when the wind stops | when the breeze dies down

windoom a bad sight [+ window]

wind mall the ongoing-ness action of people in a shopping centre, in and out of shops, up and down levels [+ windmill]

window bender one who sticks their head out the window and looks left and right [*dogs are very good at this*]

windown a window on the ground floor

window pain a painful outlook

windowse to watch the dowsing of a pendulum

windowse cook to watch the screen of an oven | to watch food being cooked, e.g. we would windowse cook every time nan baked a cake

windowse wash to watch the washing machine washing your clothes

windrim to treat [insp. the winter's bank tree]

windter to get cold | a cold blow

wine-make a lowimpact process

wing pin dra when a drawing pin goes flying

wing pin drat to sit on a drawing pin – to sit on the pin that went 'wingpindra'

wing span of attention

wing wok to keep hearing loud noises | to hear a noise that comes and goes [Na. wok: loud] [*a wing sways in and out*]

wingding to flap about bingo wings

winge a damaged wing

wingspun to move the arms in circular motion

winkly sharp-pointed

winnate to inherit by winning

winput a good input

wint winter

winter to hide

wintimidate to informally or flirtatiously intimidate someone

wire w-yr-h

wires veins

wiris to try and wire into what someone else is thinking

wise act to pull away in sexual activity before discharging inside

wise eye to look into

wise man den to huddle under a bus stop when it's raining

wise mandala to look always see good in something

wisholate to wish to be alone

wisk to wish for a risk

wisolate to be wise and be alone | to be wise and do it on your own

W itch an itch W of the back

witch an itch from wearing a watch

wit fart toilet humour

wit hat a magicians hat

wit hut a comedy venue

wit woo to be woo'ed on in comedy

witnest the next witness

witter with thanks

witter watter to give humour to a dry conversation

wit plus watt moisture [energy + pitter patter]

WMP wake me please

wo way out

WOA work of art

wof what of

wog thirteen years | the beginning of being a teenager [insp. the game 'Wolf & Goats' having 13 pieces]

woke a week of hard work [yoke + week]

woki to *Wikipedia* a lot

wol wallet

wol pel change in the wallet

wolder to look in the wallet

wolf to grow the hair

wolf cry for things to then grow in the hair

wolf parade people eating at a buffet restaurant

wolver a very hairy womb to tomb

womage an image of a woman

wombledon The Wombles slang for their turf

wombmans people who live for impregnation

women red women troubles

womengage a meeting of women

WON wave of noise

won to want now

wonderarms instant biceps and triceps, (a mens version of the wonderbra for the arms)

wonderiff to try and remember the name of a song or the band's name

wong-pong a slightly bent or damaged ping pong ball

wonky table a little error

WOO window of opportunity, e.g. there's a WOO ready to jump out of or into

woo ble indigestible [insp. wood blewit]

wooc who's in charge?

woo cry completely absent [insp. the wood crickets' hindwings are completely absent]

woo hed cracked [insp. wood hedgehog]

woo hut an entertainment venue

wood pig pigs do fly [insp. wood pigeon]

wooden dry skin

wooden lag something not able to come forward and flow [wooden leg + lag]

wooden spoon a bit stiff on accepting liquidity and movement, e.g. he's a wooden spoon on the dance floor

woodpecker a hole in furniture from woodworm

woods words of nature

woolypeck to pull frayed string

woosh to wish a lot [oppo. **washing**]

wootput a good output

wopar to wake up in the middle of an operation after being anaesthetized

word jacket to use words to fabricate

wordshippers worshippers of words

wordy-gurdy to get the words mixed up

wor-kin a family business [+ kin]

wo will to be amazingly willing

W (past) one letter past V, two letters past U, three letters past T, four letters past S, five letters past R, six letters past Q, seven letters past P, eight letters past O, nine letters past N, ten letters past M, eleven letters past L, twelve letters past K, thirteen letters past J, fourteen letters past I, fifteen letters past H, sixteen letters past G, seventeen letters past F, eighteen letters past E, nineteen letters past D, twenty letters past C, twenty one letters past B, twenty two letters past A, twenty three letters past Z, twenty four letters past Y, twenty five letters past X

wranicker to put a pair of pants on the head

wrappliance to install set-up programs for an appliance to be recognized

wrecktangle a wrecked frame-of-mind [wreck + rectangle + tangle]

wrecto a terrible recto [*recto is a right handed page of open book/manuscript*]

wrench warrant for it to be official that someone is a wrench | to award someone the the title of 'wrench'

wrept to have walked in water [wept + crept]

wring wiring mangled and tangled together wires

wring wring to squeeze very hard | to wring well

wrist to handwrite

wristen to carve in the wrist area | of depression | cave paintings | physical

poetry of emotion [+ written]

writer's black to only write dark poetry

writer's buck to write for money

writer's clock writing with a deadline

writer's lock the character the writer gives off

writhe-watch to have the arm twisted as in having a chinese burn

WTD walk the dog

W (to) one letter to X, two letters to Y, three letters to Z, four letters to A, five letters to B, six letters to C, seven letters to D, eight letters to E, nine letters to F, ten letters to G, eleven letters to H, twelve letters to I, thirteen letters to J, fourteen letters to K,

fifteen letters to L,
sixteen letters to M,
seventeen letters to N,
eighteen letters to O,
nineteen letters to P,
twenty letters to Q,
twenty one letters to R,
twenty two letters to S,
twenty three letters to
T, twenty four letters to
U, twenty five letters to
V

WWF where went fire,
world war flame

WWI-FI where went
fire, in went world, fire:
inn [see **SITUATION**]

www three in a row
[see **O's and X's**]

www row ron three
people in a row, all
called 'ron rowing a
boat

wwww four in a row
[see **FIAR**]

WWYS watch what
you say

wyre why higher?

w-yr-h wash your
hands

Xx

X *pic* a vote without its box | a free right

x 2 tims Z

X it cot a toxic bed

x out to cross out

x pulse unknown pulse

x ray the ultra violet light rays of an electronic sun bed

x ruler an unknown size

x shaped hourglass

x time unknown time

x well whatever's good, it's all good

X, Y & Z to change outfits many times

x-act an unknown show

xalar a fake laugh

xancine TV-therapy | to treat yourself by going to the cinema | to indulge in lots of TV watching

xang speaking in a multiple languages

xant warning

xant warrant a warrant warning

xanthang to have no saliva in the mouth | a dehydrated mouth

xanthe sashy

xanthen unknown now and then

xapch contaminated water(s) [+ sap]

xarabat to hit someone with a bat

xarnic a spot of arsenic

xath to cross the path

xatho to cross paths with someone

xav to not have

xcl exclude

xdown head down

xe experience

xen before there was electric

xeno a day of no electric [Gk. xeno: alien]

xerd a person who used to have intelligence [+ nerd]

xero to not copy something | original | the only copy

xeroo cat to not be an **xerox cat**

xerox to copy

xerox cat one who copies everything and does not think on own behalf

xest to fail at everything apart from existence [exist + exit]

x-fact an unknown fact

x-factor commercialism

xfan to miss being admired

x-flakis a flaky area

xian a river and a palace

xing missing

xingaling to report someone **xing** | to report something as stolen

xingro to get rid of something before it grows or becomes bigger

xintro to move from the introductory [+ exit]

x-isle an unknown path

xit an itch that needs scratching but you can't get to it

x-itch an itch you can't reach | something you can't come to terms with

xixi an unknown coward | someone who does not own up to what they have done [+ sissy]

xl car a big car

X li no liberties

xmas a merry kiss

xmassian christmassy

xmessian the post-mess of a celebration

x miss to miss

xmyth to make up that somebody kissed you or you kissed somebody

xorous x a no, cause identity, no; every

xov no vox

XOXOXOXO alternating four in a row of **XXXX** and **OOOO**

X (past) one letter past W, two letters past V, three letters past U, four letters past T, five letters past S, six letters past R, seven

letters past Q, eight
letters past P, nine
letters past O, ten
letters past N, eleven
letters past M, twelve
letters past L, thirteen
letters past K, fourteen
letters past J, fifteen
letters past I, sixteen
letters past H,
seventeen letters past
G, eighteen letters past
F, nineteen letters past
E, twenty letters past
D, twenty one letters
past C, twenty two
letters past B, twenty
three letters past A,
twenty four letters past
Z, twenty five letters
past Y

x-ray to used to be
called ray

x-rray when array lost
its arrr-feel

x-ray lay to lie in
position ready for an x-
ray to be conducted

x-ray stray to be
missing an x-ray

x-road a cross road

x-rug a piece of floor
which used to be
covered by a rug

x section crosssection

X (to) one letter to Y,
two letters to Z, three
letters to A, four letters
to B, five letters to C,
six letters to D, seven
letters to E, eight letters
to F, nine letters to G,
ten letters to H, eleven
letters to I, twelve
letters to J, thirteen
letters to K, fourteen
letters to L, fifteen
letters to M, sixteen
letters to N, seventeen
letters to O, eighteen
letters to P, nineteen
letters to Q, twenty
letters to R, twenty one
letters to S, twenty two
letters to T, twenty
three letters to U,
twenty four letters to V,
twenty five letters to W

xulong forest [Gk
xulon : wood] [+ long]

xup head up

xutbutch a very large house [+ hut]

xxx three in a row [see **O's and X's**]

xxxx four in a row [see **FIAR**]

xylan tones of language [+ xylophone]

xyle to carry water, e.g. when going for a run it is always good to xyle to avoid dehydration [insp. *xylem: the part of the wood in the tree that carries water and minerals from the roots*]

xylitol gumtree

xylol to laugh so hard you pee a little

xylumb to destroy a forest for unnecessary purpose [xylostroma + lumber]

Yy

Y yellow

Y *pic* a set of scales

yacht a dozen [insp. **yarcht**]

yada same same

yaddakin a family member who non-stop talks

yaket to boil the kettle for lots of cups of teas | for a kettle to be filled to its maximum capacity [oppo. **kayaket**]

yakult yack

yaled no delay

yallow a loud noise

yam may not

yam yam never | more unlikely than **yam**

YAN you are nice

yann tiersen the male voice full of passion

YAPMO you are pissing me off

yarcht twelve rounds [insp. *game of 'Yacht' has twelve rounds*]

yardigan to carry a cardigan on the shoulders

yaw row to row unsteadily or irregular

yaw-dawdle go dawdle unsteadily [insp. **yaw row**]

yaw-row zone the euro zone [see **yaw row**]

yb 'your blood is the ink'

yeah, yeah, yeahs to always say yes | to always agree

yearyearyearyear year after year after year

yeast good

yee-hah to be sarcastic

yellebration a loud celebration

yellow history [insp. the game 'Trivial Pursuit']

yellow box an american cab

yendill a pile of money

yendolin to count money

yendoll to check your balance at the ATM machine

yen-yen money money

yen-zen priceless

yes-show to display all

yes-zon plenty of space

ye thing everything you need to know

yetidal to straighten (out) wavy hair [yeti + tidal]

yeye the love of yeast extract

yib yab a bobs boot to barter for a pair of ankle boots at the market

yimorota yeah, I'm In my car

yink positive thought [oppo. nink]

yip to talk

yips yes please

yip yap hat a sales talk

yip yip to talk forever | to go on and on and on

yipday a day of celebrations

yipzip to be the compare | to open and close an event

ylang ylanguage romantic language

y/m years mould

ymbli blimey, oh my!

yo to bend | to flex

yo gun a young one with a gun

yodaphone a prank call [yoda + vodaphone]

yoga to communicate

yogate to calm down

yogatoe a flexible toe

yogatoga loose clothes | light clothes worn for yoga

yoghurt a yoga injury

yog-hurt to be pinched

yoglog a long bendy or flexible tube

yogo able to go two directions | for there to be two directions on offer

yogo pog to toss a coin on two options

yogo pogo to choose any one of the two directions

yo-hetty a big hello [hefty + yeti]

yoink yoink a spoilt brat | to squeal and cry when somebody takes something of yours away

yola hola a colourful hello [+ crayola]

yolky the aroma or smell of armpits on sweat patches, e.g. we called them the yolky folk because they really did work hard, after all you could smell it

yomorotaway yeah, I'm on the motorway

yop to read the **YP** [see **YP**]

yopipe to bend a pipe

york self [insp. **nerve york**]

yot not yet

you spin me right hound dear dog, you spin me right round when you chase your tail like that

you thin me right round you're thin, I'm right round (said the plum to the wooden spoon)

youtopia space for the self [+ utopia]

youwillC the cat inside of you

yow you know how

yoyacht to wriggle the toes

yoyo gun flexibility

YP yellow pages

yppah sad | unhappy

Y (past) one letter past X, two letters past W, three letters past V, four letters past U, five letters past T, six letters past S, seven letters past R, eight letters past Q, nine letters past P, ten letters past O, eleven letters past N, twelve letters past M, thirteen letters past L, fourteen letters past K, fifteen letters past J, sixteen letters past I, seventeen letters past H, eighteen letters past G, nineteen letters past F, twenty letters past E, twenty one letters past D, twenty two letters past C, twenty three letters past B, twenty four letters past A, twenty five letters past Z

Y (to) one letter to Z, two letters to A, three letters to B, four letters to C, five letters to D, six letters to E, seven letters to F, eight letters to G, nine letters to H, ten letters to I, eleven letters to J, twelve letters to K, thirteen letters to L, fourteen letters to M, fifteen letters to N, sixteen letters to O, seventeen letters to P, eighteen letters to Q, nineteen letters to R, twenty letters to S, twenty one letters to T, twenty two letters to U, twenty three letters to V, twenty four letters to W, twenty five letters to X

yumnum a competition to see how many you can eat

yup to nod

yup yup to nod the head multiple times

yyy three in a row [see **O's and X's**]

yyyy four in a row [see **FIAR**]

yyyyyy a nodding person anxious and wanting to get it over with

Zz

Z a bingo dash-score | 2

zadibble the dribble which occurs when you sleep

zambelt a skinny belt [insp. **bambelt**]

zanzle to sprain the ankle

zap a broken zip

zap code a broken code [computer]

zap-fix to fix a broken zip

zappish a little creative [oppo. **zapposh**]

zapposh very creative [insp. Frank Zappa] [oppo. **zappish**]

zat to ask *what is that*

zaz-bus a new bus | good quality bus

ZAZUMBIC zero a zilch until more before initial coma

z car slow car

zealouse one who is devoted to slugging away at work [zealous + louse]

zeb crass a racist person [zebra + crass]

zebals B&W barcodes

zebbID a black and white uniform, e.g. a mime has zebbID [+ zebra]

zebratio B&W ratio

zebvibes B&W vibes

zebvid B&W film

zen-dive to discover

zenergy zen energy | the energy of zen

zenga to incur boredom when playing the game of 'Jenga'

zen-yen priceless

zephan to refuse an OBE

zerran couldn't have ran | was unable to run

Z-faced two-faced [see **Z**]

zhem a boring song which seems to go on and on and on and on and on and on and on [ahem + hymn]

zhues protective footwear [Zeus + shoes]

zi to see [oppo. **nazi**]

zina warrior a zine based on war

zinada no peeking | no looking (see **nazi**)

zinada piñata to be blindfolded | to have the eyes covered up

zinch not much sleep had [zzz + inch]

zipholt a zip that is stuck | will not move

zip-pad a place with good security

zircon natural air conditioning [insp. zircon: birthstone for December]

zish the noise of a wasp flying away

zist 'that's it'

zistwich an unappetising sandwich [+ zit]

zit an inner beauty spot | unique character

zitilitios to de-pus a zit

zitwatch a time where many zits occur

ziz to say 'it is'

zoe so easy

zn Benjamin Zephaniah

zokwok to add too much in the cooking pan

zolast to last forever

zombie nation when people do not think for themselves

zone allowed

zone a mainstream

zone b in fashion

zone c popular buy

zone x never heard of

zone y not much known about it

zone z has not been made yet

zong to save a file on the computer [Na. zong: save, defend]

zonga wonga to save money

zoo to cage the **wilde**

zoo-bus a noisy bus

zoocralose when you intake too much sucralose and you turn into a wild zoo

zoom when an animal escapes from a zoo

zoomatron to babysit wild children

zoom voom a quick kiss

zonba a field of sheep
[zone + bah]

zoo zag lag to travel
a lot

zoozit to have zits
everywhere

zoozitsu to try and
get rid of the zoozit

zouch to catch your
skin in a zip

Z (past) one letter
past Y, two letters past
X, three letters past W,
four letters past V, five
letters past U, six
letters past T, seven
letters past S, eight
letters past R, nine
letters past Q, ten
letters past P, eleven
letters past O, twelve
letters past N, thirteen
letters past M, fourteen
letters past L, fifteen
letters past K, sixteen
letters past J,
seventeen letters past I,
eighteen letters past H,
nineteen letters past G,

twenty letters past F,
twenty one letters past
E, twenty two letters
past D, twenty three
letters past C, twenty
four letters past B,
twenty five letters past
A

Z-sided two-sided [see
Z]

z tent the person who
always gets left behind
| an unknown band at
a festival

Z (to) one letter to A,
two letters to B, three
letters to C, four letters
to D, five letters to E,
six letters to F, seven
letters to G, eight
letters to H, nine letters
to I, ten letters to J,
eleven letters to K,
twelve letters to L,
thirteen letters to M,
fourteen letters to N,
fifteen letters to O,
sixteen letters to P,
seventeen letters to Q,
eighteen letters to R,
nineteen letters to S,

twenty letters to T, twenty one letters to U, twenty two letters to V, twenty three letters to W, twenty four letters to X, twenty five letters to Y

Z-time second time [see **Z**]

Z tone two-tone [see **Z**]

zuruzulu a drag queen who entertains [*jap* zuruzure: sound or act of dragging] + zulu

zxcv to have mastered learning the computer [insp. **qwert**]

zycock to tease the cock | to cock-tease

zyfly to have flown by

zylock to play around and pretend to be locked in or out | pretend to lock someone in or out

zyvag to tease the vagina (a vagina-tease)

zyway to have flown away [insp. **zyfly**]

zzz three in a row [see **O's and X's**]

zzz bed three in a bed sleeping in a row

zzz sleep three sleeps in a row

zzzz four in a row [see **FIAR**]

Misc |Pic| Sym

! the leg and the foot

noughts and crosses grid (game)

$ the making of a 'figure of eight' track

& et | ate

& @ ate at

& @ restaurant ate at restaurant

(/) a wonky bum

(|) a flat bum

('} facing Eastwards

* a compass point

* D the star of David

***** five star

, a nail sticking out of a floorboard

; to hammer down a ,

@ a snail

] a pocket flap

].,: stuff falling out of a pocket

{'} facing Westwards

~ a lonely wave

≈ the lonely wave found companionship

('}{'} two people kissing

1o1 one on one

4j forge

4jr forger

6 F U six feet under

™ to mate

Ω in o(h)m is a head and shoulders of a portrait

♪ a single cherry

♫ two cherries
a goal post

∫ a walking stick

ζ the serpent (let us call her "Zeta")

Ï conjoined twins

Ψ candela

Θ a person with sunglasses on

Д a table on top of a table

Ÿ the innder bird

Щ a cat walking on the ceiling

Ħ a fireplace

¥ a zip done up half way

ō a halo on the head

ų two unlit candles on a shelf

№ a very difficult yoga position

ð a piece of phone cord
| to cut the phone cord

♣ a tree

Δ no musical experience

§ hangers at dawn

Many Thanks To

Microsoft Excel for alphabetically arranging the 12,000 entries, Wittgenstein for language games, Spike Milligan's rewriting of Bible stories to keep the head sane, Bernstein's Backward dictionary, Ivor Cutler's phonic poetry, Douglas Adam's Meaning of Liff, Viz's Roger's Profanisaurus, The Furby Dictionary, Gertrude Stein's Alphabet of Names, Voltaire's Alphabet of Wit, The Yellow Pages, The free pdf dictionaries available on the internet, Miles, Jackie and Charlotte for the donation of a sum of 150 mental-words, The Isle of Arran for relieving stress, The lolly pop light flashing outside the window I was working from, The bed that put up with me and the laptop in it for nearly a month when creating the words, The film Kung Fu Hustle for a break away from long type-setting sits, Cobbing's work, Bruce Andrew Ex, Why and Zee, The kettle and bourbon biscuits, Bananas and the movements of the last two months I have been inspired to make words from.